D1348250

NEW WORKS
IN ACCOUNTING
HISTORY

Richard P. Brief, *Series Editor*

Leonard N. Stern School of Business
New York University

A Garland Series

WA 1126174 9

ACCOUNTING
THEORY

**UNIVERSITY OF GLAMORGAN
LEARNING RESOURCES CENTRE**

Pontypridd, Mid Glamorgan, CF37 1DL
Telephone: Pontypridd (01443) 480480

Books are to be returned on or before the last date below

2 4 NOV 1999

15 MAR 2000

– 5 FEB 2003

996

1126174|9

657.
072
ACC

Introduction copyright © 1996 by W.T. Baxter
All rights reserved.

Library of Congress Cataloging-in-Publication Data

Baxter, W.T.
  Accounting theory / W.T. Baxter.
    p. cm. — (New works in accounting history)
  ISBN 0-8153-2246-1
  1. Accounting. I. Baxter, William T. (William Threipland), 1906–. II. Series.
  HF5625.A239   1995   95-45924
  657—dc20   CIP

All volumes printed on acid-free, 250-year-life paper.
Manufactured in the United States of America.

Design by Marisel Tavarez

22·10·96

CONTENTS

ACKNOWLEDGMENTS

"What is Wealth—Nursemaid versus Accountant" was reprinted by permission of the *CA Magazine*.

"Asset and Liability Values" and "The Realization Rule—An Optional Aid to Sound Finance" were reprinted by permission of *Accountancy*.

"Asset Values—Goodwill and Brand Names" and "Discount and Budgets—with Constant Prices and Inflation," research papers that were originally published by the Chartered Association of Certified Accountants in 1993 and 1986, are reproduced with kind permission.

"Goodwill—The Misconceived Asset" was reprinted by permission of the *The Times*.

"The Future of Company Reporting" was reprinted by permission of Harvester Wheatsheaf.

"Income—A Wil-o'-the-Wisp?" was reprinted by permission of van Nostrand Reinhold.

"Early Critics of Costing—LSE in the 1930s" was reprinted by permission of the Academy of Accounting Historians.

"Depreciating Assets" and "Accounting Research—Academic Trends versus Practical Needs" were reprinted by permission of the Institute of Chartered Accountants of Scotland.

" Depreciation, Replacement Price, and Cost of Capital" was reprinted by permission of the *Journal of Accounting Research*.

"Depreciation and Probability" was reprinted by permission of the LSE Foundation.

"Accounting Standards—Boon or Curse?" was reprinted by permission of *Accounting and Business Research*.

"Early Accounting—The Tally and the Checker Board" was reprinted by permission of the Clarendon Press.

Ann Cratchley did splendid work as secretary.

INTRODUCTION

One can be a competent book-keeper and yet know next to nothing of theory. Bookkeeping demands care and accuracy; but usually it sticks to old routine, and poses few searching questions. Only when we come to its end products—a firm's published accounts or a factory's cost summaries—do problems and doubts arise. What do the total figures *mean*? To what uses can they properly be put? Could they be improved? What effect have they on the outside world? Such questions are the concern of accounting theory.

Particularly at universities there are now innumerable researchers who try to improve our body of theory. But, as you can see by looking at their journals, they have mostly wandered a surprisingly long way from practical accounting. They are concerned with intricate statistical studies (of e.g., the movement of prices on the stock market); they ponder over the accountant's role as agent of various parties; they venture into decision theory and information economics; they lengthily cite and criticize the earlier literature in their own special field; and so on. Such work may in time prove fruitful. But so far it has given disappointingly little help to the professional office: indeed, most of the office staff would be hard put to understand the articles.

As the pronouncements of Standard Boards show, the practicing accountant too now finds himself confronting problems of theory—but in areas that are nearer home. He is being forced to ask how he can improve his published reports, and especially their income and asset figures. Academic researchers ought surely to help with this work, by seeking a framework of principles that would lead to better published accounts (and, incidentally, would vastly enrich the training of accounting students).

Because of my own early immersion in office work, and sad limitations of my education, my interest has stayed with the balance sheet and income statement. Rather belatedly, I have tried to see these from the standpoints of thoughtful outside critics; their ideas—about wealth, and growth in wealth—are central to the articles that follow.

Early training in an accounting office left me with a passable understanding of bookkeeping and some parts of the law. But it instilled an excessive respect—almost reverence—for established ways; in those days, no-one suggested that there could be big improvements in our work, or that underlying principles existed and were worthy of debate. The brain-washing was so thorough that I later was profoundly upset when university colleagues (economists) questioned me about accounting's principles, and put forward objections that left me abashed and tongue-tied.

From the 1930s onwards, several outsiders criticized accounting, and I was lucky enough to know some of them. The first economist to help with my education was Kenneth Boulding, later to win great distinction at the University of Michigan.

For some years, we shared a room as assistant lecturers (the lowest of the low) at the University of Edinburgh. Among other things, he introduced me to the view that income is not primarily a matter of costs and revenues, but rather is growth in wealth; the costs and revenues are not much more than bookkeeping entries that explain details. This idea still seems compelling; it pensions off "matching," and asserts the supremacy of the balance sheet over the income statement.

In the late 1930s, two of my young friends at the London School of Economics, Coase and Edwards, began to publish in the weekly *Accountant*. They looked at accounting through the economist's clear spectacles. Their articles seemed shocking to many traditionalists (including me). Ronald Coase, later of the University of Chicago and Nobel-laureate, argued among other things that cost should be defined with an eye to decision-making (then a novel idea): decision budgets should therefore contain marginal and not fixed costs, and the splitting of fixed costs (allocation of overheads) is foolish (ideas re-launched by A. L. Thomas in the United States some forty years afterwards).

Edwards (later Sir Ronald Edwards and head of Britain's nationalized electricity and car-making industries) developed the same thoughts. He pointed out too that wealth can be viewed as either (1) assets and liabilities (the *ex post* accounting approach), or (2) *ex ante* as the present value of expected cash flows. View (1) yields more objective figures, and is much the better for routine records. But our major decisions (e.g. on whether to buy or sell firms or shares) are swayed by (2); and increase in (2) underpins our ideas on income—a notion that LSE's senior teacher of accounting denounced as "sheer insanity."

At the same time, Professor James Bonbright of Columbia University (a scholarly and delightful man) published his *Valuation of Property*. This clarified the idea that has since become gospel to enlightened students of value theory: an asset is valuable because it obviates outlays; if it ceased to exist (e.g. if stores were used up), the owner would face the unpleasant need to spend on replacement. This view was seized on by UK's Standard on inflation accounting, as "value to the business"; in my own work, I thought up instead "deprival value," which points to the underlying logic.

The 1950s saw the publication of Edwards and Bell's *Theory and Measurement of Business Income*. This enlivened accounting thought immensely. Among other useful things, it stressed the advantages of providing alternative income figures that contrast realized with unrealized gain, and the current year's income with earlier appreciation. Bell spent a year at LSE, and discussion with him was illuminating. His book's benefits grew still more obvious a few years later, when inflation accounting brought its new and fascinating problems. After several false starts, I was led to think that good inflation accounting must look to *both* general and special index changes, i.e. must be "current cost constant purchasing power accounting" (the phrase used by my former colleague David Solomons, to whom also I am greatly in debt).

Inflation accounting became important in the 1970s, and provoked much discussion among both practical men and theorists. The Standards on it were a big step forward (especially as they had to jettison historical cost). But, presumably because scholarly thought was ignored, the British version was marred by various faults, including a depreciation adjustment that was a marvel of perversity and complexity. The study of inflation accounting grew less important as inflation abated; yet it still provides excellent mental training, useful for understanding topics far off from inflation.

Some words by John Hicks (another Nobel-laureate in economics) have had a surprisingly big effect on accounting, and have swayed even Standards Boards. His helpful idea that a man's income is "the maximum value which he can consume during a week, and still expect to be as well off at the end of the week as he was at the beginning" was adopted eagerly; and students were soon calling his amplifications "Hicks (1)," "(Hicks (2)," and "Hicks (3)." Yet he was concerned with *ex ante* values of cash flows rather than assets; and he pessimistically concluded by asking whether income does "in the last resort, stand up to analysis at all."

The economist's central tenets concern scarcity and therefore the need for rationing. In accounting, this means that the most useful calculations often take the form of alternative budgets.

In other words, we must approach each problem by asking "what difference does it make?" (the question stressed by another helpful colleague, Harold Edey). For instance, an asset's value is most clearly explained *via* "Have" and "Have Not" budgets of its expected cash flows. Figures common to comparative budgets do not affect their answer, but do obscure the facts—one more argument for ignoring fixed items and concentrating on marginal ones.

Another fruitful idea (again from Hicks) is that the chief role of income figures is to help us with our consumption problems. The best income figure for this year is the one that best foretells our spending options in coming years. Inflation accounting is useful because, when prices are in turmoil, it lets the owner of assets see more clearly how his wealth has changed, and therefore how much he can wisely consume. Likewise sound depreciation figures give guidance on long-run patterns of income and consumption.

In time, I was won over to the economist's way of thinking. It certainly colours the articles, and has improved them immeasurably. And some of them were influenced too by another LSE colleague, the philosopher Karl Popper. He tells us that we can never be certain that we have found truth; we must never cease to test ideas vigorously. To aid our quest for truth, ideas should be allowed to compete in our minds on equal terms; we should not invest some with extra prestige, and "authority" should refrain from backing any of them. So the accounting theorist would here seem to be on collision course with Standard Boards. Well . . . . perhaps his wisest plan is to distinguish between *commands* (which, by imposing comparability on accounting, may possibly bring gain even if they are wrong-headed) and their underlying *principles* (about which we should never cease to doubt).

At any rate, I trust that you will read my articles in a highly critical spirit.

WHAT IS WEALTH?

Nursemaid versus accountant

What is Wealth?

Nursemaid versus accountant

When we were young, a good fairy-tale had a happy ending. The hero won romance and riches. Nurse or mother told us of his wedding to the princess; and of her dowry, itemised as palace, land, herds, jewels, and so on. Later experience may perhaps have made us dubious about having a princess in the family. But we still picture wealth as desirable objects that can be listed and counted in a stock-taking. If you are asked how rich you are, your first inclination is to list your assets one by one, put a value on each, and add up these figures: the total is your wealth.

When we assess wealth in such an inventory, we are still following nurse's method. And the accountant does much the same when he drafts a firm's balance sheet. He too lists assets, and adds their separate values. True, he subtracts negative assets (ie, the liabilities); and he dignifies the answer to his sum—the net total—with some such name as "capital" or "proprietor's interest" or "equity". His childhood memories (strengthened by his training as an apprentice accountant) buttress his belief that a balance sheet is a sensible measure of the business.

In some ways, no doubt it is. But the impressions gained at mother's knee still sway him if he tries to see his work with a fresh and critical eye. Sometimes those first impressions are a handicap. At other times, they are a help: the common-sense and plain speech of the child (and, for that matter, of non-accountants) may be better than the set ways of the specialist. In what follows, I shall try to see how far the innocence of his childhood is an abiding nuisance to the accountant, and how far it should aid him.

Achievements to date versus hopes for the future

Let us go back to our fairy-tale's list of fields and flocks. Note that an economic statistician, asked to measure a country's wealth, can hardly do better than draw up a similar list. He makes an inventory of the factories, houses, cars, etc, and adds their values. In doing so, he soon runs up against problems. When listing mineral resources, for instance, should he count seams that are still untouched, or only minerals that have been detached, or those that have been raised to the surface? More important, how should he compare a country like Finland, whose people have limited physical resources but high education and skill, with, say, a South American land where potential resources abound but education and enterprise are scarce? The odds are that the Finns will, in coming years, enjoy the higher flow of wealth. Lists of assets cannot allow adequately for *expectations*; achievements to date do not mix with hopes for the future. The statistician will of course cheerfully concede the limitations of his sum. It gives one kind of picture—the best that is practicable; imperfect though it is, it is better than no picture at all. He is on the side of the nursery and the counting-house.

The real foe of the nursemaid is the economist. With flawless logic, he points out that we should prize a thing because it will give us future advantages. Only the miser gloats over money for its own sake; a more balanced man esteems it for what it will some day buy. An asset is the title-deed to future benefits. Sometimes these benefits are satisfactions; sometimes cash to be received as rent, dividends, etc, or when the asset is sold; sometimes cash outlays obviated. Moreover (and this is a point to which I shall come back often), the asset's physical characteristics—kilos, litres, etc—here mean nothing unless they signal forthcoming flows of benefits.

These are notions that most children, and many adults, find hard to swallow. Even the patron saint of valuation theory, Professor J C Bonbright, of Columbia Business School, admits to reservations:

"A squirrel which betrays a high valuation for the nuts that he stores in the ground cannot confidently be said to base his conduct on the discounted present value that he attaches to the opportunity of securing a series of nourishing meals therefrom during the winter. Instead, the squirrel is apparently motivated by some impulse of a non-anticipating nature to get that nut, to avoid eating it now, and to bury it in the ground.

"Human beings are doubtless more anticipatory than squirrels in their valuation processes. But it is an open question whether even men and women do not base their bids and offers for commodities partly on a similar impulse of desire for or aversion from the commodity itself, rather than on a process of valuing the prospects of a flow of future benefits. Can we be confident that the impulse of a woman shopper which leads her to pay a certain price for a pretty dress or a delightful bottle of perfume is governed by her calculation of a series of future receipts of warmth and decoration, and a series of future receipts of pleasant smells and favourable social responses?"[1]

But there can in fact be no doubt about the economist's logic. Just as Molière's Monsieur Jourdain used prose all his life without knowing it, so we have used the economist's forward-looking (*ex ante*) approach—often to guide us in most fundamental decisions. We buy house X rather than house Y

---

[1] J C Bonbright: *Valuation of Property*; McGraw-Hill, New York 1937; (reprinted) Michie, Charlotteville, Virginia, 1965, p 222.

because we think X will better meet our future needs. The stock market tumbles at news of impending strikes.

Now, if value hinges on future benefits, then the value of a farm or business must usually hinge, not on the separate assets, but on what these will yield when working as a team. In other words, a company's value depends on what the owners expect to draw from it (nowadays, as dividends and eventual sale money). So, in principle, the best valuation is not made by listing assets, but by summing expected future cash flows; and the latter must be discounted to allow for waiting time and risk. Thus, when an economist tells his children a fairy-tale, he presumably does not end with a list of lush fields, fine horses, and overflowing barns; instead, he must delight his young with prospects of cash flows from future harvests, appropriately discounted. Less fortunate children will continue to be misled.

The *ex ante* value of a firm can be very different from the sum of its separate assets. True, just conceivably the flows and the assets may add to the same amount, by a fluke or because the assets belong to some peculiar type. But normally one asset cannot earn by itself; the assets make up a team, and it is the team that earns; the baker's flour is not much use without his oven, and vice versa. Consider a farm, where the assets must work together, and whose separate values add up to £500,000. What will the whole farm fetch when sold as a going-concern? If its future net receipts are expected to be £70,000 per annum and such receipts are valued in the market at a 10:1 rate, the whole is worth £700,000, ie, £200,000 more than is shown by the list of separate assets.

But, you will reflect, there is something to be said for the asset-plus-asset view. It makes the valuer's task much easier, and his figures much more reliable. To be sure, the valuation of even a single asset is not free from troubles and uncertainties. When an appraiser estimates its market value, he thinks back to actual sales of similar assets, then tries to picture this asset's fate in his mental market. But markets are fickle; and this asset may differ somewhat from those sold earlier. Appraisal is thus an exercise in imagination, very different from measuring a length of string with a foot-rule. Yet, however dubious the valuation of separate assets, the valuation of future cash flows is far more so. Our guess about the size of next year's dividends may be wildly uncertain; and that about each later year becomes wilder. Moreover the choice of discount rate brings a host of further troubles.

And so, despite the logical beauty of the economist's forward-looking concept, in practical affairs we must at times content ourselves with the list of assets. Sureness of calculation often outweighs intellectual appeal, even if the result is incongruous or unfair. This is obvious with tax calculation. Take the suggested wealth tax. Because the future is so hard to reduce to crisp £s and ps, Treasury pundits propose that the wealth in question should be defined asset-plus-asset rather than discount-your-future-receipts. This practical but crude approach must inevitably lead to crass injustice. Suppose a father has two sons, bright A and dull B. He invests half his fortune in A's education as a surgeon, the other half in a mansion and its furbishings for B. If the wealth tax is imposed, B's list will land him with a big bill. A's education cannot be appraised, and his stock of knives and saws is worth little, so he may pay nothing; yet his hopes of high future earnings constitute great wealth by the forward-looking test; this would be patent if the Treasury could auction him as a slave, or transfer him like a football star.

We have by no means exhausted the subject when we say that wealth can be assessed either as expectations or asset-by-asset. Each of the two concepts has its sub-concepts. For instance, if we opt for asset-by-asset market value, we have still to choose between (at least) buying price and sale price. Worse, from the accountant's standpoint, we have to choose between today's prices and what we paid for the asset when we bought it (historical cost).

The economist tells us, again with impeccable logic, that our past sacrifice when buying the asset is now useless as a guide ("it's no good crying over spilt milk"; "bygones are bygones", etc): we shall make better decisions on what to do now with the asset if we forget what we paid for it in the first place. This truth is extraordinarily hard to stomach. Suppose I am sitting in the theatre, and find that the play is so bad that I should get more pleasure at home watching TV. Do I go home or not? My decision (and, I expect, yours too) will alas be much influenced by whether the tickets were complimentary or cost me £5 apiece. Again, there are no shouts of derision in Parliament when ministers assert that it would be folly to scrap the Concorde after we have spent £1 billion on it—ie, that we now ought to chuck good money after bad.

Accounting has been very tender towards historical cost. The fledgling accountant learns with great pains how to record today's outlays. Such figures are useful as a record of stewardship; without them, indeed, a firm's finances would soon be in a disastrous mess. But today's outlays must tomorrow become feeble guides to current value. The accountant is then reluctant to admit their limitations, and to replace them with more topical figures; to do so would seem to be an admission that his work and training have been in vain.

The accountant's attachment to historical cost has become all too obvious with inflation; historical costs of assets are now weak guides to current values; but proposals for reform excite bewildered resistance. Again, cost accountants must have done immense harm where managers use the stale data for decisions.

If there are so many values—past, current and future—which is the right one? Do we see the truth more clearly through the child's eyes or the economist's? The answer is that words like "true" and "right" are here misleading. The asset-by-asset and the forward-looking methods are both defensible; both look at the same thing, though at very different facets. For "true" and "right" we must here substitute "useful" or "helpful". The truest measure is the one that yields the most helpful information to the given user in the given circumstances. For one's private decisions, the misty impressions of the forward-looking method are normally best. Where other people have a stake in wealth, we usually need figures that are less speculative and subjective, and then the asset-by-asset method is preferable. But only in very odd circumstances, and for very limited purposes, are historical costs defensible.

What is Income?

I now turn briefly to *change* in wealth during a period, ie, to income. Our childish impressions of this are vivid, thanks to the delight of receiving cash (in my case, a Saturday penny and the occasional present from a benign aunt). So we grow up thinking that income consists of cash: a business-man "makes money". But the accountant finds this nursery concept narrow and uninformative. For instance, our company may sell on credit; thus cash is owed to us, but not yet paid. Does this debt not swell our income? Again, our stock may go bad, and our machines wear out. Such loss is not marked by cash movement, but does it not eat into our wealth? Reasoning on these lines, accounting has come to define income, not as inflow of cash but as increase in the whole range of assets less liabilities. (However, often the snags of asset revaluation make such an income figure contentious. Accordingly, some academic accountants bid us revert to the nursery viewpoint, which they call the "cash flow concept" of income.)

Obsolescence and Depreciation

Let us now move to something else—economic versus physical attributes. From childhood onwards we gain lively impressions from the physical world, and we learn measurement with physical things as our subjects. But, alas, it is not safe to transfer this learning to the economic world. Why, for instance, do we feel that the word "obsolete" is useful? To be more specific, how far do you think your car's loss of value over its life is due to depreciation, how far to obsolescence? What is the difference between these two? Can you quantify them, and is there any point in doing so? Once again nursery experience illuminates the problem. If little Johnny takes his hammer and smashes the radio to smithereens, the change in physical state gives a clear explanation of the asset's value fall: here is depreciation incarnate—wear and tear, or at least tear. But if the radio becomes less attractive after father buys a TV, its decline in esteem is harder to explain. It is physically intact, and will still work; but no one wants to hear it now. In the same way, a machine's life may be ended by its physical wearing-out—and we think this natural enough. Or its life may end because the firm no longer wants to use it (because a better machine has been invented, or customers' orders for the product have dried up); and then we find it a trifle odd that the asset loses value with no physical symptoms of senility—perhaps indeed when it is still "as good as new". To reassure ourselves, we use "obsolescence" for this non-physical form of value loss. But both forms have the very same economic consequence—a worsening of cash flows—and there seems little point in distinguishing "depreciation" from "obsolescence" in our calculations and bookkeeping.

Glue or Goodwill

Another lesson that we learn from the physical world is that the whole equals the sum of the parts. Any exception to this rule would affront our sense of fundamental logic. Suppose I measure the width of a room, and find it to be 20½ feet. I then measure it plank by plank, and find there are 20 planks, each 1 foot broad; the total is 20, not 20½. Clearly either I have bungled the measuring, or I have left something out—say, glue between the planks.

But things are not always so simple in the economic world. Earlier I gave you an example of a farm whose separate asset values add up to £500,000, whereas the whole is valued (thanks to prospects of high receipts) at £700,000. Here, the whole does exceed the sum of the parts—at least, when they are valued from different viewpoints. How does the accountant deal with the disparity? Happily he can at most times ignore it: his ledger embraces only the separate assets, ie, accounts for the £500,000 but not the £700,000. Sometimes, however, he must willy-nilly accommodate both whole and parts in his ledger—as when he works in a company that buys another, the price being £700,000 but the assets' book-values (which he enters one-by-one in his accounts) only £500,000. His books now fail to balance—the worst thing that can befall an accountant. He reasons, on the physical analogy, that there must be an extra asset that has somehow escaped from the list. So he opens an account for this maverick, and enters it at £200,000; he does not however call it "glue", but "goodwill".

Honour is thereby satisfied; but common sense is not. You, the ultimate consumer of accounts, have every right to feel aggrieved if you are puzzled by "goodwill" when you read your company reports. The notion of goodwill as a missing asset is unsound. The usual example for proving this point is a pair of shoes. Alone, the right shoe has hardly any value; likewise neither has the left; but the two together have a considerable value; and this certainly does not mean that a third asset is skulking out-of-sight.

The accountant confuses both himself and us when he talks of "goodwill". He should substitute something else. But there is no one word in English that meets his need. To be clear, he must be clumsy, and use a lengthy phrase—for instance: "Difference between the sum of the separate asset values of subsidiary Y and the price paid for it as a going concern".

Names and Things

As my last topic, let me elaborate on this matter of wording. It has often been said that a child gets a flying start in a home where the grown-ups use words competently, and encourage questions and discussion. This holds where the child is destined to be an accountant. One of my pet theories is that nothing helps the student of accounting more than having heard the Alice tales at his mother's knee. The conversations with Humpty Dumpty and the White Knight teach two truths of immense importance: first, words are our servants, and we may adapt their meaning to suit our needs; second, to perceive the true nature of a thing, we must look at the thing itself, not its label. Humpty Dumpty's pronouncements are too well known to bear repetition; but let me remind you how the White Knight distinguishes between label and thing, à propos the song with which he is about to comfort Alice:

"The name of the song is called 'Haddocks' Eyes'.
But that's what the name is called. The name really is 'The Aged Aged Name'.
The song is called 'Ways and Means'—but that's only what its called, you know.
The song really is 'A-sitting on a Gate'."

Now, one of the reasons why accounting is a splendid mental discipline is that its names can be at odds with its things, so that the student is forced to look critically at the things, and ask himself whether the label fits. Here again the nursery can help. A child's stamp album teaches him that, should he acquire a black Victorian stamp that is labelled 1d, it is nevertheless worth something very different.

The student should apply this analogy to, for instance, par value—the money amount that forms part of a share's name. Thus one of your shares may be described as (say) a £1 ordinary share; £1 is printed in bold letters on your share certificate, and is used in the company's balance sheets and other important papers. But £1 need not be:

(1) the price at which the shares were first issued;
(2) the price that you paid when you bought your shares;
(3) the price at which you could sell them;
(4) the sum that the liquidator will pay on each share at eventual winding-up.

So £1 need not be the share's market price at any date in the past, present, or future. The label is an anachronism that causes immense confusion and heart-burning, and it should be abandoned. The clear-sighted laws of some US States permit instead the better label "share of no-par value". But British governments, partly because of trade union opposition, have always shrunk from this desirable reform.

Thus, when he is dealing with share values, the accountant must look away from the impressive money sign, and listen to the White Knight: the share is called £1—but that's only what it's called, you know; the share really is. . . . Well, what is it? If the company's capital consists of 10,000 such shares, a share is a right to 1/10,000 of future dividends and eventual liquidation proceeds. We are back to the ex ante concept of wealth, and this is far too volatile to be captured by any fixed sum on a label.

The White Knight's logic serves also to debunk bonus shares (that is, save where men's politics make them impervious to reason). If your company doubles the number of its shares with a bonus issue, you get more labels; but both numerator and denominator of your fraction double, and you are in reality no better off; the company cannot increase wealth by change of labels. If twins each have a one-half share of a teddy-bear, they will not expand the bear by talking of their 2/4 shares.

I could give you many more instances—notably from inflation—of how our first impressions linger on, for better or for worse. A good accountant will strive to adapt them in the light of economic reasoning; but he cannot shake them off. The child is father to the man . . . even when the man is an accountant.

ASSET AND LIABILITY VALUES

I. ASSETS

Assets are worth having (we all agree) because they will yield benefits. So it is odd that accounting does not look directly to these benefits when it values assets. It looks instead to the market, i.e., uses historical or current cost.

Benefits *versus* Market Values

To a private consumer, the benefits will normally take the form of utility. But a firm can often view them as cash flows— from the asset's sale, use, hire, etc. For instance, a firm may expect that a machine's use will yield future revenues (or, more likely, savings of wages, etc.) whose discounted present value is £9000. We accept that £9000 is the right figure to put into budgets for finding whether the machine is worth buying (i.e. for comparing benefits with price). But, once the machine is bought, it will be put in accounts at its price of (say) only £5000. Thus the balance sheet does *not* show the maximum price that the firm, if pressed, would pay for an asset (i.e. benefits); it is blind to "consumer's surplus."

There are sound reasons for this. The familiar balance sheet would change its function completely if it recorded hopes for each asset rather than the firm's solid achievement to date. And figures for future cash flows must often be highly subjective guesses. They will vary from day to day with the valuer's mood and with new information; they will vary too from person to person; and the discount rate must be debatable. Again, the benefits from each successive unit of an asset (e.g., materials) are not constant. So a valuer can seldom feel at all sure about a figure such as the £9000.

Jointness

And benefits often depend on "jointness." Many assets work as a close-knit team, and then the benefits from each asset are inextricably blended with those from the rest; they cannot be unscrambled. (What part of the firm's receipts are earned by the office typewriter?)

So, where there is jointness, any attempt to assign benefits to a given asset would fail, and would lead to absurdity. Suppose a firm is a team of two assets, A and B. and its market value (discounted future cash flows of the whole) is £14000. Suppose too that the firm is "deprived" of A (a machine wears out, material is used up, etc.), and that it would, if pressed, pay up to £9000 for another A; likewise, if deprived of B but still owning A, it would be willing to pay £9000 for another B.

Here a calculation would go wildly astray if it added the two sets of benefits to produce £9000 + £9000 = £18000; the value of the whole team is only £14000. Similarly, if a balance sheet perversely showed benefits, it would go still further astray if it tried to record the benefits from each asset in a team.

Benefits versus Market Values

In other words, we can look on benefits and market value as answers to two very different questions:

(1) What is the benefit of my owning (say) a car, compared with owning no car at all? This is the question that a capital budget should ask; and such a budget should embrace all benefits.

(2) How much would I have to pay, if deprived of my car, for replacement of its remaining services? This is the figure for current value accounts; and it looks not to benefits but market prices.

Values from Comparative Budgets

Current values can best be explained and justified by comparing two budgets of cash flows:

> *a.* if the firm still has the asset, and
>
> *b.* if the firm were deprived.

(*a*– *b*) is clearly the advantage of possession, i.e., the asset's deprival value. Normally the difference between *a* and *b* is that, as a deprived firm would need to restore the lost asset's services, *b* includes payment for their restoration; so this potential payment— *outlay obviated thanks to possession*—emerges as value. "If you didn't have it, you'd have to buy another."

Thus the budgets' inexorable logic shows outlay obviated (usually replacement cost) to be a better value figure than not only benefits but also historical cost or an exit price. It justifies the accountant's seeming indifference to benefits; he in effect compresses these into obviated cost. He looks to the market not expectations.

Benefit Sets

To get a full picture of the flows, we can of course put benefits into the budgets. We must however do so not only in *a* but also *b* (because, where a deprived firm would replace, deprival does not bring benefit loss).

Often the benefit flows in *a* (from the existing asset) and in *b* (from the replacement) will be the same; so the two sets cancel one another. We might just as well have stuck to our rule that accounts ignore benefits, and left them out.

Sometimes however the benefit sets in *a* and *b* are not the same. A "replacement" (as distinct from a "reproduction") may differ from the existing asset, and yield different benefits; thus a new model of a machine may have improved features. Or (notably with a depreciating asset) a younger replacement would give services to a later date. Here "replacement cost" should allow for the sets' differences in size or timing. Cost is not always the same as price.

Where the valuer's budgets stretch forward in time, they must discount future figures. His discount rate should presumably be the usual return that the firm expects on investment.

If there is not a good market for the asset (e.g., there may be few transactions in an unusual kind of machine), the valuer must try to guess what the price would have been if transactions had in fact taken place. Thus (as a judge has put it) he may have to envisage an imaginary market "peopled by the indeterminate spirits of fictitious and unborn sales."[1]

Physical versus Non-physical Assets

But (it may be objected) the argument has so far assumed the asset to have physical form, e.g., is a machine or stores. Here the valuer can disregard benefits because they are covered by the obviated cost of a machine with a given output or of x tons of stores. But suppose instead that the asset does not have physical form, and consists of rights to future cash flows (e.g. shares in an unquoted company). Here surely the valuer must look to the future flows?

He must indeed— and thus at first sight seems to be valuing benefits directly. But the market deals in flows (e.g., from shares and bonds); and a buyer of flows again contrasts price with benefits. A gap between the two figures may depend on (i) the buyer's own peculiar hopes or fears for future flows; (ii) (more fundamentally) opportunity cost— i.e., the returns that he can get from other investments.

So the valuer of flows can still (as with physical assets) use price rather than benefits; and there seems no reason why he should not do so. He must find the cost of alternative assets that would in a wary market's view yield a similar flow (e.g. bonds of comparable companies). Despite appearances, his concern is again the obviated cost of "replacements" rather than direct benefits.

Value Diagram

When he disregards benefits, the accountant must have at the back of his mind some such notion as that explained in the simple diagram below. OD shows time, AO shows benefits and values. At an asset's acquisition date, the benefits are AO; thereafter they can be shown by points on ABCD. In this example (to give a complete picture), the benefit expectations fall while the asset (say, a ton of stores) awaits use; the fall could be due to e.g., change in working methods at this particular firm (not reflected in market prices).

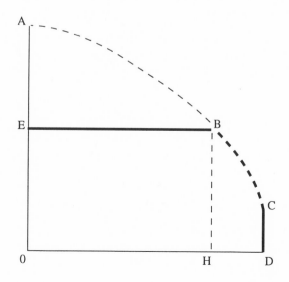

Till date H. accounts ignore AB, and deem the most practicable value to be outlay obviated, i.e. the benefits' replacement cost EB (here constant)— or, as a handy substitute, historical cost. So value starts at EO, and thereafter (despite the decline in expected benefits AB) is shown by points along EB.

Low benefits

Next consider what happens at date H. when benefits collapse further to some point on BC. They now are so low that a deprived firm would not replace. But they are still above the exit figure CD (possibly scrap price); so the firm will keep the asset, and use it in whatever way is least disappointing.

Our conventional wisdom is that the accountant now at last looks to benefits (BC). He must (to quote the UK Accounting Standards Committee) show the asset at "the present value of future cash flows to be derived from the asset,"[2] i.e., at "use value."

(Presumably because they were overawed by marginal calculations and the discounting arithmetic, earlier generations of accountants gave the name "economic value" to use value at this stage. But surely all the other values are equally "economic"?)

Later still, at date D, the benefits sink to below C. The asset will shortly be discarded. Benefits now are the expected sale proceeds CD (strictly, net realizable value). Deprival would rob the firm of these, and so they constitute value; here this is indeed based directly on benefits. And the owner, notionally regarded hitherto as on the buyers' side of the market counter, now shifts to the seller's side.

The Three-part Formula

By the above resoning, "the recoverable amount" (the asset's value after H) is the higher of benefits from continued use or sale.

This view has been promulgated by many writers (including me) as the basis for current value accounting; it was adopted (as "value to the business') in the UK inflation accounting standard (SSAP 16); and no doubt several generations of value students have been indoctrinated with it. Often the steps in the argument are reduced to the neat three-part formula: deprival value is the lower of

> cost obviated, and
> the higher of
> > benefits, and
> > net realizable value.

But many accountants have found this bafflingly complex, and I myself now doubt whether it is in fact right in principle.

Doubts on use value

The doubts hinge on the BC stage. As we have seen, our invariable rule for normal assets (on AB) is that we must value at obviated outlay rather than directly from benefits. Is there any sound reason for abandoning this wise rule when we appraise assets on BC?

Such wilting assets may sink to some 'inferior' role. Thus materials may end up being used in products that are normally made from cheaper materials. A semi-obsolete machine may be retained as a mere standby, to be brought back into service at times of peak activity; or it may be kept churning out a product that has failed to sell well but still is just worth making.

Deprival of such assets would not always affect benefits (on BC); a deprived firm might— as with AB assets— obtain these with "replacements" (stretching the term somewhat). Without the materials, the owner would have to pay for the cheaper materials. Without the standby machine, he would have to pay for, e.g., overtime work or the occasional hire of a relief machine.

Even the machine with a disappointing product can be viewed as outlay obviated. Like the flows from unquoted shares, etc., its net revenue has a market value, namely the cost of investments that would in the market's view yield the same cash flows.

In other words, the owner's BC assets, like his AB assets, still yield benefits above "replacement" cost; consumer's surplus persists. Comparative budgets again equate deprival value not with benefits but outlay obviated. The only new circumstance (irrelevant to value) is that the BC "replacements" look still less like the existing asset than do AB replacements.

There thus seems no sound reason why we should not continue to value at cost (suitably defined). Our contrary rule is wrong.

And of course jointness is again likely to obtrude (a fact conveniently ignored by those who hold forth on economic value). Where it does, no asset in the team yields separate benefits; so value cannot be based on benefits. "Replacement cost" would seem to be the only sensible measure left; and the argument against use of benefits becomes even more compelling.

The diagram should thus be amended. Where benefits have sunk to just below B. value can be shown by a new cost obviated line such as FG (for perhaps very different assets or services, e.g, overtime wages). If the benefits shrink still further down GC, a lower version of FG will show whatever obviated cost has now become relevant.

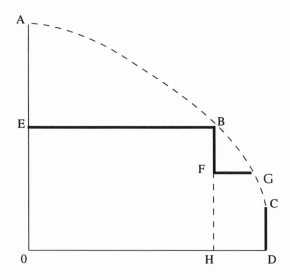

Conclusion on Assets

If we adopt this idea, we can scrap the three-part formula, and use something much more simple and congenial: value is outlay obviated (replacement cost very broadly defined), save where assets are about to be discarded, when it is net realizable value.

II. LIABILITIES

The current value of liabilities can be important where the balance sheet is to be refurbished in up-to-date terms (a process that surely should cover liabilities as well as assets), and in certain business transactions, as when a third party takes over liabilities as part of a deal.

A Mirror Image?

Since liabilities can be regarded as negative assets, it seems logical to start by asking whether the value rules for assets have some sort of mirror-image when we come to liabilities.

We can certainly say that a liability has "disbenefits" (of emotion and cash flow). They are the burden of the debtor's expectation of paying (say) so much interest each year and a sum at final settlement, discounted at his subjective interest rate. This burden will for instance seem worse to him when he foresees deflation or higher interest charges.

Further, we can contrast the burden with the market price of liabilities— perhaps arguing that the debtor must usually rate the burden at less than price, for otherwise he would pay off the liability forthwith. But, to get a clearer view of these matters, we need to look further afield.

Liabilities Bring Earnings

When a firm raises loans, it does not weigh burdens in isolation. It is impelled by hopes of putting the new funds to good use: it will buy assets whose benefits outweigh the loans' disbenefits.

So borrowing is a double-barrelled affair, and creates a second set of cash flows—the earnings of assets financed by the loan. A firm should be concerned with the *net* benefits of borrowing.

While the firm is still about to borrow, it may well compare the loan's disbenefits with the benefits from a particular asset whose purchase the loan will finance. But, once the loan has been raised, it should probably be looked on as part of a financial pool that provides all the assets. Normally a loan's continued existence is justified if its disbenefits are less than the benefits from whatever assets would have to be given up to finance its repayment.

Disbenefits versus Market Prices

But do a liability's disbenefits (and the related benefits) affect its value? I shall argue that, as with assets, they do not— save in the sense that benefits must exceed disbenefits if the liability is to be kept. The valuer should again look to market prices.

14

In some situations, a liability's market value is obvious. Thus if loan is issued without discount, etc., its value may well for a while be the same as its face value. Again, when the liability is about to be settled, its value will approach the pending payment; thus many current creditors, bank loans, etc., present no problem.

Comparative Budgets and Values

In less simple situations, liability values (like asset values) can best be understood with the help of comparative budgets. These should contrast the present values of the firm's future cash flows

a. if it still bears the liability; and

b. if the liability ceases to exist.

In other words, if the firm were relieved of the liability, it would be richer by (b - a); and so (*b-a*) is the liability's value. We might, as a counterpart to "deprival value', call it "relief value'.

But "relief' suggests two possible situations: (1) the liability is deemed to have vanished (as where a kindly outsider has assumed it); or (2) the firm has itself paid off the liability.

With (2), budget *b* omits not only the outflows of interest etc., but also the earnings of the repayment cash; so comparison of *b* with *a* shows the net benefit of borrowing— and certainly not the liability's value. With (1), asset earnings continue, and can be put in both *a* and *b* (thus cancelling out) or can be ignored; outflows of interest, etc., are in *a* but not *b*, so the comparison gives the liability's value— and is not affected by earnings.

The Valuation of Outflows

The assets that come nearest to a long-term liability's mirror-image are investments in fixed-interest loans. Like other assets, as we have seen, these should normally be valued at market cost to buyers.

There appears no reason why the same reasoning does not apply to liabilities. Relief would spare the debtor payments (such as annual interest and the final settlement); it is thus equivalent to whatever sum of money would be needed to get rid of these outflows by the cheaper of buying or repaying the liability. So this market figure is the liability's value. The debtor stands on the buyer's side of the notional counter, i.e., uses entry price.

Where the debtor plans to pay off the liability before the contractual date, the argument still holds. Relief equals buying price; the debtor stays on the buyer's side of the counter. Whereas, if the owner of the corresponding asset expects to sell it before maturity, he must shift to the seller's side, and substitute exit for entry values. Here the mirror-image gets blurred.

Much of the above discussion implies that liabilities are quoted in the market. In fact, probably most of them are unquoted, i.e. are private loans or trade credits. Here the valuer's task is harder. He must presumably continue to accept the market's su-premacy, and (as with assets) look at an imaginary market. He should use any market data that are available, but then try to allow for factors such as the liability's non-tradability and the debtor's obscurity. He should continue to disregard subjective estimates (e.g. the firm's internal discount rate), and concern himself only with the cautious figures that his hypothetical market would use.

The Replacement Loan Fallacy

I argued earlier that the respected three-part formula for asset values is faulty. It certainly does much mischief when we try to twist it into a rule for liabilities. Beguiled by love of symmetry, I made this attempt. "Replacement cost" plays a big part in most versions of the asset formula; I therefore had to excogitate the liability's equivalent of that cost. With misplaced ingenuity. I hit on "replacement loan."

Suppose that the firm, if relieved, would raise a fresh loan in exchange for the same burdens of (say) £x of yearly interest and £y at final settlement. Valuation budgets— the argument ran—will still show £x and £y, but also the receipt of the fresh loan (less costs); this potential net inflow—truly a "replacement loan"—would be the benefit of relief, and so is the value of the existing liability.

I now think this argument wrong. The prime consequence of loan relief is acquittance from payments such as the £x and £y; this direct improvement— and no more— is surely what should be put into sensible budgets, and what the balance sheet should show to the outside world. Relief would indeed bring all sorts of less direct changes in cash flows. The firm might or might not raise a fresh loan. If it did, there would be further changes: the new money would increase asset earnings, etc., etc. Where should we stop? The remote flows hardly seem relevant to the immediate valuation of £x and £y. Replacement loan is an unconvincing guide to value.

So the phrase "replacement cost" led me badly astray. Had I instead used "cost obviated," I should have seen that the asset's mirror-image is a "cost incurred" and should not have fumbled with notions of replacement.

High Risk Liabilities

A worrying factor emerges where the liability's value falls because the market deems the firm a bad risk. If the accounts now show this lighter burden, they give a more cheerful view of the firm's net assets and growth. (The improvement is in one sense real enough; if the firm were reconstructed, etc., it might have to pay only a fraction of its liabilities.) Such accounts could grossly mislead.

So, where liabilities are suspect, current values bring a disturbing problem. Should we here stick to market figures despite the dangers (which could be lessened by giving the full legal figures as notes)? Or should we for the sake of safety abandon market figures, and instead show liabilities at their full legal amount? (And where would one draw the line between risky and safe firms?)

Conclusion on Liabilities

To sum up. A liability should be valued at its market purchases price. Talk of "replacement loan" is a confusing irrelevance.

Previous Discussion on Liabilities

W.T. Baxter, *Accounting Values and Inflation*, London, McGraw-Hill, 1975, p. 138.

Deepak Kulkarni, "The Valuation of Liabilities," *Accounting and Business Research*, Summer 1980, p. 291.

Jean St. G. Kerr, "Liabilities in a Current Value Accounting System," in D.M. Emmanuel and I.C. Stewart (edits.), *Essays in Honour of Trevor E. Johnston*, University of Auckland, 1980, p. 223.

Notes

1. Mr. Justice Danckwertz in Holt vs Commissioners of *Inland Revenue* [1952] 32ATC402.

2. *Guidance Manual on Current Cost Accounting*, London, ICAEW, 1976, p. 7.

ASSET VALUES

"Goodwill" and Brand Names

Introduction

Very soon after they start work on advanced accounts, students find themselves facing problems of value. How (for instance) should we value the assets in a balance sheet? How should a manager cost inputs? Why does a firm's value differ from the sum of its net assets? And so on. Further, they find that "value" has many meanings; they must distinguish between these, and ask which is the right one for particular accounting uses.

In what follows, I try to introduce such topics as these in as simple a way as possible. But even a simple approach soon runs up against puzzling problems to which accounting has yet to find good answers. You should view all suggested solutions (including mine) with profound scepticism. If you do so, and make up your own mind on the answers (regardless of what "authorities" say), then accounting will be giving you an excellent mental training.

CHAPTER I

BENEFITS AND VALUES

The task of the accountant is to keep track of wealth. In recent years, this has more and more meant that he has also to measure the size of the wealth, i.e. that he must find values - of both individual assets and the whole firm.

Valuation has proved remarkably difficult and controversial. Accountants have approached its problems in conflicting ways, and have indeed attached conflicting meanings to "value". Thus a valuer must perforce take sides in controversies and choose between rival meanings.

Asset recognition

One obvious preliminary problem is that of recognition. Before he can value an asset, the accountant must make sure that it exists.

An asset is an asset (we mostly agree) because it is the source of future benefits. But in some cases these are hazy and unpredictable. At what point do they become sufficiently sure to justify the accountant in putting an asset in his ledger? Thus a firm may hope that its research or prospecting will yield future benefits; but by what tests should it decide whether or not such hopes constitute an asset?

Accountants have still to find a convincing answer to this problem, to which we shall return later.

Historical or current figures?

If he decides that an asset exists, the accountant's next problem is whether to value it at historical cost or a current figure.

Historical cost (HC) has a long and respectable pedigree. Accountants have always tended to leave assets' values frozen at the levels of their acquisition dates, i.e. to value in a backward-looking way. HC is familiar; it saves trouble and

thought; and it often has the merit of being objective. Many accounting rules (e.g. in the UK Companies Acts) seem to take its use for granted.

However, an asset's price usually changes over the years (during inflation, far and fast). So historical figures are likely soon to give a poor picture of a firm's present size and structure, and therefore to deceive users of the accounts. In particular, they can mislead a manager when he makes decisions; if he is choosing between rival plans with the help of budgets, he should cost the "using up" of existing assets not with out-of-date figures but current ones.

Current values admittedly have their weak points (e.g. they may be subjective, and they entail extra work at revaluation dates). If however an asset's existence depends on future benefits, then surely we should link our value figure as closely as possible to the benefits and their market prices. These can be seen more clearly at valuation date than earlier. So the case for current value (CV) is very strong.

Because of inflation, we have come to assume that HC is more cautious than CV. But this is not always so. When the US "thrifts" (building societies) were on the brink of wholesale collapse, their weakness was hidden by their valuation of mortgage portfolios at HC rather than the lesser CV. Our attachment to HC has here had profoundly unfortunate economic and political consequences.

It is moreover hard to see how anyone can explore accounting principles without reasoning from CV. Historical figures are cut off from the benefits now anticipated and their prices; they thus lack any logic for solving problems dependent on such data.

In what follows, I shall therefore assume that only with CV reasoning can the accountant reach solutions to his value problems. Of course, he may then have to adapt his solutions to practical ways, e.g. by trying - as far as possible - to fit in historical figures as surrogates.

Sub-divisions of current value

"Current value" can mean several things, notably market value or more personal estimates. And market value must be further sub-divided according to whether the asset is bought or sold. (Consider for instance a grocer's wholesale and retail prices.)

Because these current values depend on expected future benefits (e.g. share prices fall if dividend cuts become probable), they can be described as forward-looking. For a simple arithmetical illustration of the relations between backward- and forward-looking values, turn to Appendix I.)

Personal value

Personal value is one's private estimate of worth - the maximum that one would be willing to pay for an asset's benefits. It is sometimes also called "economic value", though surely the other forms of value are equally "economic".

Such an estimate is usually made when a purchase or sale is being considered. If for instance a businessman decides to buy a machine for £1000, he probably thinks that its future cash contribution - extra revenue or (more likely) savings of expenses such as wages - is worth more than £1000; its purchase will yield him a surplus. If a shopper in a foodstore decides that £3 is too high a price to pay for a melon, he must rate the melon's benefits below those to be got by spending £3 in other ways. In each case, the person concerned makes his subjective estimate of future benefits - cash or utility - and contrasts this personal value with market price. Such appraisal may be no more than a vague feeling. But it can take the form of a detailed calculation. If I am valuing my holding of shares in company X, I may guess their yearly dividends and eventual sale price, and then discount these cash flows and so get a present value - for instance, 120p. per share. This may well differ from the market price (because my guess at the future flows and also my interest rate can differ from those of other marketers). The discrepancy may prompt me to buy or sell; I am likely to buy if the price is below 120p. and may sell if it is above. The retention of an asset argues that personal value exceeds sale price.

Here then are two contrasting current values. Neither is an all-purpose figure. Accounting uses both, but in very different contexts. Personal value is of course the essence of the capital budgets used for testing whether an asset is worth buying. Normally however market values (current or historical) are more suitable in routine accounts such as balance sheets.

There are several reasons for this. Personal values are shadowy, depending on the valuer's skill, tastes and mood; thus they may be contentious and impossible to verify. More important is jointness; where assets A and B work as a close-knit team, the team's benefits cannot sensibly be split between them. And a list of personal values (e.g. in a balance sheet) would probably add up to an extravagantly high total; as we have seen, an asset's retention argues that personal value exceeds market value (perhaps by a big amount); inclusion of all these surpluses would yield a very high and meaningless figure.

Values from alternative budgets

Much the same arguments might be set out in a rather different way. We could say that value is the answer to certain questions. These may take different forms, and get different answers.

If I am valuing my car, two possible questions are:

A.   What are the benefits of having a car (compared with having no car)?

B.   Why am I better off owning this car than if I ceased to own it (but could get a replacement)?

Question A sometimes (but not always) deals with a potential newcomer to the asset list. B always deals with a particular asset that is already owned.

Both questions make us compare alternatives; with each, we should ask "what difference does it make?" if various things happen, i.e. if various scenarios are followed. Thus we adopt the marginalist way of thinking that has proved so useful in solving economic and business problems.

To compare scenarios clearly, it helps if we set out the figures as alternative budgets. For instance, I can best answer question B by drafting two budgets that show my cash flows if (1) I continue to own the car, and (2) I no longer own it. Examples will follow.

Kinds of market value

The budgets must often include market transactions in an asset. But, as we saw earlier, market price varies according to whether one is buying or selling. So valuation budgets should distinguish, in the light of the firm's actual plans for the given asset, between

(1)   buying ('entry') price, i.e. replacement cost (RC); and

(2)   sale ('exit') price - or more precisely (as sale may bring future expenses such as delivery costs) net realizable value (NRV).

Circumstances can vary greatly from asset to asset, and for a given asset over time. (Compare a machine that still has a long and useful life with one that has become obsolete and will shortly be scrapped.) I shall therefore argue that we cannot rely on some hard-and-fast valuation formula such as "current value is NRV". The right formula must make us look at the particular asset's current circumstances, and then choose whichever figure now fits these. It must be selective.

The case for and against NRV

Some accountants reject this selective view, and argue strongly for the general use of NRV.

There are several arguments in its favour. It tells creditors how far their claims could be met by sale of assets. It is at least a rough indication of how much more cash the firm could raise from creditors, mortgagees, etc. It can draw attention to assets that the firm ought to sell (because their price is higher than their contribution in use). And - a gloomy thought - the sum of the sale prices may show that the owners would gain by selling off the assets piecemeal and going out of business.

But the counter-arguments seem weighty. They include:

-     RC tends to give some assets (e.g. machines) a higher value than NRV; everyone knows that a car's value (if defined as NRV) drops at once after purchase. The drop will be big where the asset suits the owning firm but not others ("specificity"), as replacement may here be costly yet sale proceeds negligible. Use of NRV in financial accounts may then result in (i) a savagely high depreciation charge in the year of an asset's purchase; (ii) thereafter depreciation charges and balance sheet values that are misleadingly low; and (iii) - where directors fear that such distortions would affect the firm's market status - decisions to buy less suitable but non-specific assets.

-     If cost accounts used the low NRV figures rather than RC, managers would tend to under-cost products and then to price them too low.

-     Often prices of new goods are easier to find (and more reliable) than those in the second-hand market.

-     When an insurance claim is made (say, for fire loss), the values in the firm's own books are to some extent evidence of the size of the loss. NRV's low values would weaken the claim.

3

CHAPTER 2

DEPRIVAL VALUE

Now let us see how the argument of earlier pages can best be applied when an asset is revalued, e.g. for the annual balance sheet.

Finding the advantage of ownership

The valuer should in effect frame a question on the lines of B on page 2, i.e. "by how much is the owner better off with the asset than if he ceased to own it (but could get a replacement)?". The best answer is surely to be found by comparing the owner's positions (1) with, and (2) without the asset. In simple circumstances the amount may be obvious; one can then say, without more ado, that value is e.g. replacement cost. But to deal with complex figures, and to explain the reasoning behind them, one should set out the two scenarios in comparative budgets:

(1)   The "Have" budget, i.e. the owner's cash flows as they will be if he continues to own the asset; and

(2)   The "Have Not" budget, i.e. the flows as they would be if he had just ceased to own it (= deprival), as for instance if he had used up material in production.

Such comparison seems the clearest way of explaining just why the asset makes the owner better off. The excess of (1) over (2) measures this benefit; it is called "deprival value" (DV) or "value to the business".

The DV concept comes largely from the work of the late J.C.Bonbright of Columbia University. In his **Valuation of Property** he tells us:

> The value of property to its owner is identical in amount with the adverse value of the entire loss, direct or indirect, that the owner might expect to suffer if he were to be deprived of the property.[1]

DV appears by far to be the best measure of value. It is the answer to our fundamental question "what difference does it make?". Its budgets are a framework that enables us to adopt whatever kind and size of value emerges from the latest comparison of the two scenarios: thus it reflects current prices, and it changes from e.g. RC to NRV when new circumstances or intentions make this appropriate; it meets the test of being selective. It is unquestionably the right costing basis for many of a manager's decisions (see below) - which is an extra reason for using it also in financial accounting. It was the value prescribed by the Accounting Standards Committee in its standard on inflation accounts.

In what follows, I shall rely on the DV reasoning, and its Have and Have Not budgets. If you are not familiar with these, you will be helped by looking at the examples in Appendix II. These cover various likely circumstances that influence as asset's value.

Deprival value example (with replacement)

However, one set of illustrative budgets demands a place at this point, because it shows some very important things, viz:

(1)   normally DV is RC; and

(2)   some cash flows may occur in both budgets, and so do not affect the difference between them, i.e.value; and

(3)   (perhaps unexpected) revenue can be one of these "common" items, and so be irrelevant.

As is often the case in accounting, a rather extreme example drives home the points at issue. Suppose I need a car for my work, and that I expect over the years to earn revenue whose present value is £500,000. If I were deprived of my car (say, by an accident), I should at once replace it (for £8,000). The car's value budgets therefore are:

(1) **Have** (i.e. with undisturbed ownership)

I shall earn £500,000

(2) **Have Not** (i.e. without this car)

I shall replace the car for.. £(8,000)
And then continue to earn 500,000

_____

492,000

_____

(3) **So the advantage of ownership is** ....£ 8,000

Thus DV is here replacement cost. The £500,000 revenue is in both budgets, and so its figures cancel out; we might as well have omitted them.

Value as cost obviated

This omission of revenue (receipts or saving of running costs) is perhaps the hardest bit of the argument. It is completely at odds with much of our thinking about value - which, in the guise of personal value, often envisages all future benefits, notably revenues; for instance, the capital budgets for testing whether to acquire an asset must include revenues.

If it seems surprising that revenue forms no part of DV in the above example, one may look once again at questions (A) and (B) on page 2. If we were answering (A), my personal value of £500,000 would indeed be relevant; it shows what I should lose if I were never allowed to own a car. But (B) seems the right question for routine valuation of assets already owned. It deals not with "a car" but "this car". If the latter can be replaced speedily, deprival would bring no loss of revenues: I shall earn these anyway. Both Have and Have Not budgets can include them - or, more elegantly, omit them.

We readily accept this view in some familiar situations. If my car is wrecked, I should not dream of asking my insurance company to pay me £500,000 Plainly £8,000 is adequate compensation; it will "make me whole".

So - where the asset would be replaced - DV must be defined in terms not of future revenues (or savings of working costs), but of **replacement cost obviated**. Because a firm's machines, stock, etc., have already been bought, its future outflows will be less. This reduction in outflows is the relevant advantage that ownership here confers; it is what justifies the accountant in recognizing the asset, and it explains why valuers should mainly use RC (or, as a poor surrogate, historical cost). "If you didn't have 'em, you'd have to pay for 'em".

However, figures derived from revenues may become relevant if the flows of the asset and its potential replacement vary because they have different ages. Here the future flows are not "common" **in date**, and the budgets must allow for the timing differences (important with discounting). Thus if unreliability lessens an old taxi's earnings, the budgets should contrast the revenues (for each future year) of the existing machine and a younger replacement. Likewise where a machine's repair bills mount as it ages, the budgets should compare the two cost flows. (See example 5 in Appendix II.).

The three possible forms of DV

The car in our example seems not untypical of assets, since deprived owners would normally buy replacements. But how does DV behave in less typical cases - where "economic" value is less than replacement cost, i.e. where the asset is not worth replacing? Here the Have Not budget will ignore RC; deprival would not obviate that cost, but would instead rob the owner of the best contribution that the asset can still make (the "recoverable amount"). "Best contribution" covers two possibilities - sale or continued use:

(1)   The asset will soon be sold (and not replaced).

-     Here the **Have** budget contains the sale proceeds. The **Have Not** budget is blank. DV = NRV. Or

(2)   The asset will be kept for a time (and then not replaced).

-     Here the **Have** budget has traditionally contained whatever benefits the asset will still yield (often explained as economic value); these benefits are for a time the asset's revenues or costs obviated (use value), and then sale proceeds.

-     The **Have Not** budget is blank. DV is thus the value of the remaining benefits.

The owner will naturally choose the better of these two courses, i.e. DV is here the higher of the answers to calculations (1) and (2).

Summary on deprival value

This description of DV is sometimes boiled down to a neat formula:

Deprival value = the lower of

-         Cost obviated

                or

-         Recoverable amount, i.e. the higher of

    -         NRV

            or

    -         Use value (=Benefits from use)

But, if we are to be consistent with our normal way of valuing, use value should not be linked directly with future benefit flows, but measured as their replacement cost. If for instance an old asset is kept as a standby, deprival might make the firm occasionally hire another machine or pay more wages; the machine's value would be the cost of these very different "replacements" (and not the benefits of use as a standby). So the formula can be simplified; DV is:

-     (So long as the asset would be replaced) replacement cost.

-     (Where the asset will be kept but not replaced) cost of the most suitable "replacement" - perhaps of a very different type - of the remaining services'.

(Where the asset is about to be sold) net realizable value.

DV and management accounting

So far, we have tended to cast the argument in terms of financial accounting, as if our prime concern is the firm's balance sheet. But often DV is also the right figure for help with management decisions. This is important; indeed it is one of the strongest arguments in favour of DV.

Suppose for instance that a manager is drawing up an estimate of the minimum price at which to accept a job. The inputs include materials already in stock. Historical figures (e.g. our old textbook favourites FIFO, LIFO, and average cost) may completely fail to represent the sacrifice of the inputs, particularly during inflation. Likewise NRV is irrelevant. The material's "using up" on this job will normally make the manager pay for replacements, so the sacrifice is replacement cost. If he would not replace, he must think about the materials' scrap value or their value (cost obviated) as substitutes for other kinds of material. The DV logic gives him the right guidance.

Last thoughts on asset valuation

We must always remember that the valuer's figures usually are attempts to predict a hypothetical market price. He "must enter a dim world peopled by the indeterminate spirits of fictitious or unborn sales" as a judge said when he had to value unquoted shares. Thus many values (DV or any other) must be no more than arbitrary and uncertain estimates, which can never be proved to be 100% "right" (or, for that matter, "wrong").

A valuer's estimates must be particularly dubious where market prices are on the move, and where there are few dealings in like assets. Thus work-in-progress can seldom feature in market dealings; we therefore seem doomed to value it by some rule-of-thumb routine.

In practice, because of the uncertainties and to avoid undue effort, the valuer may well be justified in taking short cuts. Thus he may review fixed assets only at longish intervals. And he may deal with like assets in blocks, raising all the items in a block with the same index.

It is right for us to accept these qualifications on the valuer's accuracy. Yet, properly interpreted, his figures still can improve accounts.

8

CHAPTER 3

A FIRM'S VALUE

Cash flows versus assets

When we think about the value not of separate assets but a whole team - the firm - we must choose between two very different approaches, yielding two very different kinds of values. We can either:

(1)   Look to the future benefits from the united team, i.e. estimate the market worth of the firm's expected cash flows (discounted); or

(2)   Sum the separate assets one-by-one (using either historical or current values) and deduct liabilities - as in the familiar balance sheet.

The two resulting values may not be close to one another, and may indeed be far apart. Let us as shorthand call them DCF (= discounted cash flow) and BS (= sum of the separate net assets in the balance sheet). What follows is largely concerned with (DCF - BS), i.e. the **difference** between the two values.

Pros and cons of the two values

Accountants can rightly take both DCF and BS seriously. Both have their merits. But unfortunately both have faults too.

Thus, though DCF's logic is clear and is helpful with the solution of problems of principle, its figures (of future cash flows) must usually be a matter of surmise. The discounting rate also can be debatable. So the discounted present value must be very much a shot in the dark. Moreover the concepts and technique call for some sophistication.

The asset lists used by BS look simple, are familiar, and have common-sense appeal. But unfortunately BS is lacking in the logic that helps with the solution of many economic problems.

Moreover it usually plays only a supporting role when the really important decisions are to be made, e.g. on the firm's sale.

The unimportance of the balance sheet

This last sentence will affront some readers. Accountants devote much care to the balance sheet, which may indeed be the culmination of their work for a year; thus surely (they must feel) it deserves respect when major decisions are made on the firm's fate. Even the layman may be biased unconsciously in favour of assets; first impressions last, and our childhood's first notions of wealth envisaged the beautiful princess's castle and lands and flocks and gold, not her DCF expectations.

But there is plenty of evidence to suggest that, when the prices of a firm or its shares are at issue, rational investors look to the future benefits being sold (e.g. dividends and eventual capital repayment); the market seems to treat DCF as the key to price. So budgets, and not asset lists, should be the main concern of anyone who is valuing firms and shares.

It is salutary to remember the innumerable private investors who buy or sell shares without looking at accounts. And one recalls successful takeover predators who claim to act solely on their beliefs about the victim's prospects, i.e. without recourse to balance sheets.

Perhaps we should ask ourselves a naive question: why should we think that there is any connection at all between the DCF and BS figures? The most plausible answer probably is that we expect investment to earn a "normal" rate of return; so the size of the investment (i.e. BS) is a guide to DCF. If many small firms are trading in a very competitive market, there may indeed be a tendency for each to earn a "normal" profit, and for DCF to equal BS. But, in the absence of such textbook conditions, actual profits of different firms can be dispersed far and wide around the "normal", and DCF may often be far from BS.

So, when firms are to be valued, would it be reasonable for the valuer not to look at the balance sheet, i.e, has it no part at all to play? I think that it has at least minor uses. Thus it can draw the valuer's attention to an excess or shortage of liquid assets (and thus to hiccups in the future flows). It helps to show whether the "tools" are adequate to produce the expected flow (e.g. what replacement costs have been obviated, and for how long). And it suggests (to a limited extent) how much may be retrieved if disaster strikes. In short, it can improve the quality of DCF budgets, even where it plays no direct part in them.

The genesis of "goodwill"

Usually the ledger has to deal only with routine transactions and the separate assets, and so has no concern with DCF. But some unusual transactions - notably the purchase of another firm - shatter this happy state, and force the accountant somehow or other to accommodate the incongruous DCF in his records.

Two types of firm may be affected. Firm A may buy and absorb B; then A's ledger must be made to digest B's asset figures and (DCF - BS). Or company A may keep B as a legally-separate subsidiary; then similar problems arise over the consolidated accounts at each year-end.

Suppose A absorbs B, paying £100 for it; and that A's accountant puts all B's obvious assets (less liabilities) into his books at "fair values" that add up to only £80. He will then tend to assume that he must have overlooked an elusive extra asset worth £20. And the prim logic of double-entry forces him to enter £20 in a ledger account (to balance his books), just as if in fact there were an overlooked asset.

His alien figure is a source of much confusion. Unfortunately he usually makes things worse by not labelling it accurately as "Excess of B's purchase price over the sum of its net assets". Instead he calls it "Goodwill". This noun - at once reassuring yet vague - strengthens the notion of an extra asset (perhaps linked with popularity); it suggests too that the "asset" can and should be treated like ordinary assets, i.e. that it brings its own flow of benefits, which can be valued separately. The next chapter looks critically at this notion.

CHAPTER 4

THE WHOLE AND THE SUM OF THE PARTS

Is (DCF - BS) indeed an asset? Accountants think that it is. But we should (I believe) consider an alternative view - that it is not a separate asset (with its own stream of identifiable benefits, capable of being valued like the other assets), but instead is a slice of the general investment in the acquired firm.

One reason that prompts us to regard (DFC - BS) as a separate asset is our ingrained belief that the whole equals the sum of the parts. Accordingly if the whole is 100, and the known parts add up to only 80, there must be a 20 part that we have failed to see. But let us look hard at this whole-and-parts proposition.

Example - services

Suppose that two clowns - call them Laurel and Hardy - can each earn a fee of £100 if they act separately. Thanks however to a rare skill in combined acts, they can earn a joint fee of £350. These figures suggest some arithmetic:

	£	£
Whole: Joint fee		350
Parts: Laurel's fee	100	
Hardy's fee	100	
	200	
Missing part?	150	
		350

But in truth there is no missing part. By bargaining jointly, the clowns create a **new economic unit** that is detached and different from the separate parts and their sum (£200); the market treats their joint act as a unit in its own right, with a price struck by its own supply and demand forces. The £150 is thus not the price of anything, but a mere arithmetical residual.

Example - tangible parts

The same reasoning holds when tangible things are combined into new market units. Take the example of porcelain ornaments. A Dresden shepherd and shepherdess probably command a far higher price if sold as a matching pair than separately. Our explanation is that a buyer's satisfaction from seeing the complete unit on his mantlepiece is more than double his satisfaction from one piece. We do not argue that the pair's price embraces a mystical third something ("pairness"?). Right- and left-hand shoes are another example.

Where an object (say, a bicycle) is made specially for a customer, he and the maker may amicably agree that the price will be the sum of the parts' costs (including the maker's time); thanks to the contract, the whole-and-parts argument here has some validity. But if the customer decides to sell the bicycle, the market will be blind to both contract and the parts; the assembled bicycle has become an independ-

11

ent unit, and its price will hinge on market forces (scarcity of bicycles and buyers' eagerness for them); and if (say) eagerness and the price fall, we cannot argue that the input prices were less. Here again a new "whole" has been made - different from, and with more market reality, than the whole that is merely the arithmetical sum of the parts.

Example - a firm and shares

A portfolio of investments is a revealing example. If the owner can deal in them separately, the market value of his whole portfolio may well equal the sum of the parts' values; any unusual skill that he may have in winning capital gains may make him feel happy, but is not reflected in the whole's market value. Likewise the value of units in a unit trust is linked to the value of the sum of the parts, because of a government rule forcing the managers to buy and sell units on that basis.

But if the shares' owner reorganizes his portfolio as an investment trust, the latter and its shares are new market units, detached from the portfolio in the eyes of the law and the stock market, and subject to their own demand and supply forces (e.g. the shares' price reflects the directors' dividend policy and skill at spotting winners). Notoriously a trust's "whole" (market capitalization) tends to be less than the sum of the underlying investments' values; and, whatever the reason for the shortfall, it is not an overlooked liability or "badwill".

Exactly the same reasoning must surely apply to other kinds of business. When a firm is sold, the price will most likely differ from the sum of the net assets' values. We may reasonably speculate about the causes of the gap (e.g. we may guess that a shift in fashion is boosting sales), but we are less reasonable if we go on to argue that whole-and-parts turns such causes into assets.

The analogy of a ship's tonnage has perhaps some point. The tonnage can be measured either by weight (displacement) or by volume (gross tonnage). The two measures yield somewhat different figures. Suppose the **Queen Mary's** displacement tonnage is 50,000 and its gross tonnage is 51,000. We do not argue that the 1000 gap points to the existence of a chunk of material somehow overlooked by the surveyor. It merely shows that two different things were measured.

A philosopher might at this stage suggest that a firm's parts constitute a **system**: they work together as a whole, like the parts of an engine; they produce a synergy that shows in the whole's behaving in ways remote from the behaviours of the parts. "A scientist in his analysis, evaluation and synthesis of systems is not concerned primarily with the pieces of hardware that make up the system, but with the concept of system as a whole".[2]

The whole-and-parts idea misleads because a firm can be measured as two different "wholes" - a list of separate assets, and the future receipts from the composite of assets. And a gap between the measures of two dissimilar things does not prove the existence of a third thing.

Assets that contribute jointly

The relationship between the parts and the whole can influence our reasoning in yet another way. A valuer may try to find a value for one asset by asking how much it contributes to the whole. Here he is in great danger of shifting from market value to an "economic" value; his figure may be at odds with all the other values. He becomes embroiled in further difficulties where assets contribute jointly.

Thus suppose a firm is by any test not worth more than £100; that it has three assets - A, B, and C; and that these work as a close-knit team. The valuer could argue that with no A (but still with B and C) the firm's net revenue would fall, reducing the firm's value to (say) £40; so A is worth £100 - £40 = £60. But then, looking at A and C without B, he could similarly adduce a value of (say) £60 to B, and likewise £60 to C.

There may well be occasions when such marginalist thinking is useful. But it could certainly lead to absurdity if applied to all the assets in a balance sheet; in our example, the list would show £60 + £60 + £60 = £180, though the whole firm's value is only £100. By becoming a team, the three assets have in effect merged into a single productive unit that makes a joint contribution.

If one of a firm's assets clearly contributes its own revenue stream (e.g. an investment in stock exchange securities), we can sensibly argue that its value is a function of this stream. But most assets contribute jointly; a given asset has no independent link with cash flows (save as replacement cost obviated). We cannot sensibly attribute so many £s of the firm's revenue flow to this typewriter or that lathe. Likewise we cannot work backwards and argue that such-and-such part of the revenue flow proves the existence and value of such-and-such an asset.

Probably (as we shall see) the same argument can with good reason be used by those who oppose the recognition of novel intangibles. A firm may indeed benefit from intangibles such as image, promotion slogans, entry barriers, scale advantages, etc. But attempts to give each of these a separate value may run into impossible difficulties of interconnection and double counting.

CHAPTER 5

Goodwill

The word "goodwill" has been used for a long time, and with various shades of meaning. The OED cites a 1571 will: "I give....my whole interest and goodwill in my quarry". Again the Vicar of Wakefield paid "an hundred pounds for my predecessor's goodwill"; here the word perhaps means a price paid to win the blessing of a seller. In **Dr. Bradley Remembers** (Francis Brett Young's semi-autobiographical novel), a young doctor prefers to buy an existing practice, rather than add to the competition, in order to secure the goodwill of the district's other doctors.

Meanings of "goodwill"

It may be as well to look at three senses in which "goodwill" is now used in the context of value:

(1)   In everyday speech, the "goodwill" of a firm can mean much the same as "popularity with customers".

(2)   In the accountant's technical speech, as we have just seen, "goodwill" means (DCF - BS), i.e. the figure needed to balance the accounts where DCF has crept into them. The firm may or may not be popular.

(3)   "Goodwill" can be approached in a somewhat different way, as the value of "super-profits", i.e. of profits in excess of what is deemed a "normal" rate on the firm's net assets.

Late developments have forced accountants to qualify meaning (2) with adjectives - to distinguish between

-       purchased "goodwill" - arising, as earlier pages have assumed, when another firm is bought; and

-       non-purchased (or "home-grown") "goodwill", arising where the firm revalues itself at DCF level - a step that would till recently have been regarded as too shocking to contemplate.

Would a phrase be preferable to "goodwill"?

(DCF - BS) can arise from many causes other than popularity (e.g. the firm may be a hated monopoly). So the word "goodwill" is clearly inept. As a judge said recently, "to call it 'goodwill' can only be confusing"; use of the word by the Accounting Standards Committee was "most undesirable and unfortunate".[3] And the use of this - or any similar - word must foster the notion that an undetected asset exists.

No single word gives a clear picture of (DCF - BS). A descriptive phrase seems preferable, and would make for clearer and more cautious thought. The EC's Seventh Directive uses "consolidation difference". A longer phrase is still better; "excess of Company X's purchase price over the values of its separate net assets" is an improvement, and was indeed found in some consolidated accounts until misguided EC pressure substituted "goodwill".

This matter usually becomes important in discussions of whether accounts should rid themselves of "goodwill", and, if so, how. When we are faced with these problems, it sounds eminently wise to say "'Goodwill' is an asset like other assets, and so should be depreciated over its useful life like other assets". If instead we said "This figure is the difference between two different meanings of value", the easy analogy with an extra asset would seem a good deal less plausible; we should think twice about what (if anything) "depreciation" and "useful life" here mean.

"Goodwill" and partnership

Dealings between partners popularized the use of "goodwill" in sense (2). If, as is usual, the firm's

15

BS does not equal DCF, a partner's capital account (linked with BS) will not tally with the market value of his share (linked with DCF). Thus awkward problems arise when a new partner's in-payment or a retiring partner's out-payment has to be accommodated in the books. These problems can be eased by the insertion of a "goodwill" account for (DCF-BS), and the consequent writing up of the partners' capitals.

Even where those changes are not made, the word has come in handy, e.g. a new partner, perturbed because only part of his in-payment is credited to his capital, may be overawed by being told that his payment consists of "£x as capital and £y for a 1/nth share of goodwill" - hardly the most lucid of explanations.

"Goodwill" methods of valuing

As accountants are now perhaps forgetting, the relative importance of DCF and BS was mistakenly reversed in what used to be a popular method of valuing firms and shares. For long (till perhaps about 1960), many accountants valued these in three steps. (a) They listed the net assets; (b) they calculated the "goodwill" by methods described below; (c) they then found a value figure by adding (a) to (b). "Goodwill" was thus not a residual gap but an ingredient in its own right.

This procedure begs many questions. What kind of values should be ascribed to the assets at stage (a)? At stage (b), "goodwill" has to be found by capitalizing some version of profit. The cruder methods did this by taking so-many-years' purchase of it. (How many years?) A more high-flown method (sense (3) on page 15) first found "normal profit" (notional interest on the assets - at what rate?); it then subtracted normal profit from total profit, to yield "super-profit"; and it then capitalized this, at a higher rate because of its supposed extra risk. (How much higher?) The late P. D. Leake went a stage further: arguing that competition must soon wipe out super-profits, he explicitly summed them as an annuity of short life.

The main criticism of these methods is that they are not squarely based on future cash flows, but rely unduly on the idea that the balance sheet is

a direct ingredient in the firm's market value; they put the cart before the horse. Also their rates of capitalization may have no clear market counterparts to serve as bench-marks. And their assumptions about normal profits' permanence and super-profits' transience are too simple.

It is significant that the supreme forum for business valuation - the stock market - ignores such methods. Today's analysts would probably laugh at them.

Thanks presumably to the younger generation of accountants - schooled in capital budgets and finance theory, and armed with computers - the "goodwill" methods of valuing seem to have quietly given way to DCF calculations.

"Goodwill" and monopoly

Phrases such as "super-profit" may lead one to think of "economic rent", and to speculate on whether "goodwill" is a sign of monopoly. It may well be. An obvious example is a firm with an exclusive licence. More often, a firm wins an exclusive position and high profits by a mix of good management, research, luck, and some of the many other factors that come to mind.

But consider the very usual case in which a firm earns little in its early years, and gradually works up to its best profits. (A restaurant is said not to break even for two years.) Suppose that such a firm over its whole life earns only the competitive rate of profit. In the later years, profits will grow high, thus raising DCF to more than BS, and so creating "goodwill".

Other difficulties with "goodwill"

In trying to treat "goodwill" like ordinary assets, the accountant has opened a Pandora's box and created enormous difficulties for himself, including:

-    If "goodwill" is carried forward in yearly accounts, major troubles arise. Practice and law both expect that it will in time be written off, like depreciating assets, on a "systematic basis not exceeding the useful economic life". This idea raises perplexing problems: "if you can write it down, you need not; if you cannot, you should." And what is the "life" of (DCF - BS). Why should it not in some cases stretch ahead indefinitely? To force directors to find the life (as the UK Companies Act does) is patent absurdity. The position grows worse where the firm uses current values; if the subsidiary has been kept as a separate entity, presumably its DCF and BS could be revalued to yield a fresh figure for "goodwill" - though whether this would in time shrink to zero is doubtful.

The gap between DCF and BS may point to the existence not of "goodwill" but of genuine assets not hitherto recognized in the accounts. A well-trained group of academics has convincingly argued that much of so-called "goodwill" should be described instead as e.g. trade-marks or brand-names, or explained as the payment of too high a price for the bought firm.[4]

Most accountants hold that, if an asset is to be recognized in the accounts, it should be **separable**, i.e. capable of being bought or sold without the rest of the business. (DCF - BS) is part-and-parcel of the whole, and cannot be sold separately. To treat "goodwill" as an asset is at odds with the rule.

If purchased "goodwill" is to appear in accounts (some accountants hold) why not the home-grown variety too? Is not the latter just as real as a "goodwill" produced by a sale contract? Home-grown's historical cost can be found - the argument runs - by adding various sums that have been spent to enhance the firm's value, e.g. expenditure on training, advertising, and research; but this line of thought soon runs into troubles (how much of the expenditure is wealth-enhancing and how much just normal? What about the costs of unsuccessful advertizing?) And (DCF - BS) may grow for reasons remote from conscious striving: different firms can have different revenue patterns and cost curves (some creating "goodwill") for a multitude of reasons, many of which cannot be untangled with any certainty. What for

instance is "cost" where the chairman is popular in his golf club and so makes contacts that increase the firm's profits? Or where these are sheltered by government barriers?

Getting rid of "goodwill"

We earlier took as example a payment of £100 for a firm with assets worth £80. Most accountants (and the UK Companies Act) regard the resulting £20 "goodwill" as a grating and discordant figure, and therefore as something that must be got rid of quickly. Paradoxically a holding company's own accounts can keep indefinitely the whole £100 as an asset ("investment in subsidiary...,. £100").

In Britain, there are three well-known ways of suppressing the £20:

(1)   It can be set off against ordinary "reserves". This is the most usual method.

(2)   It can be written off against "premium reserve".

(3)   It can be kept for a time as an asset, and gently written off each year against profit.

All three methods may be objectionable:

(1)   The reduction of "reserves" reduces the equity (i.e. the shareholders' investment). This fall may be quite unjustified if the purchase of the subsidiary was sound business; and it may make the gearing seem high. Again, "reserves" may be too small to absorb all the "goodwill" (a situation that Saatchi and Saatchi have surmounted by brazenly putting a "negative reserve" of £125 million into the balance sheet).

(2)   Premium write-off requires costly legal proceedings, and seems wrong in principle, since premiums are in fact capital under another name.

(3)   The yearly write-offs cut profits in a way that may be hard to justify. And over how

many years should the burden be spread? If we accept the argument of earlier pages - that "goodwill" is not in fact an independent asset - then (DCF - BS) has no logical "life". Nor are annual revaluations guaranteed to get us out of the wood; (DCF - BS) might stubbornly refuse to sink to zero, and might indeed share the group's good fortunes and grow. So rules on this point can only tell us to use some completely arbitrary period for the write off, the suggestions ranging from 5 to 40 years.

Conclusions on "goodwill"

Because there have been so many takeovers, etc., in recent years, "goodwill" has grown enormously in importance. The methods of getting rid of it have therefore become a hot political issue, arousing fierce feelings among directors and managers.

As we have seen, some or all of "goodwill" and its write-offs could be lessened where part of (DCF - BS) consists of admissible intangibles that have so far been ignored. These can be given the status of separate assets; and they may not need to be written down. Further, in the unlikely event of the managers' admitting that part of the "goodwill" comes from payment of too high a price, this part should obviously be written off at once. The problem is what to do with the residue.

For the reasons set out earlier, accounting has no clear solution to offer. My suggestion is that the case for treating (DCF - BS) as a pariah, and for getting rid of it fast, has been somewhat over-stated. We may agree that the use of the word "goodwill" and the notion of an independent asset are both objectionable, and yet think that, if the whole subsidiary is valuable, so must part of it be. The fact that a holding company carries forward DCF ("investment in subsidiary") for an indefinite period must surely suggest that its consolidated balance sheet should likewise carry forward (DCF - BS).

In other words, the most logical solution to our problem is to reject the view that (DCF - BS) is a separate asset, with its independent and short-lived benefit stream, and to describe it as what it really is - as e.g. "Part of value (in excess of the net assets) of investment in subsidiary". And, if the investment is not written down, neither should the part be.

If this view is rejected, there seems no basis in logic for deciding how to treat "goodwill". The outcome of the present disputes will therefore probably not be based on reason but on the convenience and political muscle of contenders who, to suit their own circumstances, back one or other of the possible methods.

CHAPTER 6

THE BORDER-LINE ASSETS E.G. BRAND-NAMES

The widening definition of assets

The balance sheet might be described as an inventory whose scope has widened over the centuries. In medieval days, manorial stewards drew up inventories of the obvious assets such as cows and horses; and merchants might list their ships, consignments, and also invisible assets such as rights backed by contract (debtors). In time, manufacturers included their machines and stocks; and then a more sophisticated statement added intangibles such as rent receivable or payable, or rights backed by patents, etc.

Often the assets came into being as a result of transactions with the outside world (e.g. the firm buys a machine). Such a transaction, especially if coupled with tangibility or a legal contract, is a clear test of the asset's existence, and the payment is evidence of value. But accounting is ready to admit also some non-purchased assets, such as a farmer's calves and lambs; a machine made on the premises is acceptable too (and the payments of wages, etc., can give a historical value figure).

Our problem is that we are now under pressure to extend the definition of "asset" much further. Powerful companies are conferring asset status on home-grown intangibles such as brand-names, and so at a stroke of the pen are adding (in some cases) hundreds of millions of pounds to their asset list. And unfortunately there seems to be no clear logic for deciding just how far our list should stretch. Here lies one of the most difficult accounting problems of our generation.

Our training in economics makes it harder to resist claims by the intangibles. Economics teaches us that we should not make physical qualities the touch-stone for wealth recognition, that wealth is not wealth because of its substantial qualities. It is wealth because it is scarce.

We cannot define wealth in physical terms as we can define food in terms of vitamin content or calorific value.[5]

Yet, if money is spent on e.g. research salaries and research equipment, we incline to write off the former and keep the latter. Our somewhat lame defence is that tangibility here adds to the likelihood of future benefits and the obviation of expense.

Reasons for recognizing new kinds of assets

The pressure to expand the asset list has not come only from the vanity of directors. These men may have had other and better reasons. In particular, they argue that the acquisition of subsidiaries and the raising of extra finance gets easier if asset lists are inflated. A sceptic may doubt whether bankers, etc., are so naive as to be impressed by such creativity; but perhaps they are bound by house rules about ratios of debt:equity, etc.

We now face a much weightier argument for BS expansion. Company accounting grew up in an age when the productive assets were familiar things like stores, machines, and the shop or mill. But new forms of organization, science (notably the micro-chip and cell engineering), and the change from manufacturing to service industries are now making that simple picture much less typical. Many benefits no longer come from tangible sources; an electronics company, a firm of public accountants, an advertising agency, a publisher, etc., may have enviable benefit flows yet few old-fashioned assets. Their benefits might loosely be described as coming instead from one or other (or a mix) of research, know-how, training, brand-names, the client list, publisher's titles, and so on. These will rise even further in importance as e.g. markets become more global, TV advertising gets dearer, and the economies of scale continue to grow. Increasingly a balance sheet limited to the traditional assets will fail to describe the firm; BS will be far less than DCF. Then the streams of unrepresented benefits will demand places in the balance sheet (rather like **Six Characters in Search of an Author**). Pressure for fancy new assets may become overwhelming.

The definition of assets

So the problem of defining "asset" is growing harder and more important.

How sure must the future benefits be? Because I hope it will bring me services, my car is an asset. I hope too that my aunt will leave me a legacy; but such hopes are not normally deemed an asset (even though they may already influence my life style). So what is the difference between the two types of hope - between wealth-in-the-hand and prospective-wealth. What turns the latter into the former?

Economic statistics provides us with an intriguing analogy. The statistician who measures a nation's wealth finds totals for rents, profits, etc. from tax data; he then capitalizes these, using market rates. But he cannot put capital values on the earnings of men and women; thanks to the statistically unfortunate fact that slavery has been abolished, this part of the income flow escapes his survey.

So, although a country may be more prosperous if (say) a singer earns high fees, this prosperity is not normally reflected in the wealth statistics. If however the singer turns himself into a company, its shares can be traded in the market, i.e. his fees can now be capitalized. He is promoted into a national asset - not because of improved benefit flows, but because a legal arrangement creates a new marketable unit.

In statistics, then, assets depend on measurable category, and the category list can be lengthened by trivial changes in institutions. To some extent, the same is true of accounting, e.g. the acquisition of a patent can let a firm extend its asset list. Now accounting threatens to extend the list much further on the basis of much weaker evidence.

Official definitions

How do accounting bodies define assets? The FASB tells us that assets are

-   probable future economic benefits obtained or controlled by a particular entity as a result of past transactions or events.

The IASC changes this to

-   an asset is a resource controlled by the enterprise as a result of past events and from which future economic benefits are expected to flow to the enterprise.

Professor Solomons in his **Guidelines** says

-   assets are resources or rights incontestably controlled by an entity at the accounting date that are expected to yield it future benefits.[6]

None of these help us much with our problem. But Professor Solomons goes on to say *inter alia* that the benefits' uncertainty may be so great as to cast doubt on the asset's recognition; and this may well be the decisive factor.

Deprival value reasoning suggests that we should recast the definitions somewhat by stressing the role of the **market** in distinguishing between assets and non-assets, between wealth-in-the-hand and prospective-wealth. The market can provide replacements for the former, but not for the latter; and the former's prices are known and can serve as values. So, while there may well be exceptions, in general we can say that an asset is (1) separable and tradable, (2) at a price that can be predicted with fair accuracy.

Valuing brand names

Is then a brand an asset? It "is simply a collection of perceptions in the mind of the customer", who expects branded goods to maintain a standard of quality.

To the owning firm, a brand's benefits may on occasion be separable and real enough. Usually however the value figures are highly uncertain. Any links with historical costs (past payments for advertizing, etc.) may be very vague. And a current value (based on future receipts) is hard to prove. The valuer must (as with unquoted shares) try to estimate replacement cost, i.e. the price that the market would pay for a similar net receipt stream. He presumably drafts a budget of the yearly revenue that a well-informed market (not the optimistic owners) would expect the brand to yield - having regard to extra units sold thanks to branding, price premium on each unit, less advertising costs, etc.; and he then discounts these figures (at the market rate for equally vague and risky income) and so finds a net present value. Various firms of consultants are already (for a fee) producing impressive documents that purport to do something of this kind.

But such a document will remind the critical reader of the Emperor's New Clothes. Every one of each year's figures must usually be a very dubious guess. The number of years is also highly unsure; some brands (Hovis) seem to last indefinitely, but many (beauty aids) are ephemeral. The discount rate (and its reciprocal the "multiplier") is likewise debatable. In short, the brand's value could lie anywhere in a vast range of plausible figures.

It may also be true that the new asset sometimes breaches the separability rule. Could a brand-name be sold without wrecking the business? Are the extra revenues in fact due solely to the brand-name, or are they not in fact provided jointly from other resources such as training or the distribution system?

So the old-fashioned accountant can claim, with some reason, that to recognize brand-names is to violate time-honoured rules of procedure and prudence.

CHAPTER 7

CONCLUSIONS

In this paper, I have tried to explore some of the problems that face accounting. I have distinguished personal value (e.g. my high hopes of future dividends from my shares) from market value. I have argued that solutions to our problems cannot be found from reasoning based on historical cost; we must use current value, preferably in the form of deprival value. I have discussed the sum-of-the-parts and the whole firm's value, and suggested that a gap between them cannot be explained by conjuring up something with an asset's attributes, but is due to their being almost unrelated market units. And I have described the other intangibles that now press for inclusion in the asset list.

Argument over these intangibles centres on both principle and certainty of measurement. Principle probably forbids us to think of "goodwill" as a separate asset (I have suggested) but might permit us to call it part of the investment in the subsidiary. Principle does not seem to forbid us from treating some of the other intangibles as assets; but lack of measurement certainty may in many cases do so.

Possible roads ahead

Faced with the demands of the upstart assets, we should perhaps consider four alternative proposals:

(1)   The fundamentalist rule

If we want to define "asset" with consistency, and in a way that the lay person will understand, then there seems no choice for us but to dig in our heels and keep the balance sheet completely free of dubious intangibles. In other words, we must stick to what is in many quarters dismissed as an unduly conservative and out-of-date view - to what we may call the fundamentalist rule: no item deserves a place in the balance sheet unless it accords with a narrow

definition, common usage, and certainty of valuation. The new-fangled intangibles should appear in the accounts at most as notes.

(2)   Show assets and dubious assets apart

It would be possible to re-arrange and re-word the balance sheet in a way that distinguishes between assets-proper and dangling debits created by e.g. past expenditure on brands. Companies that want to parade their aspiring intangibles could list them below a new and emphatically marked line, so distinguishing them sharply from the sturdier assets.

(3)   Compromise

We may grudgingly extend the list of acceptable assets when the lobbyists become too importunate, without much regard to principle and consistency. In any case, principle is likely to play less part in the outcome of the argument than political muscle. If powerful companies are hell-bent on inflating their balance sheets, they will probably succeed in doing so. They pay the accountants and auditors.

(4)   Inclusion of DCF

We might take the extreme step of raising BS till it equals DCF.

Why not expand BS to DCF?

Suggestion (4) conflicts with time-honoured procedure, and is not likely to find favour. But could not a radical critic maintain with some reason that companies are in fact trying to boost BS all the way up to DCF level; and that they should do this explicitly instead of boosting it almost all the way with fanciful new assets?

Such a scheme would at least have conceptual honesty. The ordinary net assets would be set at current values; a balancing figure (suitably described) would then be put in to raise the ordinary total to DCF.

Ideally the DCF figure would be the price at which the shareholders would consent to a takeover of the whole company. But clearly something less subjective would be needed. Market capitalization seems the obvious choice (an extension of the scheme proposed by the Scottish CAs' research committee). To avoid dependence on one day's freak quotation, the average quotation for (say) the preceding quarter could be used. Such a figure is indeed wide open to criticism, but is surely far less capricious than the figures for brand-names, etc.

Would not this extreme step be better than a muddled compromise?

47

References

(1)   J. C. Bonbright, Valuation of Property, New York, McGraw Hill, 1937.

(2)   A. D. Hall and R. E. Hagen, "Definition of Systems", J. A. Litterer (ed) Organizations; Systems, Control and Adaption, II, New York, Wiley, 1969, p.43.

(3)   Re Thorn EMI plc. 1989 BALC 612.

(4)   J. Arnold, D. Egginton, L. Kirkham, R. Macve, K. Peasnell, "Goodwill and Other Intangibles", paper for the Accounting Standards Board, 1992.

(5)   L. Robbins, The Nature and Significance of Economic Science, London, Macmillan, 1949, p.46.

(6)   ICAEW, London, 1988.

APPENDIX I

FORWARD AND BACKWARD-LOOKING VALUES

A simple example of an investment can illustrate several points.

Suppose that at year 0, I deposit £100 for two years in a bank that gives 10% interest per year on such deposits. After two years, my investment will therefore realize £121. I visualize this venture with a diagram:

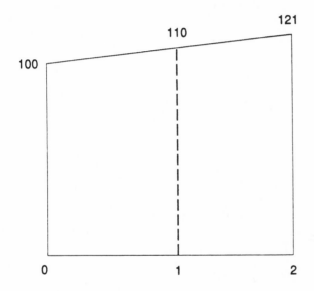

In my accounts at the end of year 1, I probably value the asset at £110. I can justify this in two quite different ways:

(1)   With **backward-looking figures,** such as those in the (historical) account in my ledger:

.... Year 0	Cash deposited	£100
.... Year 1	Interest accrued	10
		£110

(2)   With **forward-looking figures,** i.e. by discounting the £121 due a year hence, and so finding a present value of £110.

So here both the backward-looking and the forward-looking methods yield the same value for my Year 1 accounts.

Does this give any grounds for thinking that the backward-looking values of my other assets should be the same as their market values (linked with market expectations of future cash flows)? The answer must alas usually be an emphatic "no". All the figures in our example are **certain** (fixed by contract); in real life, future figures tend to be uncertain, e.g. annual revenue may rise unexpectedly; and the market discount rate may also change. So market value must fluctuate according to the market's latest estimates and mood.

The example can explain further points:

- Suppose that an escape clause in the agreement lets me close the account at the end of year 1, but with repayment cut to only £90 in full settlement. Here we have another possible value for my Year 1 accounts. But clearly such a low figure (not untypical of some "exit" prices) would give a false impression in my balance sheet - save where in fact I now intend (because of unforeseen needs) to withdraw the £90.

- Suppose the bank gets into difficulties at year 1, and announces that the year 2 repayment will be only £102. The forward-looking value (discounted) sinks from £110 to about £93. Plainly this figure is far more informative than £110; in bad times at least, the forward-looking should replace the backward-looking, even in an otherwise historical system.

30

Appendix II

Examples of deprival value calculations

The various forms of D.V. are illustrated below.

Deprived owner replaces by similar model

Suppose a shopkeeper has an item that sells for £15. He is considering using it up in an advertising display. He can replace it quickly for £10, and so still get the £15 revenue. What is its value, i.e. what will he lose by using it up ("deprival")?

The budgets run as follows:

Example 1

Where alternative budgets show DV = replacement cost.

	Future cash flows if asset	
	(1) is not used up	(2) is used up and replaced
	(= Have budget) £	(= Have Not Budget) £
Outflow Replacement cost of duplicate		-10
Inflow Sale revenue	15	15
Net inflow	15	5
Difference (= benefit of owning asset	10	

The benefit of owning (the difference between (1) and (2)) is £10, i.e. value here equals replacement cost; £10 would "make the owner whole". The budgets could just as well have ignored revenue.

Replacement by an improved model.

If the potential replacement is better than the existing asset, (e.g. has a bigger output), the valuer must try to estimate the benefit of the improvement, and set this off against the replacement price.

As example, suppose an asset costs £500. An improved version has just been invented; it costs £700, but would bring extra benefits worth £480. Clearly it is the likely replacement, and should be put in the budgets:

Example 2

Alternative budgets where the replacement has improved.

	(1) Have £	(2) Have Not £
Outflow Price of improved replacement		-700
Less: Extra benefits from replacement		400
Net outflow obviated by owning	-	-220
Benefit of owning (= net replacement cost	220	

The existing asset can be described as semi-obsolete; its book-value should be written down to the net replacement cost of £220. "Replacement cost" here differs from "replacement price".

<u>Replacement is not worthwhile</u>

Here the owner will either sell shortly or retain in use.

(a) <u>Sale</u>. Suppose that an owner is about to get rid of a stock item.   It costs £100, but is now almost unsellable because of technological change.   It will fetch £7 as scrap.   The budgets again compare the benefits of (1) still owning the asset, and (2) not owning it.

Example 3

Alternative budgets where DV = NRV

	<u>Future cash flows of a firm</u>	
	(1) <u>owning the asset</u>	(2) <u>not owning the asset</u>
	(= <u>Have budget</u>) £	(=<u>Have Not Budget</u>) £
Inflow Scrap proceeds	7 ==	- ==
Difference (= benefit of owning asset)	7 ==	

i.e. where an owner intends to sell an asset and not replace it, replacement cost is irrelevant; deprival value is here net realisable value.

(b) <u>Retention for use</u>. Sometimes an asset is not worth replacing, yet it is worth keeping, e.g. for use as a standby. Here value lies in a zone below RC but above sale proceeds.

The benefits of retention must often seem personal and hazy (what is the utility of that old radio in the attic? Should we try to assess "sentimental value"?). But a firm can often link the benefits to cash flows - as e.g. hire or wages obviated, or as occasional revenues. Then "use value" seems not so much a separate category as shorthand for replacement cost of a (possibly very different kind of) asset or service.

Example 4 deals with such an asset. Its replacement cost is £900. New methods have made it semi-obsolete, but it can at activity peaks yield high benefits ("economic value"); without the asset, these would be got by occasional hire costing £300. Scrap value is £20. The budgets are:

Example 4

Alternative budgets where DV = use-value

| | Future cash flows of a firm | |
	(1) Owning the asset (Have) £	(2) Not owning the asset (Have Not) £
Outflows "Replacement cost" (Hire rentals obviated)	-	-300
Difference (= benefit of owning asset)	300	

i.e. the asset's scrap value and replacement cost in the normal sense are both irrelevant. DV equals use value, which can be measured as the "replacement cost" of hire.

<u>Depreciating assets (i.e. postponed replacement)</u>

As illustration, let us look at yearly flows that worsen with age (probably the normal pattern for a depreciating asset). A machine has a 3-year life. Its price is £210. Repairs are (Year 2) £20, and (Year 3) £30. Earnings fall by £40 in Year 3; this can best be treated like an extra repair.

Suppose further that the replacement has this same pattern of flows. Our budgets must allow for the timing differences between the two flow series. Thus an owner deprived at the start of Year 2 would compare the second year repairs (£20) of his old machine with the first year repairs (£0) of the replacement; and so on.

The simplest way to draft the Have Not budget is to turn the potential replacement's flows into a constant yearly equivalent, much as if the replacment can be got by contract hire for an inclusive yearly rent. The "rent" is here 1/3 £(210+20+30+40) = £100.

Below, each year's actual Have flows and notional Have Not flows are in columns (1) and (2). So the yearly difference between the flows (column (3)) is the net "rent" obviated by ownership; i.e., the benefit of owning for the one year. By the year-end, this has been lost, and so must be written off (the year's depreciation charge); (4) shows the remaining benefits, i.e. the end value.

Example 5

Alternative budgets for a depreciating asset

	(1) Have	(2) Have Not ("rent")	(3) Net benefit for year	(4) Remaining value
	£	£	£	£
Year 0	210			210
Year 1		100	100	110
Year 2	20	100	80	30
Year 3 £(30+40)	70	100	30	-

The calculation could be refined by allowing for interest.*

*   For fuller treatment, see my <u>Inflation Accounting</u>, Oxford, Philip Allan, 1984.

WHAT IF THE PARTS EXCEED THE WHOLE?

Assets versus the Firm's Value

We tend to assume that a healthy firm's profits are big enough to lift its value as a whole (e.g. its takeover price) to more than the sum of its separate net asset values. Thanks to this excess, an enlightened firm that wants to raise assets to current values can usually do so with few qualms.

But an interesting question arises where a firm is in the opposite situation—where it is doing badly, so that the whole's value drops to less than the total of its net assets. Some accountants hold that here the assets—though otherwise sound enough—ought to be written down. Should they? And, if so, on what basis, and which of them should be the sacrificial lambs?

When we hear of such a firm, we naturally think that it probably should sell off its assets and close down, or put the assets to other uses. We think too that nobody would now start an enterprise that earns so little.

But sometimes the managers will not share such pessimism, and will doggedly struggle on. They may believe the firm's troubles to be temporary; they may be anxious to avoid staff unemployment, or to preserve their own pickings. So they continue to trade and to replace old assets, and they may see little need for writedowns.

To reach the kernel of our problem, however, we must suppose that the setback is indeed permanent, and the owners recognise this.

Current value

It is not unreasonable to expect that, if the firm revalues, somehow its new figures will contrive to reflect the low profits now expected. Normally however accounting does not link each asset's current value to the firm's profits but to the asset's market price. We must consider whether we should abandon this practical rule where profits are bad.

Let us assume that the revaluation will be guided by the principles of "value to the business," i.e. deprival value (DV). This does indeed stress the need to write down unfruitful assets. As we all know, it regards value as the likely ill effects on cash flow of an asset's hypothetical loss (e.g. of stores used up in production). The valuer behaves like a thoughtful manager who is costing materials-on-hand for a job. Traditionally he is said to select, in the light of the facts, from three possible figures: DV is the lower of

> cost (i.e. potential outlays on replacement). If the firm were deprived of an asset, it would usually have to buy a new one. The advantage of ownership is that it obviates this payment.

> (where the asset is not worth replacing) the higher of (a) net realizable value (NRV) and (b) value in continued use (future benefits).

If a firm intends to stay in business, it will probably replace any lost asset. So DV is normally the obviated cost of replacement (RC), and not one of the other two possible figures.

This is fortunate. While RC is not free from difficulties, it is simple and objective in comparison with the other values. By relying on the market's replacement price, the appraiser is spared the need for research (or guess–work) about prices in scrap markets, etc.

Assets that will not be replaced

In an unsuccessful firm, however, there is an obvious possibility that assets will not be replaced, and so—according to orthodox rules—will have to be shown at NRV or use-value. Accountants find this a worrying prospect. In particular, measurement of use-value is vexatious (we have traditionally assumed) because it must involve speculation about the asset's future benefits (cash flows) and then their discounting (DCF). Accountants dislike such speculation; and, till recently, most of them were completely innocent of DCF calculation; the idea of using DCF versions of wealth was dismissed scornfully, and use-value was warily given labels such as "economic value" (EV).

Ailing firms can for our purposes be conveniently classified in three groups:

(1). Firms with very short life expectancy.

Where a firm faces a gloomy future, its plans will depend in part on how much money it could raise by selling off its assets piecemeal.

Investment has been likened to a rat-trap: cash slips in more easily than it wriggles out again. Escape becomes less difficult if the assets can be sold off quickly and at high prices. Where they can, a depressed firm is more likely to turn them into cash, and to stop trading.

When such a sell-off is planned, assets should indeed be revalued. The DV of each is now its NRV. And total NRVs equal the whole firm's value.

(2). Survivors with low profits.

But suppose instead that the assets would fetch negligible prices. Here escape from the rat-trap is less easy. The owners' strategy will largely depend on the firm's patterns of cash receipts and payments.

Consider first a trading firm with cash, debtors, stocks, etc. (but no machines or buildings). With these assets, receipts and replacement payments go almost hand-in-hand in the trading cycle—which makes the possible future courses very obvious. Where profits are low, the owners should estimate the likely proceeds of a closing-down sale, and the cost of paying off staff, etc.; and then they must decide whether the net receipts from closing down outweigh the low future net receipts from staying in business.

If they decide to stay, later profit figures will look incongruously small compared with the assets. But these will still be replaced in the course of ordinary trade. Accounting rules and common sense both tell us that the cash, stocks, etc. can hardly be valued at any figure save face value or RC; there is small scope for write-offs. So here the accountant must shrug his shoulders and accept that his odd-looking figures faithfully match the facts.

The same reasoning may apply to a firm with many fixed assets where their replacement dates and costs are spread out smoothly. Here however (if the owners decide to carry on) the idea of writing down fixed assets becomes alluring; low figures seem cautious and wise. But such book-keeping would in fact flout logic. There is no reason for picking on the fixed assets except that their correct values are not obvious. There is likewise no rational way for determining the write-off from each asset; and mere rule-of-thumb deductions would be allocation at its worst. Deprival would here still lead to replacement; so DV is still RC. Again the odd figures match the facts.

(3). Survivors that will later face large outlay.

Where a weakly firm faces big payments at irregular intervals, each payment prospect brings a powerful inducement to get out of the rat-trap at whatever cost. Replacement payments for depreciating assets are an obvious example.

Suppose that revenue has fallen to a point at which profits (after depreciation) can still be earned, but at such a low level that entry to this kind of business would not be justified. Here renewal of a costly asset may well be unwise, and the firm may face closure. The grounds for closure get still stronger where the small profits sink into losses.

If the best plan of such a firm is to close quickly, assets should be written down to NRV. However, DCF budgets may show that the firm should carry on for a while—perhaps many years—enjoying its net receipts as long as ageing assets can be coaxed to work. A little is better than nothing; cash budgets here give wiser advice than income statements.

The argument for write-downs may now be strong. If the discounted benefits from a depreciating asset are less than a suitable slice of RC, then DV sinks to be the benefit's present value. There seems at first sight no escape from the need to find EV.

If however we follow the usual accounting rule, we shall value the benefits at the market price of similar flows (e.g. dividends from companies of comparable risk); probably this is implicit in the use of a suitable discount rate. That market price would "make good" a deprived owner's wealth. So again we use a form of RC, rather than EV.

Jointness

But the above reasoning may often be inapplicable. In particular, it must founder over *jointness*—something ignored by those who hold forth on this topic. A firm's assets very often work as a close-knit team. (Assets that earn in isolation are somewhat rare; firms with only one asset are still rarer.)

Suppose the ailing firm's assets include X and Y. How do we find X's value? We must distinguish between the two possibilities:

> Case (1). X and Y are not a team. Each earns separately (e.g. is an investment in another company). Here we can identify and appraise the net receipts of each.

Case (2). Where X and Y are a team (as is usual), the firm's revenue cannot be unscrambled. The assets earn jointly; the team's flows can be valued, but not those of either X or Y.

Following the normal rule, in case (1) we value X and Y at the market price of similar cash flows.

In case (2), we must go back to our fundamental question: what harm would deprival inflict on cash flows? We face trouble at once. If lack of X would force the firm to close down, we may be tempted to say that X's value is the present value of *all* the firm's flows. But we could with equal justice say the same of Y; so, by this reasoning, the sum of the two asset values would be twice the firm's value. Which is absurd. Clearly neither X nor K can be valued at EV. Likewise any other written-down figure that purports to reflect separate benefits must be meaningless.

Fortunately there may often be an escape way from this difficulty. The firm deprived of X or Y would probably find means of continuing to trade for a while, e.g. by buying a second-hand asset or using extra labour. Then deprival's consequence would be the need to pay for such "replacements"; benefits are again irrelevant, and EV gives way to the accountant's old friend RC, now defined somewhat loosely.

Thus the grounds for ever using EV seem weak. Where an asset will not be sold or literally replaced, normally it can (and should) be given a value that is not EV but a much-expanded version of "RC."

Conclusion

These arguments suggest that accountants should not embark lightly on a downward revision of an ailing firm's balance sheet. Such a write-down would in some cases be irrational, even if the assets' total exceeds the firm's going-concern value.

So can anything be done where the figures look incongruous? Probably the least unsatisfactory plan would be to leave alone the separate DVs, and to deduct a blanket provision from their sum. In this way, the balance sheet total could be cut down to the firm's low going-concern value. (But, if valuation of each asset may be difficult and contentious, valuation of the firm is many times more so.)

Maybe we here face a problem that defies tidy solution.

"GOODWILL"

The Misconceived Asset

For many years, accountants have been wrestling with the problem of how to deal with what they call "goodwill." Perhaps their problem could have been eased by wiser use of words.

"Goodwill" arises because we can value a business in two completely different ways, which can give very different answers. We may either look to the future cash receipts that the owner will get (e.g. from yearly earnings and eventual sale price), and estimate their present value; or we may look at the net assets in the balance sheet, and sum their values.

Let us give the name "DCF" (discounted cash flow) to the figure found by method 1, and "BS" (balance sheet) to that found by method 2. "Goodwill" is the difference, i.e. (DCF—BS). And traditionally accountants have regarded it with disfavour.

As we cannot see the future, the cash flow figures used by DCF must be guesswork; further, the chosen discount rate may be questionable. And many people have perhaps only a vague understanding of the notions underlying DCF. Assets on the other hand can often be appraised with fair accuracy, and seem familiar and friendly; so BS has obvious appeal.

Nevertheless there can be little doubt that DCF, despite its faults, is immensely more important than BS when firms and shares are sold in a sophisticated market. What buyers want is future cash flows; DCF governs price. Thus share prices respond quickly to news affecting the company's prospects, i.e. to changed expectations about flows; whereas good markets seem to neglect BS unless DCF is very low.

When the sale price of a firm or shares is to be estimated, some valuers have tended (thanks to training and tradition) to put much weight on BS. But, if DCF is more important, should they not try to discard this respect for assets? These are perhaps best viewed as no more than evidence of the quality of the DCF estimates. Only in the extreme case where the firm is about to be broken up (i.e. where the separate assets' knock-down sale proceeds constitute the final cash flows) are assets of much relevance.

Suppose a firm buys a subsidiary for £100. If accounting methods had been different, the subsidiary could have been put in the group's consolidated balance sheet as itself— "Investment in Company A . . . . £100." And no-one would normally have argued that there were special reasons for writing down the £100; ordinary valuation rules would have applied, and the whole £100 would usually have stayed in the balance sheet.

But accounting has in fact chosen a different method. It splits up the £100 among individual assets (e.g. if A's machinery is worth £45, then £45 is added to the figure in the balance sheet for the group's machinery).

Suppose next that BS is smaller than DCF, and A's separate assets (spread around the consolidated balance sheet) add up to only £75. To make his figures balance, the accountant must somehow or other squeeze in a new asset of (DCF—BS), i.e. of £100—£75 = £25. A logical description of this would be "One quarter of subsidiary A . . . . £25." Instead, accountants have sometimes used some such phrase as "Excess of A's purchase price over the sum of its net assets. . . . £25"—which is intelligible. But usually they call it "goodwill." And they mistrust its value, and write this off either at once against "reserves," or over a few years against profits.

The word "goodwill" is most unfortunate. It suggests something nebulous and fickle, unworthy to be put alongside trustworthy assets. It suggests too ("the whole equals the sum of the parts") the existence of another asset that has somehow been overlooked and must now be inserted. However, if you measure two quite dissimilar things (here DCF and BS), any gap between the two answers does not prove the existence of a third thing. If a right-hand boot sells for £3 and a left-hand boot for £3, but a pair for £50, there is no £44 third thing lurking in the background; the market views the pair as an economic "whole" different from the separate parts and their "whole." Attempts to value "goodwill" as another "part" would seem irrational and bound to fail.

The accountant's mistrust of "goodwill" can in part be explained by history. When earlier generations of accountants were called on to act as valuers of firms and shares, they automatically turned to BS; DCF was still a somewhat alien notion. But a BS figure sometimes proved unacceptably low; profits on assets of (say) £75 might be £10, whereas "normal" profits would have been only £7.5—suggesting a yearly "super-profit" of £2.5. Here the accountants grudgingly topped up BS with "goodwill," a cautious multiple of super-profit. But they looked askance at their creation, and recommended that it should be written off fast.

They rationalized their feelings with the following argument. If new firms can (in our example) start up in this lucrative field with capitals of only £75, then competition will soon grow and the super-profits will be eaten away.

There may sometimes be a grain of truth in this. But do new subsidiaries in fact earn super-profits for only a short time, and then have dwindling gains? Such firms will not stand still, but will strive to defend their profits by improving procedures. And potential newcomers may face many barriers; they may earn little at first, and have to invest more than e.g. £75 because of the need for training, research, etc. We may well doubt whether the argument is robust enough to justify a rule that "goodwill" is always short-lived and must be written off.

These views suggest that the bias against (DCF—BS) is a hangover from an unsophisticated age when DCF was little appreciated The bias is becoming increasingly unfortunate.

There are more and more firms (in research, advertising, etc.) with few conventional assets yet with lucrative cash flows. If (DCF—BS) is excluded here, balance sheets will increasingly understate assets.

The "life" of (DCF—BS) may well stretch forward indefinitely into an unpredictable future. So the UK law's requirement on directors to write off "goodwill" over its "useful economic life" is an absurdity. And firms forbidden to keep (DCF—BS) in their balance sheets will in its place invent dubious intangibles such as brand-names.

Sometimes a company's assets may indeed have to be written down, but there may be little reason for picking out a subsidiary's (DCF—BS) as the sacrificial lamb. A rational world would keep purchased (DCF—BS) in the balance sheet, with some such description as "One quarter of subsidiary A (being A's value less sums allocated to its individual assets) . . . £25"; and this would be written down only where DCF had shrunk.

The above assumes that (DCF—BS) is created by purchase of another business. But a firm could boost its own book-value by adding some "non-purchased goodwill" to its assets—a step that would until recently have been deemed too shocking to contemplate. How would such "home-grown goodwill" be valued? It might be given a historical cost (spending on advertising, research, etc.); but how much of that spending was for wealth enhancement and how much for normal maintenance? Radical thinking suggests that a more logical plan would be revaluation of the whole firm by DCF. Perhaps "home-grown goodwill" is best seen as a half-hearted step to that extreme.

© William Baxter, *The Times*, 07.01.93.

THE FUTURE OF COMPANY REPORTING

The future will (one hopes) see many reforms in company reporting. Accountants are arguing fiercely over possible improvements. Some sociologists like to explain collective behaviour in terms of a scrummage between conflicting forces in quest of equilibrium; and certainly accounting now lends itself to such interpretation. In the following pages, I discuss some of the major suggestions. But there are plenty of others. One of my minor pets is the share of no par value. We all pay lip service to the view that financial matters should be explained to laymen as clearly as possible. So how can we justify the use of (say) '£1' as part of a share's name, when that figure probably is not - and never was or will be - the share's market value? A government committee considered this matter in 1954, and recommended (the unions' representative alone dissenting) that no par value shares should be legalised (HMSO 1954). The report has ever since lain in its pigeon-hole. Reform is not quick.

Facts *Versus* Guesses

Many writers on accounting have concerned themselves with better ways of showing our traditional figures. They plead for statements that re-arrange, simplify, or amplify historic costs. Useful though some of these changes might be, plainly they are far less radical than those mooted by the more courageous reformers who bid us scrap historic figures in favour of up-to-date values. So let us start by asking ourselves whether (or how far) historic costs are obsolete. The question is often phrased in a different way. Should objective figures be replaced by subjective ones - or, as unkind critics put it, fact by guess-work?

Historic Cost or Current Value?

The issue has grown familiar. Historic cost (its defenders claim) makes book-keeping easy, is well-understood, and is usually reliable. On the other hand, even at the best of times, many of its figures soon cease to match current conditions; during inflation, the gap becomes plain for all to see. Then the precise may become the useless. Up-to-date figures would obviously be better - if only Heaven would give us ones that are safe, simple, and comprehensible. In fact, current values hardly meet these specifications. Many depend on personal judgment. The accountant must first judge between competing types of value (e.g. replacement cost or sale price). Then he must find the actual figures. Published quotations or catalogues may sometimes show these. Often however they demand research in obscure corners, and then perhaps adjustment for such matters as obsolescence. So the end-results may indeed be highly subjective. They become still more arbitrary where the chosen type of value (especially value-in-use) depends on estimates of future cash flows. However, we make the most important decisions of our personal lives largely on the strength of our beliefs about the future; and likewise a firm's success depends in good part on predictive skill. So we cannot dismiss current value just because it is subjective.

Here then is a contentious problem that is sure to bedevil accounting for many years. Most likely the outcome will be some sort of compromise. And we shall be helped to strike a workable mix if we are clear on the theories at stake.

Blemishes in Historic Cost

The good points of historic costs are obvious to anyone with the slightest experience of book-keeping. Their objectivity was mentioned above. They give a clear record of stewardship. They are simple, and lend themselves to neat and easy applications, such as control of stock and factory costs. And the auditor finds them eminently tickable.

What are their faults? The most patent is their inability to reflect market change. Their asset values thus get out-of-touch with reality. In the historic cost balance sheet, assets are mis-stated. In management calculations, historic costs misrepresent the sacrifice of using up assets as input; a factory's salesmen seem biased (rather surprisingly) in favour of prices that are too low, and out-of-date costs may aggravate this weakness, particularly during inflation. Another grave fault is that historic cost corrupts the income statement during inflation. It does so by subtracting old costs from current sales. When there is a time-lag between cost date and sale date, a cost £ has a higher purchasing power than a sales £; so the cost figure is too low in comparison with the sale figure, and income is over-stated. If you concede that it is wrong to subtract dollars from francs, you must concede too that it is wrong to subtract the (say) 1970-£ from the very different 1980-£; yet accountants do this when charging (for instance) historic cost depreciation.

Allocation

The artificial slicing-up of costs (the process of allocation) must suggest a likely weakness in costing and accounting. And, while an ingenious accountant can no doubt slice up current values, historic cost gives him far more scope. Because the historic cost ledger does not seriously attempt to mirror the current world, the accountant can split and re-arrange its figures to his heart's content, without the constraints imposed by comparison of figures with economic reality. Bacon tells us that the first distemper of learning is 'when men study words and not matter'. Had he known a modern accountant, he might have substituted 'figures' for 'words'.

The case against allocation was first put by Edwards (1938) and by Coase (1938) in memorable issues of *The Accountant*. Some thirty years on, Thomas (1969) re-stated the case. The arguments took somewhat different lines. Edwards and Coase relied on the plain logic of economics: if you want to find your best plan of behaviour (e.g. optimum output level), you must study the figures for the various alternatives that face you; any items that do not affect the answers are irrelevant, and can be left out; therefore costs that are fixed (i.e. that are not changed by the plans being considered) should be ignored. Further, to average a fixed cost is to mislead; for most decisions, marginal (and not average) cost is what matters. Accordingly, accountants are wrong when they split fixed costs between, for example, departments or jobs or processes, or between successive income statements. Thomas, on the other hand, centred his attack on the 'incorrigibility' of allocated costs. The different figures found by different methods of allocation cannot be tested; so which should you take as a guide? It is easy to think up very different figures for a job's cost, by allocating on direct labour or prime cost of machine-hours or whatever; and your costing text-book cannot tell you which method is 'right'.

It is hard to be sure how far today's accountants have seen the light in this matter. The growth of 'marginal costing' (and reliance on 'gross margin', rather than surplus after charging 'full cost') is evidence of progress. There seems a fair chance that, as the economists' ideas sink in, allocation will get less common — thus weakening the need for some of the reforms proposed in earlier chapters.

Matching

Historic cost gives colour also to another fallacy (as it must seem to most theorists) — namely the notion that income is best found by a 'matching' process. According to supporters of this view, costs must be matched with revenue 'on a cause-and-effect basis' or 'in a systematic and equitable manner'. Thus cost is not directly linked with change in wealth. Surely, however, costs cannot exist *in vacuo*; only a slave to the ledger can think of 'flows of cost' that are divorced from assets. To my mind, it is the asset value which is fundamental, and the sacrifice of value is secondary. That is, depreciation charges are rational if they mirror decline in the asset's value, and suspect if they are merely historic cost figures manipulated by a ledger clerk. 'Matching' hardly seems a sign of profound thought, and has been used to support many dubious propositions.

Inflation

In the eyes of most accountants, historic cost's most worrying feature is that it cannot respond to inflation. Earlier paragraphs have touched on two aspects of this fault — under-valuation of assets, and over-statement of income where costs are subject to time-lag. But there is also a third aspect, sometimes more important. Historic cost financial statements cannot show *real* change in values. Even if directors decide to modify historic cost by revaluing assets, the financial statements still do not show whether appreciation is merely in line with inflation, or greater or less. To find real change, financial statements must adopt the hybrid reform that uses both current values and the general index (i.e. both current value and constant purchasing power). Two areas then grow clearer:

(1) *Non-monetary items*

Suppose a firm starts with £100, and spends this on land. At the end of the year, the land is revalued at £130, and the general index has moved from 100 to 120. Our future balance sheet may show the end-position in one or other of these forms:

	i Historic cost £	*ii* Current value £	*iii* Hybrid end-£
Asset	100	130	130
Starting capital	100	100	120
Revaluation surplus, unrealised:			
Nominal		30	
Real			10
	100	130	130

Column *i* gives no information about the value change. *ii* recognises it, but fails to show its full significance. *iii* shows that it is in fact a modest real gain, still unrealised.

(2) *Monetary items*

It the firm instead keeps its £100 as cash, the figures change
to:

	i Historic cost £	*ii* Current value £	*iii* Hybrid end-£
Cash	100	100	100
Starting capital	100	100	120
Loss on holding money			(20)
	100	100	100

Here *ii* cannot reveal the loss in value of the cash (because
crude current value accounting has no way of looking beyond
the *nominal* values of coins, etc.). *iii* tells the full story.

Suppose again that the monetary item is negative (e.g. land
is financed with a loan). The balance sheets now become:

	i Historic cost £	*ii* Current value £	*iii* Hybrid end-£
Asset	100	130	130
Loan	100	100	100
Revaluation surplus:			
Nominal		30	
Real			10
Gain on owing			20
	100	130	130

Here *iii* is far superior to its rivals. It shows that the firm
made a modest real gain by holding land, and a bigger one by
being in debt. The two gains are not unlike in nature: both
are found when the general index is put to simple use; both

are unrealised (until the asset is sold, and the load repaid), and so — if we are at all cautious — should be kept distinct from operating gains. It is sad that *Statement of Standard Accounting Practice 16* (ASC 1980) rejects this form of gearing adjustment, and demands instead one that is convoluted and deceptive. We must hope that the simple and rational form will win in the end.

Making Current Value Workable

One can favour current value, and yet admit that its difficulties and dangers are formidable. What can we do to lessen them? Many improvements and safeguards will no doubt come in time. Better indices will be made available by bodies such as the Central Statistical Office; acceptable short-cuts will suggest themselves (e.g. less valuable machines can be revalued with an index based on the detailed re-appraisals of more valuable machines); and auditors will learn how to detect weak procedures. Theory suggests three further aids to improvement:

(1) *Use of Deprival Value*

This can to some extent curb over-optimism. More important, deprival value clarifies the problem of how to pick the best form of current value. For it must be thought of, not as an extra value, but as a system for choosing between the main contenders for the current value role — usually replacement cost, value-in-use (or economic value), and net realisable value.

To use this selective concept, one must ask how the firm's cash flow would in fact be worsened if the firm were deprived of the asset (say, by using-up as input, or loss by fire). Deprival normally leads to replacement; here replacement cost measures the asset's value to the firm. But, where

278

replacement is not worth-while, the worsening hinges on loss
of the asset's contribution in its best role. So we can define
deprival value as the lower of (a) replacement cost and (b) the
highest of its possible contributions — usually either value-in-
use or net realisable value.

It is often suggested that there is a clash between the values
suitable for management and for outsiders. Deprival value to
some extent gets rid of this problem. It relies on the figure
that a manager should use in his own budgets (e.g. when he is
costing stores to find whether a job is worth doing). Thus,
the manager's logic fashions the published report too.

(2) *Use of Holding Gain Figures*

Current cost accounting is today proclaimed as the cure for
many of accounting's ills (e.g. in *SSAP 16*). In some ways, it
can indeed bring improvement. But I suspect that its advocates
confuse two issues. They are right to recommend current
value for assets, and for costing inputs in management's
budgets. But does this mean too that current cost gives the
best charge for income measurement (i.e. that income should
not include holding gain on inputs)?

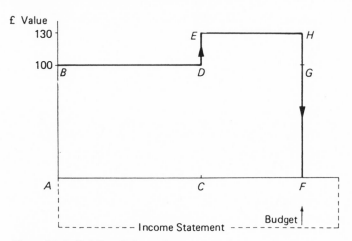

Figure 12.1 *Holding Gain on Input*

80

Suppose that I buy an asset, retain it until it appreciates, and then consume it as input. The story can perhaps be told most simply as in figure 12.1. This shows time on the horizontal axis, and value on the vertical axis. I start the year with £100 (*AB*) and spend this on the asset. At date *C*, replacement cost jumps to £130, so I make a holding gain of £30 (*DE*). Still later, at date *F*, I draw up budgets to see if it is worthwhile to use up the asset on some project. In the budgets (or a balance sheet at *F*), I should assuredly now value the asset at its current cost of £130 (*FH*). But my income statement should not look only at the one moment in time, *F*, but at the whole period, *A* to *F*; budget and income statements have different aims and time scopes. Suppose further the project's revenue to be £136. The budget should put the advantage of going ahead (as seen at date *F*) at £136−130 = £6. But the income statement starts at date *A*, and should put the period's gain at £136−100 = £36: it cannot logically record the exit of £36 (*GH*), but not its entrance (*DE*), as current cost accounts are apt to do.

The problem can be re-stated by putting the figures into alternative income statements. *i* gives the traditional form, *ii* gives the crude current cost version. A reformed income statement need not ignore current cost; *iii* uses it, and also includes holding gain, thus covering the year's events fully:

	i Historic cost £	*ii* Current cost £	*iii* Current cost and holding gain £
Revenue	136	136	136
Realised holding gain			30
			166
Input cost			
Historic	100		
Current		130	130
Income	36	6	36

iii has a merit that should command respect. As we have seen, historic cost gives precise information that may not he helpful; current value gives helpful information that may not be precise. *iii* contrives to make the best of both worlds, showing the helpful information yet ending with objective income.

(3) *Real Capital Maintenance*

But, you will rightly object, the above argument belittles the case for current cost by ignoring general price change. The firm's owners are not really richer by £36, unless £100 at date *F* will still buy them the same basket of goods as at date *A*. During inflation, 100 end-£s will buy less than 100 starting-£s, so real profit is then less than £36, and current

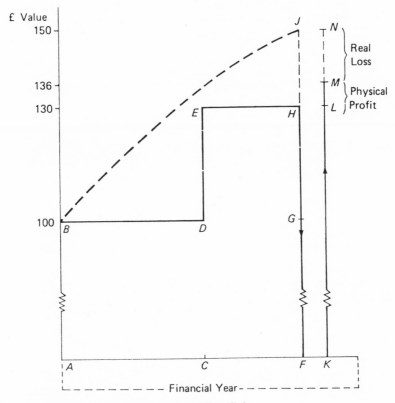

Figure 12.2 *Nominal and Real Holding Gain*

cost accounting produces — so its proponents claim — the right reduction.

Well, does it? Probably not, if the test of capital maintenance is the owners' purchasing power; the price of a given asset is not likely to move exactly in step with the general index, and may indeed move quite differently. Current cost accounting is thus not true inflation accounting, and does not meet the test of real capital maintenance. It looks instead to physical capital maintenance (i.e. replacement of the given input). But this involves great practical difficulties (e.g. how do we define such replacement if the assets are subject to fast technological change?) It involves too great conceptual difficulties. In particular, if the price of the given asset falls steeply (consider electronic machines), the current cost of this input must fall too; so operating cost tends downwards, and profit upwards, when the firm makes a severe holding loss. Can such bizarre figures be helpful?

Reformers must therefore choose between three main types of inflation accounting for their income statement. The following figures assume a 50% rise in the general index.

	i Historic cost adjusted with general index	*ii* Current cost	*iii* Current cost and real holding gain
	£	£	£
Revenue	136	136	136
Real realised holding loss £130 − £100 × 1.5			(20)
			116
Input cost			
Historic (corrected) £100 × 1.5	150		
Current		130	130
Profit (loss) by test of:			
Real capital maintenance	(14)		(14)
Physical capital maintenance		6	

Here current cost accounting *ii* is less cautious than its rivals, *i* and *iii*. And here, *iii* again shows how a subjective estimate (current cost, £130) can be harnessed to fairly objective profit (minus £14, found not by personal judgment but by the external index of purchasing power).

If you find diagrams helpful, you can set out this example as in figure 12.2. Here capital (corrected with the general index) is assumed to follow some such line as *BJ*, rising over the period to *FJ* (£150). This (and not replacement cost *FH*) is what must be recovered if real capital is to be maintained. But in fact the revenue is only *KM* (£136). So there is a real shortfall of *MN* (£14). But, by the physical test, there is a profit of *LM* (£6).

Standards

Until the middle of this century, accounting's development was due to countless anonymous men who kept trying out new methods within their own firms. If the methods proved bad, they were scrapped; if good, they became part of the fabric. But then there came — with little debate or conscious decision — a profound change. Power to make (or halt) improvement slipped largely into the hands of external authority, in the shape of standards committees or government bodies like the Securities and Exchange Commission.

Origins of Standards

The process was due in part to attacks by the financial press. This had hitherto been respectful; but, after several major scandals, it began to criticise and (far worse) poke fun at accountants. Some of the criticism concerned fraud by managers (e.g. at McKesson and Robbins), and led to improved audit methods. But some concerned accounting principles. If two carpenters reach two different answers when measuring a plank's length, at least one of them must be incompetent; and if two accountants (our critics proclaimed) reach two different values for stock or profit, likewise one or both must be incompetent.

Accountants might have countered by trying to educate the public. They could have pointed out that, in an economy with many thousands of firms and auditors, a few blunders are inevitable (and will continue no matter how much our rules and practice are tightened up). They could also have explained that planks and values are utterly unlike in nature: measurement of the physical may involve principles far different from those governing measurement of, for example, the aesthetic and economic; just as judges of ice skating can award divergent marks without incompetence, so too accountants can assess values differently. However, accountants did not try to spread understanding. Instead they sought salvation in standards. National and international bodies now issue these galore.

General Acceptance of Standards

The switch to standards has for the most part been accepted willingly enough, and even with enthusiasm. Accountants, the press, and City bodies welcome them. The general expectation is that standards must be a means to great improvement in both thought and practice. Thus a memorandum from the equipment leasing companies to the Accounting Standards Committee explains the difficulties of lease accounting, and asks for guidance; its authors apparently see nothing odd in such pleas by themselves, the experienced authorities on the subject, to outsiders.

True, protests have come from industries that feel themselves outside the general truths. Thus the UK's property companies have won a dispensation in the depreciation standard (on the grounds that revaluation of their buildings removes need for depreciation). And US oil companies are said to have spent $3 million in lobbying successfully against a standard on the tax treatment of dry holes. However, the more usual complaints come from those who want not less but more: standards emerge too slowly, the standard-makers give too little energy to their task (and should be full-time), and there should be sterner powers of enforcement.

Merits of Standards

If pressed, an accountant would perhaps list the merits of standards under such headings as:

(1) *Help with decisions on accounting methods*

Standards ease one's work. Faced with a problem, the accountant can look up the relevant standard. No need for professional judgment.

(2) *Uniformity*

Standards make for comparable figures (between companies, etc.). They make too for uniform practice, and, if he has done exactly the same as all his fellows, how can an individual accountant be found guilty of malpractice?

(3) *Help against improper pressures*

A forceful tycoon may try to browbeat associates into publishing slanted figures. Written standards stiffen the opposition.

(4) *Conceptual enlightenment*

When it is dealing with value measurement (e.g. stock values, inflation), a standards committee must first delve into abstract principle to find guidance. Knowledge thereby grows. Our figures will soon satisfy intellectual tests as never before.

Some Worries over Standards

Doubtless one should not look a gift-horse in the mouth. But I must confess that I do not altogether share the general euphoria. One worry is over the eventual scope and number of standards. No limits have yet been suggested. So where will standard-making end? Will every petty aspect of our work be governed by standards? One can picture the future accountant trying to digest and apply an endless flood of standards, ever-growing in complexity and detail, and issued by many authorities with perhaps conflicting aims and powers. The cost of making the standards will be high. Policing them effectively will be still more costly, and will stir up much resentment.

More important doubts concern the conceptual merit of standards. Can committees really solve intellectual problems that baffle everyone else? The struggles of the Accounting Standards Committee with inflation accounting are hardly reassuring. And will standard-makers be willing to recognise fresh circumstances and past errors, and then modify old standards? Can standards be combined with experiment and improvement? Reliance on standards — it seems not fanciful to suppose — must sap the individual urge to seek and apply new methods. The accountant of today is skilful and knowledgeable with given rules, less good at criticising and improving them. Standards must tend to strengthen this characteristic. And, as a glance at any up-to-the-minute text-book will confirm, standards are already giving a bias to education; students are being taught to respect the official rules of measurement rather than the economic facts.

History and Standards

Accountants are not unique in this matter. Our societies are much like the guilds into which merchants and craftsmen organised themselves for many centuries. And those guilds were at pains to prescribe standards — again like us, largely because of scandals. Thus the clothiers were denounced in a 1552 Act as being guilty of 'many subtle sleights and untruths'; among their 'great defects and frauds' was the use of coarser yarn for the middle than for the (more visible) ends of cloth. Therefore uniform standards of quality and dimension were prescribed in the utmost detail. Enforcement was 'committed to men of gravity' within the guilds, and often backed up by the state. Over the centuries, Parliament passed 311 laws for the wool trade alone.

And what did these well-meant standards achieve? They are now remembered chiefly for their faults. In the end, they tethered production to obsolete methods. They hampered mobility. They hindered response to the 'humours' of customers, especially foreign customers. They confused businessmen: 'there are now many laws in force' the government confessed in 1622, 'which for their number and contradiction do perplex and entangle the makers of cloth, and make it hard to be discerned what the law is'. The era of *laissez faire* and the Reform Act swept most of the standards into the dustbin. So history is hardly encouraging.

A Conceptual Framework

One often-heard comment is that standards committees ought to publish an agreed conceptual framework; and the US Financial Accounting Standards Board is indeed making some attempt to do so. The argument runs thus. So far, standards have been drafted on an *ad hoc* basis (i.e. as convenience and clamant need dictate). They do not follow a clear scheme; nor do they fit neatly into any all-embracing set of high principles. If only such a set could be enunciated, many of our vexing problems would vanish, standards would become still better, and mavericks would rejoin the herd.

We all agree that the quest for truth is a good thing, and that research should be encouraged. But is there not some contradiction in the preceding argument — and a contradiction that strengthens one's doubts about standards? Mankind's experience in other spheres suggests that the best way to establish principles is to experiment and test. It follows that accounting should freely and actively test new ideas and methods. So ... good standards depend on good principles; principles need experiment; experiment needs freedom; standards limit freedom; ... and therefore we cannot have good standards?

Wary Ending

This book has tried to sketch desirable reforms for the future. But the one sure thing about the future is that it is unsure. Accounting is likely to develop in ways beyond our imagining. For instance, when we talk of financial reports, we tend to think of printed paper sent by big corporations to many owners. This picture may soon be false. The 'many owners' are already dubious: the share-holdings of individual investors are said to be falling fast, and by 1979 to have sunk to only 27% of the total. Many of the 'big corporations' (both state-owned and private) now look sickly; these dinosaurs may have to make way for back-bedroom firms that can flourish thanks to the new information technology. And 'printed paper' may well turn into flashes on a screen, powered by electricity from windmills. Another possibility: small firms may revolt against costly reports, and win the right to dispense with all complexities and even the audit.

The Ultimate Limitation of Reports

Many of the previous chapters have enlarged on the usefulness of financial statements to investors and other users. Their authors have told you in particular about decision-making, and stressed the role of financial statements — in their present form, and still more with future embellishments — as aids to the prediction of the all-important cash flows.

No doubt the facts and reasoning are sound; and we should not dampen the enthusiasm of reformers. Many worth-while improvements are within our reach. But perhaps a note of caution — even of pessimism — will not come amiss. We must look at the original function of accounting, and ask ourselves whether its structure can in fact bear the weight of all the tasks that we now propose to pile onto it. Do we expect too much? We should not ask a faithful old cart-horse to learn the violin.

The basis for book-keeping was laid in medieval Italy. At first it was single-entry, probably developed as a means for keeping tabs on debtors and creditors. This job is always important; but it was of exceptional importance when lack of good coinage led to elaborate barter transactions and credit transfers between several parties. Later would come accounts for assets, and then for the merchant's side-ventures such as consignments and voyages. Lastly, the book-keeper achieved full double-entry by adding accounts for expenses and revenues. However, businessmen for long showed scant interest in the results of the whole firm, and annual financial statements — or even an annual balancing of the books — were rare until (say) the Victorian age.

Up to this age, accounting could do its work supremely well. It was indeed praised as the perfect science. Nearly all its figures were historical, and were endowed with certainty and objectivity by legal contracts or links with physical quantities (e.g. cash). There were few problems of income measurement or asset valuation. For centuries, the trial balance remained a mere check on arithmetical accuracy, and the profit and loss account a mere bonfire — used, say, when the ledger was full — for getting rid of figures that could be of no further service.

When companies and income tax grew important (from the mid-nineteenth century onwards), annual reckonings became necessary. The ledger then proffered a ready-made set of figures: the trial balance blossomed into the balance sheet, and the profit and loss account was promoted from bonfire to income statement.

The twentieth century saw many minor improvements. The items were marshalled and grouped, fuller detail was shown, secret reserves grew rare, etc. But the annual figures remained the unintended by-product of a system designed for another end.

The limitations of this system have grown increasingly clear. They have indeed given academic accountants and financial journalists much of their bread-and-butter. They have prompted analysts and journalists to demand improvements in both quality and quantity. They have irked the accountant himself, who naturally would like his handicraft to command respect.

The criticism has led to a grand debate on the future of reports. For which users are they intended (managers, shareholders, workers, the government . . .)? What do these users want the figures for? How much can they understand? Should reform tinker with existing methods (e.g. superimpose current values, and adjust for inflation), or should it scrap the whole system in favour of some brave new substitute (e.g. cash flow budgets)? And so on.

As we have seen, the most widely-accepted answers to these questions base themselves on decision-making: reports are good when they help us select our strategy in such matters as consumption and investment. Knowledge of the future helps these decisions. Thus reports should be judged by their ability to shed light on cash flow prospects.

A Minor Heresy

Worthy people exhort us to maintain open minds. So perhaps we should wonder for a moment whether this stress on decision is wholly justified. After all, mankind fortunately takes interest in all manner of odd things, including things that are useless for decisions. We like to acquire, and are even willing to pay for, information about quasars, Australian

290

cricket, and the Emperor Claudius, though we are not likely
ever to face decisions about any of them. The more intelligent
the man, the keener his curiosity. So why should we not take
interest in a company's story, whether or not it affects our
decisions?

Your keen reformer will brush aside this quibble. And he
has at least one sound argument for his impatience. When
accountants are trying to improve reports, they must have
some compass to direct their course. The notion of help-with-
decisions has served well. So, even if we have reservations about
that notion, we shall be wise to act as if it is unquestionably
right. 'As if' (the philosophers assure us) can be a respectable
aid to sound thought.

How do Reports Aid Decision ?

But now another question presents itself. In what sense
exactly can reports — however much improved — help with
decisions? I suspect their scope must be limited. Their assets,
income, etc. are unlikely to predict future cash flows in any
direct sense. Only a cash budget could give direct help; and
of course even it may be completely falsified by later events.

What accounting can do however is to give a framework of
background information. And this may help decisions, even if
it seems to have no direct bearing on them. A map of Germany
does not tell me explicitly whether to have a meal in Frankfurt,
or to go walking in the Black Forest; yet I shall be less able
to make such holiday decisions if I lack the framework given
by the map. In this limited sense of background information,
financial statements *are* an important (though indirect) aid
to decision.

(Those who belittle financial reports should remember
Miss du Maurier's tale *The Scapegoat*. Its hero, travelling in
France, chances to meet a Frenchman who is his double.
The Frenchman is tired of his life, and forces the hero to
swap identities — to take over an unknown home, family,
mistress, and factory. Next day, the hero — among other

embarrassments — suddenly has to visit his factory and decide its future with watchful subordinates. He has only a few minutes to brief himself for the ordeal. How should he have done this? If he had been trained in business, he would have known that his very best sources of quick information were the annual financial statements. They might not provide ready-made answers to the firm's problems, but would give a good starting point by depicting its size, assets, and recent history; and they help to ask the right questions.)

The Original Purpose is Still Fundamental

However, even if reports help decision in only an indirect way, we have no cause to feel apologetic about them. They are important. Their original task, as we have just seen, was to provide evidence that the accounting records have been kept properly, and to show what has happened to the owners' wealth. This they still do. They are the culmination of complex and exacting work. Much of it may have become routine, yet it is essential for business survival. A firm may very well find itself with no future cash flows to predict if its accounting records are not in order.

Conclusion

It would be agreeable to end this chapter with firmer conclusions. But accounting theory must often be better at seeing difficulties than finding solutions. At least we have established that tomorrow's accountant will take part in important and interesting debates whose outcome will affect his work profoundly. Our future will not be dull.

292

References

Coase, R.H. (1938), Business organisation and the accountant, *The Accountant*, (various articles in issues between October and December).

Edwards, R.S. (1938), The nature and measurement of income, *The Accountant*, (various articles in issues between July and October).

Thomas, A.L. (1969), The allocation problem in financial accounting theory, *Studies in Accounting Research 3*, American Accounting Association (AAA).

Accounting Standards Committee (1980), Current cost accounting, *Statement of Standard Accounting Practice 16*, ASC.

Committee on Shares of No par Value (1954), Shares of no par value, *Report of the Committee on Shares of No Par Value*, HMSO Cmnd 9112.

INCOME
A Will-o'-the Wisp?

INTRODUCTION

Forgive me if I start by reminding you that former generations of students were happily ignorant of all ideas about income concepts. Much the same could be said of their teachers. Hatfield's *Accounting* (1927) introduces the topic; but awareness was slow to spread. The subject was still given only a sketchy and naive treatment in the textbooks of the 1950s.

One reason for this deficiency is that the study of income is so difficult. If you get an assured wage of £x in cash per week, you may not unreasonably say that your income is £x per week. But as soon as the facts get less plain—as they will in even a simple firm—the difficulties start to pile up. Both the concepts and the task of choosing the figures are beset with doubts. So you must approach this part of your course with limited hopes. You will find yourself faced with many alternative ways of viewing income; and the accountant must again and again make arbitrary choices between different figures that all have some merit and some defects. You may well in the end conclude that the accountant's best efforts must be only a poor attempt to weigh the imponderable.

The aim of income measurement

Why then do we struggle to find such an elusive quantity? We use it for many tasks: to show a firm's progress; whether further investment is justified; and how much tax is payable. More important, it is a guide to the owner's consumption. A reasonable man may decide to spend more or less than his income; but he knows that over-spending now will lessen his future welfare, and under-spending will raise it; so he needs a baseline that reveals the "over" or "under".

That notion gets support from Sir John Hicks' much quoted definition: a man's income is "the maximum value which he can consume during a week, and still expect to be as well off at the end of the week as he was at the beginning".

II. INCOME AS GROWTH IN WEALTH

Flows and capital maintenance

The fun starts when we try to measure "can consume" and "well off". A highly abstract approach looks to flows of satisfaction: "psychic income" is a person's flow of utility from consumption. Accounting must needs content itself with something more down-to-earth. It equates "well-offness" with capital (wealth) measured in money. And it then links income with "that amount which can be consumed without encroaching on capital" (Adam Smith's words). Which means that we must use ideas of *capital maintenance*; and that to measure income we must first know how to measure capital.

This may seem somewhat at odds with the helpful analogy of the stream and lake—the view that income is a flow during a period, whereas capital is wealth at a given moment (such as the year-end). But there is in fact no contradiction. If not dissipated, the flow adds to wealth. So, with straightforward facts, we may say that income for a period is the difference (after allowing for the owner's drawings and in-payments) between opening and closing capitals.

97

Whole firm *versus* separate assets

Now for the first source of confusion. When we approach the task of measuring wealth, we must be explicit about the contrast between measuring the whole firm as a composite unit, and measuring the separate assets one-by-one:

A. *Whole firm.* Here the firm is valued on a forward-looking (*ex ante*) basis—much as if it is to be sold—by discounting its expected future cash flows. (You will recall the rather similar DCF budgets used to find whether a new asset is worth buying.) The individual assets do not enter directly into the calculation.

B. *Asset-by-asset.* Here the accountant in effect looks around and draws up an inventory (his balance sheet) of all the separate assets and liabilities that he recognizes.

Clearly A's figures for future flows must be highly subjective (indeed, often wild guesses); sometimes indeed they may be only vague impressions at the back of the mind. B's figures often are relatively sober and clear; they emerge from the respected processes of book-keeping; and we find them friendly because they echo our childhood's notions of wealth. (We were told of the Sleeping Beauty's castles and fields and flocks and jewels, not her DCF expectations). The paradox is that we use A—despite its uncertainties—for the really fundamental decisions (e.g. on the firm's price at a takeover, or whether to close down a branch), and B for lesser tasks (routine yearly accounts). Or, to put the matter in another way, A's concepts satisfy an elegant logic, though its figures must be shaky; whereas B's logic is crude, even if its figures are fairly sure and objective.

Ex ante *income*

Routine accounts do not use A. But perhaps we should in passing ask what balance sheets would look like if A were used.

Suppose that, at date O, the owner of a firm expects it to yield a net cash flow of £1,000 at the end of each year, and his capitalisation (interest) rate is 10%; opening capital is thus £10,000, as in column *i* of Table 1. If all goes as expected, the end balance sheet (date 1, column ii) will duly put income at £1,000.

But suppose instead that the owner's outlook changes at date 1, and that his DCF value jumps to £12,000. This could be because he now foresees future receipts of £1,200 per annum. However, let us consider a more interesting possibility—that he still expects to get £1,000 per annum, but his interest rate shifts to 8.3%; £1,000 divided by .083 = £12,000. He could now draft his balance sheet as in column *iii*, raising income at a bound to £3,000. Egged on by this lush figure, he might then—e.g. with the help of a £2,000 loan—withdraw £3,000 in cash for a consumption splurge. But mark the aftermath. That big withdrawal would reduce future net receipts (say, by interest on the loan) from £1,000 to about 10/12 x £1,000 = £833. Yet his capital would still be £833 divided by .083 = £10,000. So this system of income measurement maintains a "well-offness", not of future receipts, but of their capital value. Hicks seems to have this interpretation in mind when he amplifies his words quoted earlier to re-define income as the maximum amount which can be spent during a period if there is to be an expectation of maintaining intact the capital value of future receipts (in money terms)"—("Hicks 1") .

TABLE 1

Opening and closing balance sheet—wealth measured *ex ante*

	i	ii	iii	iv
Date	0	1		
		Expectations do not change	Expectations change	
			"Capital" not revised	"Capital" is revised
Cash		1,000	1,000	1,000
DCF value	10,000	10,000	12,000	12,000
	10,000	11,000	13,000	13,000
Capital: original	10,000	10,000	10,000	10,000
gain				2,000
				12,000
Income		1,000	3,000	1,000
	10,000	11,000	13,000	13,000

99

Maintainable Consumption level

But most of us would think accounts less than perfect if they told us to spend £3,000 this year and only £833 thereafter. We should prefer a system that keeps this year's income at a maintainable £1,000 per annum. We can do so by giving capital a £2,000 boost (as in column iv) to £12,000—which, after all, is the figure that the owner would have used from the start if he had been a smarter prophet. The extra £2000 can be labelled "capital gain", if we use that overworked phrase in the sense of capital revision.

To stress constant consumption rather than its present value, Hicks offers us an alternative to his earlier definitions. Income becomes

> the maximum amount a man can spend this week, and still expect to maintain future spending at this week's level. ("Hicks 2").

A third definition again stresses constant consumption, by allowing for change in the price level (as during inflation): "future spending must then be defined in *real terms* ("Hicks 3").

Forward-looking income calculations (like Table 1) are almost unknown to routine practice, and probably always must be. Yet the thinking behind them has influence. Hicks' words are, for instance, quoted as gospel by advocates of inflation accounting. And the notion of *maintainable income*—useful as a guide to both investment and consumption—has forced published reports to show a "profit on ordinary activities" that omits capital gains and also "extraordinary" items (not from ordinary activities) and "exceptional" items (from ordinary activities, but abnormal in size). But the selection and measurement of these items must often involve arbitrary judgements.

III. GROWTH IN NET ASSETS

If we brush aside psychic flows and *ex ante* aspirations, we came to familiar ground. We link income with growth in the sum of the net assets, listed item by item.

Balance sheet *versus* profit and loss account

The income figure appears in both balance sheet and profit and loss account. But we can choose which of the two calculations to deem senior. Do we put our main stress on comparison of:

> *a.* net assets at the start and end of year, or

> *b.* costs and revenues?

In principle, the two yield the same answer. But in fact each is apt to colour the thinking of its votaries—sometimes to the point of varying the answer. The framework that I shall later use depends on *a*; in my view, generally *a* is simpler, clearer, and less prone to fallacy. *b* is more fashionable. But I believe that it brings several dangers. Thus it may treat the balance sheet as a mere depository for awkward figures, with scant regard to their significance and values. Again, it can confuse the clerkly processes of book-keeping with observations of actual events. Fine phrases, such as "distributing cost in a systematic and equitable manner", and "matching costs with revenues", hint that symbol transfer in the ledger is an adequate substitute for regard to economic fact. In the real world, I have yet to run into an expiring cost.

When does an asset exist?

The approach *via* the balance sheet forces us to ask "what constitutes an asset?", i.e. when does a possible item merit inclusion in the list.

Tangible things (such as machines and cash) may present few problems. Rights to future receipts, if quantifiable and backed by a legal contract, also seem worthy (e.g. debtors). But how about hopes of getting a dividend? Or research, or an advertising campaign, or a reconstruction? These dubious candidates are the cause of much debate; many of the topics discussed later could be regarded as sub-heads of the inclusion problem. Unhappily, our item-by-item method seems to lack a logic that can solve the problem much better than would the tossing of a coin. We must often rely on custom rather than reason.

Comparison over time: capital measurement units

If we are to compare wealth over time, then the measurement units are important. In other words, we should ask whether the £s used for valuing the opening capital have the same worth as the £s used for the closing assets. Ideally they should of course be the same; but inflation destroys the likeness. ("Opening capital" is shorthand for all items in the owners' equity, e.g. share premiums.)

The need for like units should be the starting point for many reform proposals. Failure to correct opening capital with the *general* index helps to explain why our profession's proposals for inflation accounting foundered so ignominiously.

We must consider three possibilities—money units, real wealth units, and physical units:

(1) *Money units.* The usual accounting method is based on these. If the ledger puts January's capital at £1,000 and December's net assets at £1,100, then income is £100. But does this make sense if the year's inflation has cut the £'s value by e.g. 25% as in 1974?

(2) *Real wealth units.* Where this is the basis, the January £s of capital are brought up-to-date for the December balance sheet, i.e. the starting figures are rained into units of current purchasing power (CCP) with the general index. Thus like is compared with like. To my mind, there is an unassailable case for such clarity and caution if income is to be a serious guide.

(3) *Physical units.* This sounds an improbable basis for ordinary accounting. But it is in fact used sometimes, in disguised forms. If opening stock is 100 tons valued at £1,000, LIFO still values 100 tons of closing stock at £1,000, and adds or subtracts £s only if there are extra tons or "decrements". The proposal to tackle inflation with "current cost accounting" (CCA) relies on much the same trick. If your studies in economics have sunk in, you must feel that wealth is more a matter of satisfactions and

market values than physical characteristics, and so you will look askance at such methods.

Having disposed of capital, we can now move on to the other items in the balance sheet, and ask when and how their growth should be measured, i.e. how they should be valued. There are quite a lot of ways, and so quite a lot of income figures are conceivable; if there are n ways, it follows that—as there are also the three possible capital units—there are $3n$ methods of measuring income.

Recognition stages for change in asset values

From the standpoint of a book-keeper, growth concepts hinge on the point in time at which he is prompted to update his asset balances to current level. But which point should he choose? Income does not in fact burst forth at one clear moment, like the hatching of a chick. Usually there is a long series of stages, during which the income grows ever more sure and measurable. For instance, the main stages may include:

(1) Having glimpsed the far-off possibility of gain, the businessman starts to deploy his assets (e.g. by investing in securities or raw materials).

(2) His assets mature in a demonstrable fashion (e.g. securities appreciate, raw materials become finished goods).

(3) He becomes entitled to payment (perhaps postponed) say by performing services or selling goods.

(4) He receives cash.

(5) He at long last becomes sure that the receipt of cash cannot be nullified by e.g. allowances for bad work, return of faulty goods.

Each of these stages has some claim to be regarded as the point at which income arises. In an ideal world, an income statement would have a number of columns, each based on a different stage, and each putting profit into a different period. The rival figures would all contribute to the general picture. In fact, each firm chooses only one of the stages, most often (3). But let us next touch on other possibilities.

IV. Growth in Current Value Recognized

Suppose first that a daring book-keeper puts in new figures as soon as value changes, i.e. at stage (2) of our list. In deference to my liking for income measurement *via* balance sheets, let us arrange these in a series of columns that reflect successive book-keeping steps. Forgive me if, to keep my mind clear, I take insultingly simple examples. Suppose first that a firm's transactions are:

Date *a*   it starts with £10 in cash;

"   *b*   it buys an investment for £10;

"   *c*   the investment appreciates to £13;

"   *d*   the investment is sold for £14.

Table 2 shows the whole history at a glance. A form of income (preferably qualified as "unrealised") emerges already at date c, when value rises.

Alternative forms of current value However, "current value" turns out to be more complex than our Table 2 suggests (as the accounting profession found when it tried to up-date its figures during inflation). A valuer has four main possibilities:

a *Entry value*. Often this is buying price. But "replacement cost" is a better term; for instance, it justifies the use of a net value where a higher-priced replacement brings lower running costs.

TABLE 2

Successive balance sheets, income recognized at appreciation date *c*

Date:	a	b	c	d
Assets:				
Cash	10			14
Investment - at cost		10		
After appreciation			14	
Owner's wealth				
Starting capital	10	10	10	10
Growth - unrealized			4	
- realized				4
	10	10	14	14

b. Exit value, i.e. sale price—or, where sale brings charges for commission, delivery, etc., net realizable value (NRV). This has the merit of alerting owners to the possible advantages of selling off under-exploited assets; and, where the firm will in fact sell the asset and not replace it, no other figure seems pertinent. For most firms, however, the sale of fixed assets is out of the question; indeed, when assets are essential links in a productive chain, sale of one would spell disaster. So sale price often has scant relevance. Moreover, where assets are designed specially for a particular firm, but do not suit firms with other methods, NRV may be absurdly low or negative; its use would then entail initial write-downs of great size, which might indeed make the firm buy less efficient assets with higher scrap prices. So exit values have many faults.

c. Use value (or "economic value"). This looks to the benefits—often cash flows—that the asset may yield. Thus, when a firm considers buying an extra machine, it may draft a DCF calculation to compare *c* with *a*; it will buy if *c* exceeds *a*. But routine revaluation of all assets on this basis would be laborious and highly subjective; and the summing of their separate marginal benefits must tend to result in a meaninglessly high total for the whole team.

d. Deprival value (or "value to the business"). This selects judiciously from *a*, *b* and *c* according to the actual circumstances of the particular asset. It does so by asking how much poorer the owner would be if he no longer possessed the asset (e.g. if he uses up stores or wears out machines): its value is the difference between having it and not having it. Normally "not having" would make him replace, and so replacement cost is by far the most usual answer. If however the asset is not worth replacing, the owner will follow the more rewarding of two courses: he will either

—keep it in use, or

—sell it

so its value is here the higher of use value or NRV.

In short, *d* seizes on the good qualities of *a*, *b*, and *c*, but avoids their defects. It seems to me the right choice.

Extent of CV's use in practice

Historical cost accounts (HC) involve less work than current value, and are deemed to be more objective. So, despite the extra information given by up-to-date figures, the accounting profession has for the most part set its face sourly against them. You may therefore suppose that CV has no relevance save in radical schemes of reform (e.g. inflation accounting). But, as you will see, it is in fact used where circumstances make HC difficult. Farm accounts come at once to mind. I shall return to them later.

V. Historical Cost

As you know, most accounting is founded on historical cost. Value is frozen until stage (3) of the page 102 list is reached. If the transactions are as in Table 2, except that the sale is for credit, then HC balance sheets assume the familiar forms of Table 3.

TABLE 3

Successive balance sheets, income recognized at sale date *d*

Date	a	b	c	d
Assets:				
Cash	10			14
Goods		10		
Debtor			14	
Owner's wealth				
Starting capital	10	10	10	10
Profit			4	4
	10	10	14	14

Obviously the book-keeper's job is kept simple and easy if he makes no change before stage (3). But then external transactions force activity on him. If for instance he does not record credit sales in customers' accounts at date c, the whole process of collecting cash may break down.

Merits of HC income

Though our respect for stage (3) grew originally from book-keeping convenience, HC has other merits. It is familiar. It is easy to understand. It recognizes the importance of increased liquidity (i.e. the asset's march towards more objective values and finally cash). Because its figures are somewhat more certain than current values, the auditor can tick them happily, and they leave less scope for dispute over the size of e.g. tax, dividends, and commission on profit. And, when general prices are rising, HC gives a cosmetic flush to the income statement (which helps to explain the rejection of inflation accounting).

But the system is not free from faults. In particular:

—the historical cost of an asset (column *b* in Table 3) may be debatable.

— the moment for recognizing growth ("profit realization", i.e. progress from column *b* to *c*) may also be debatable.

We next consider these faults in turn.

VI. DIFFICULTIES OF FINDING HC

Sequence troubles

Suppose my transactions are:

Date 1. I buy an asset for £7

"   2. I buy an identical one for £13

"   3. I sell one for £30

Here HC puts my profit at either £(30-7) = £23, or £(30-13) = £17, according to whether (actually or notionally) I happen to pick up assets by the FIFO or LIFO sequence. Yet an onlooker who does not suffer from the "trained incapacity" of accountants might well put profit at £40:

£

Closing assets:

Cash -- 30

Asset, at current value ------------------------------------- <u>30</u>

Total -- 60

Opening capital -- <u>20</u>

Gain -- <u>40</u>

106

He would argue that my closing wealth depends on what is actually there, not on such a triviality as past physical sequence. The HC system lacks any inherent logic with which to refute him. Accounts that contain HC stock values can be defended only for their convenience and caution.

Ingredient troubles

A factory accountant can gather all the obvious costs, and—making brave assumptions—split them between products. In consequence, he can beget a "cost" for each item of stock, and a "profit" when it is sold.

Here again HC can be justified by its convenience. But a critic trained in the marginalist tradition of LSE will look askance at the slices of overhead charged to various products; he will argue further that the figures depend on choice of allocation base (direct labour costs or hours, machine hours, etc.), and that we have not—and never shall have—any convincing logic for showing which of the bases is "right."

Current value used where cost is unknown

In some enterprises, HC is impossible to apply. Farms are an example.

Both farms and factories produce and sell things. Yet their accounts must be very different, and it is worth-while to ask why.

Farms and overhead

A farmer may not be a meticulous compiler of figures. And, even if he were attracted by the claims of cost accounting, probably he would soon have doubts about allocation. How should he split local taxes between a calf and it's mother, and interest between bees and barley? How should he allow for the difference between winter and summer activity? Experts sometimes try to devise a system for him; but the trouble and absurdity usually cause even a hardened cost accountant to falter. Thus much of a farmer's stock cannot be valued at HC. He must use other figures—probably some form of current value (and part of his income then accords with Table 2).

Physical accretion

There is another contrast between farm and factory: animals breed and machines do not. So farm accounts will include calves, etc., as well as their parents, i.e. recognize assets that have no purchase cost. Where asset numbers grow, there is a strong case for increasing the income figure; farm accounts would be a poor guide to the year's doings if they left out the births.

However, the argument can hardly stop at animals. When crops are ripening, the farmer's wealth is growing just as surely as when calves are born; so his income should allow for this appreciation too. The same reasoning can be applied to forestry, on which Hatfield makes a further point:

> The product is becoming yearly more valuable. The increased value, if unquestioned, is akin to the increasing value of a discounted note which by most authorities is counted as income available for dividend even though it has not as yet been converted into cash.

On the other hand, notes and crops usually become cash in a matter of months, whereas trees take decades. So prudence should perhaps dictate a dividing line —admittedly arbitrary—between fast- and slow-maturing flora and fauna.

Other breaches with HC—plantations and mines

Some exotic plantations and mines also value their stock at NRV. Possibly they too would have trouble in finding cost. And their products may sell (indeed by balance sheet date have already been sold) in assured markets at quoted prices; in former days at least, some governments would take any quantity of gold and silver at fixed prices.

VII. HC AND THE REALIZATION RULE

Under HC, growth in value is at last recorded when the asset is realized (date *c*, Table 3).

Observing such records of a multitude of transactions in a multitude of firms, theorists have generalized with the *realization rule*: the book-keeper should enter value growth at stage (3) (page 102), though not sooner, because the new figure is then vouched for by an external transaction, and the cycle from investment to liquidity is rounded off (Table 3).

The nature of realization

"Realization" thus suggests four things:

(1) Completion of an *external transaction*, i.e.

      a. A contract with an outsider (e.g. for sale of goods).

      b. An earning process (activity and expenditure that enable the firm to fulfil its side of the bargain).

(2) Resulting *liquidity*, i.e.

      a. Conversion into cash, or at least into "near cash" assets (debtors, securities, etc.).

      b. Easy and sure valuation of "near cash" assets.

There are plenty of firms where transactions involve all these four "legs" of the full rule, and accountants have come to accept it as part-and-parcel of HC. But the full rule is unworkable, or at least highly inconvenient, in some circumstances. Then accountants have few qualms about modifying it (i.e. ignoring one or more legs) or abandoning it. It is not a Procrustean bed into which, with resolute stretching and snipping, we can fit all firms and transactions.

The law and the realization rule

This picture gets some confirmation from company law.

Thanks probably to the influence of standards and the second EEC Directive, in 1981 the rule was enshrined in the UK Companies Act:

> Only profits realized at the balance sheet date shall be included in the profit and loss account.

That sounds forthright enough. But nearby words show that the rule is in fact very much the junior in a team of three:

(1) True and fair

(2) Prudent

(3) Realized

Moreover, a later paragraph further emasculates the rule, with a seeming *volte-face* that must surprise the non-lawyer; realized profits are such profits

> as fall to be treated as realized profits in accordance with principles generally accepted with respect to the determination for accounting purposes of realized profits.

In cruder words, the rule is to be thrown aside where it offends "true and fair", or prudence, or accounting ways.

We saw earlier how the accountant discards the rule when dealing with farms. Let us next look at some of the circumstances in which he uses a modified version, e.g. by chopping off one or more legs.

The external transaction

Leg *a*: contract with an outsider.

Sometimes the contract tends to be only notional. Every student learns how to change profits by allowing for *accrued* rents and interest. Such change makes for more useful profit figures. But are we not stretching words if we plead justification by the objective test of an external transaction?

Here the difficulty stems from our definition of assets. As was said earlier, an "asset-by-asset" approach to wealth must in effect look for the assets at some date, and list them in an inventory. Thus one can imagine an estate steward of earlier days itemizing fields, flocks, and other assets that were obvious and tangible. Later his more enlightened successors came to hold that, if the estate accounts ran for the year to (say) March, and a tenant was sure to pay a £12 annual rent at the end of the following June, a £9 asset had already emerged by March, despite lack of an external happening; and likewise a liability for expenses could exist ahead of cash payment. Thus was born what in recent years has come to be called the accrual system: at his year-end, the accountant looks around for over-lapping contracts, and writes up his ledger *as if* they produced actual cash movements for (say) each month till his year-end. The resulting accounts give a fuller view, and are a useful check on the efficiency of "stewards".

But, when looking for accruals, where does one draw the line? Rent receivable— under a precise contract and from a solid tenant—can reasonably be added to the asset list. Similarly some impending payments are so certain that they can reasonably be added to the liabilities. But other over-laps may be less sure and less quanitifiable. The accountant must in each case draw a very arbitrary line—with which others might warmly disagree—to separate the admissible from the inadmissible. Thus he tends to allow for expected receipts of interest but not of equity dividends, and to include expected payments more readily then expected receipts.

Leg *b*—Earning

Looking at the list on page 102, you might reasonably think of income as growing gradually over the five stages. But, as you know, the book-keeper records all the growth at one stage (as in Table 3). Some theorists say that his entry marks a "crucial event", presumably the culmination of the *earning* process.

In most firms, venerable practice leaves little doubt about the date of this entry (e.g. the delivery of goods to, or their earmarking for, a debtor). But, as tax cases show, there are circumstances in which lawyers can disagree about the earning date. Thus a firm of underwriters at Lloyds wrote risks in return for a percentage of profit. If risk was underwritten in Year 1, work had still to be done in Years 2 and 3 (e.g. re-insurance, payments of losses). Commission was not calculated or paid till the end of Year 3. The firm argued that, as there was "nothing ascertainable, demandable, or payable" till year 3, the profit was not made till then. But the House of Lords held that it was made in Year 1.[1]

Again, consider the earning process where there are *long-term contracts*. If the firm agrees to manufacture 5,000 widgets at the rate of 1,000 a year, the delivery of a year's batch may not unreasonably be deemed a realization. But where the contract is not physically divisible into yearly slices (as with the building of a skyscraper), strict doctrine must put off realization till final completion. This might make the contractor's profit fluctuate wildly over the years. Accordingly most accountants are willing to soften the doctrine, and—with cautious provisos about future risks—to write up an asset account (e.g. by the "percentage of completion" method) as if separable units were in fact delivered. An architect's certificate may give some objectivity to measures of completion. "True and fair" here overrides prudence.

But which asset account should the contractor plump up? Increase in the HC of work-in-progress would be too blatant a breach of the UK Companies Act. So the Accounting Standards Committee tells us, in it's Jesuitical exposure draft 40, to rebaptize the increased asset as "amounts recoverable under contracts", a kind of debtor. A rose by another name can smell a good deal sweeter.

The earnings leg justifies our treatment of *revenue received in advance* (by e.g. magazine publishers and insurance offices). In the balance sheet, cash grows; but this revenue cannot yet be regarded as earned. So we include also an offsetting liability until the firm discharges it's side of the bargain. There may however be arbitrary decisions over the size of the liability, e.g. the proportion of insurance premiums to be carried forward into next year.

Liquidity

Here again, two legs are often present at realization but we do not treat them both as essential.

110

Leg *a*—Conversion into cash

The stages of page 102 led up to growth of cash. Without the cash—or at least "near cash" assets that enable the firm to borrow from it's bank—a profit figure might be a poor guide to possible out-payments and hence consumption; again, payments of tax could bring disaster if assessed profit bore no relation to means of payment—one of the objections to a wealth tax. (But of course a firm may, after realizing cash, reinvest it in fresh ventures, and so wipe out the liquidity. The income figure merely points to liquidity at same stage during the year. Its usefulness falls unless cash budgets are respected.)

Not every external transaction leads to liquidity. Early accounting textbooks gave instruction in barter, and perhaps today's writers are giving us weak generalizations by dealing only with cash flows in their theories. Payment in kind still persists. Consider for instance a well-known transaction of the 1930's. An oil company sent crude to Germany, and refined it in a subsidiary there. The Third Reich lacked the foreign exchange needed for normal payment. The company instead took new tankers from German yards, and added them to it's fleet (fixed assets). So here was realization (or something very like it) without liquidity. Should value gain from such deals be treated as unrealized? Prudence would seem to say yes; but "true and fair" must surely argue no. Omission of the gain would cause the accounts to give a poor picture of the year's trading, and would belittle the subsidiary's operations; and, if the company has other sources of liquid assets, there would seem to be slender grounds for with-holding dividend.

Leg *b*—Easy and sure valuation

Liquid assets can normally be valued more readily than fixed assets. But a seemingly sure figure—especially for debtors—may in fact be undermined by risk of non-payment or by claims for defective work, etc. A cautious firm offsets such an asset with a provision—whose size must often be a matter of personal outlook. In extreme cases, the firm may postpone growth recognition till cash reaches the till—the "cash basis" of measurement.

Risk and the cash basis

If you are not too weary, you will have noticed that so far I have not mentioned stage 4 on our page 102 list.

Our text-books should be more explicit about the effect of risk on methods of income measurement. Two firms may operate in much the same way, and yet feel impelled to use different methods because they perceive different degrees of risk, or react differently to the same degree of risk. Thus, where debtors' payments are capricious, a firm may feel that sale contracts (even with bad debt provisions) are a poor proof of asset growth. The firm will then ignore growth till the cash comes in, i.e. use the cash basis of stage (4). Examples way be found in retail trades where customers pay by instalments.

Long delays and high interest rates are another reason for choosing stage (4). They make (3) unsuitable unless discount is deducted from remote debts (and gradually

111

written back aver the years to maturity). High "after costs" of collection also argue for (4).

In many professional firms, risk can hardly be important. Yet some of them (even prestigious legal and accounting giants) reputedly cling to the cash basis. Their reason may be not unconnected with tax. And they may wish to show what can safely and conveniently be paid out to partners each year or at retirement.

Value decline without realization

A sound economic rule tends to be symmetrical (e.g. applies alike to supply and demand, to production and consumption). We might therefore expect the realization rule to apply to value *fall* as well as growth. It does not. Consider two obvious cases of inconsistency:

Lower of cost and market

When the current values of stock items sink below their cost, our general practice is to write them down (on the "pick and choose" basis). This asymmetry is defended on grounds of prudence.

Depreciation

In Victorian times, there was still a belief—particularly gratifying to tax officials— that depreciation ought not to be treated as a cost: it could be shrugged off as a "capital loss". This may not have mattered where assets had short lives, so that costs of renewals could be charged against profits. But it did matter with long-lived assets such as buildings and mines. Critics have blamed the omission, and the consequent lack of replacement funds, for the dilapidated state into which many British factories fell; and it has enabled South African gold mines to show higher profits and thus mislead investors. Now there is a general belief that all assets with finite lives should be depreciated.

But an industry with enough political clout seems able to bend principles. Our property lobby—displeased at the thought of lower profits—has wrung a dispensation from the Accounting Standards Committee. "Investment properties" need not be depreciated, but are to be shown in the balance sheet at their open market value; value changes are to be kept in an "investment revaluation" account (though a deficit on that account is to be charged against profit).

This breach of the rule seems sadly inconsistent with both the "true and fair" and prudence criteria, and may bring much odium on accounting at the next slump in the property market.

VIII. Conclusion

Scientists hold that, if a principle is sound, it will repeatedly yield consistent results when different persons apply it in different circumstances.

It would be gratifying, and good for public relations, if accounting had an "income principle" of which the same could be said. But accountants have to measure something that differs from the subject-matter of science. The wealth of a firm—let alone the well-offness of its owners—has many facets; and we are surely not unreasonable if we in each case judge which facet best suits the given firm's nature and risks. This means that we must retain some variety of methods, and be ready in each case to justify an income figure that may have respectable rivals.

To be sure, laws and standards have to some degree narrowed the variety; and no doubt this process will go on. But we may well doubt whether the wisdom of future standards committees, or the brilliance of future researchers, can ever give us a principle that does away with variety and arbitrary judgement. You may ascribe this failure to the limitations of our (necessary) asset-by-asset structure and (perhaps unnecessary) HC values; and in part you will be right. But a shrewder explanation must also cite something still more fundamental: "well-offness" is an elusive and many-sided notion that varies from person to person and from moment to moment. Let me quote Hicks once more:

> We may now allow a doubt to escape us whether it does, in the last resort, stand up to analysis at all, whether we have not been chasing a Will-o'-the-Wisp.[2]

NOTES

1. *C.I.R.* v *Gardner, Mountain and D'Abrumenil Ltd*; 39 T.C. 537.

2. All the Hicks quotations are from *Value and Capital*, Oxford, 1939, chapter 14. The Hatfield quotation is from *Accounting*, NY, 1927, page 253.

REALISATION
A Wavering Rule

At first sight, the idea of realisation seems eminently simple and practicable: accounts should not show profit till it is realised. But, when we try to apply the rule, we find that a simple version is at odds with the activities of many firms. Also the rule raises awkward problems of definition.

Definitions

Some likely meanings of 'realisation' are:

(A)   Conversion into cash - a stringent test.

(B)   Conversion into very liquid assets, including cash and debtors.

(C)   Market transactions in assets. (Transactions make the value figure more certain.)

(D)   Provision of services (i.e. profit is not yet realised when payment is received in advance).

(E)   Appreciation of assets (without sale), provided value can be found with reasonable certainty.

(F)   Establishment of a freely disposable store of wealth (i.e. of gain that can be distributed without damage to the firm's continuity).[1]

Definition (B) is the one that is used most often, and it works well in many firms. But clearly it is hopelessly unsuitable in others, particularly those whose assets grow without external transactions: a farmer will deem his profit to be increased by the birth of calves, a landlord by the accrual of rent, a contractor by the smooth progress of his long-term contracts, the owner of interest-bearing securities (or of assets charged with interest during construction) by the accrual of interest, etc., etc.; (E) is used here. And, even where firms ostensibly use (B), they may in effect whittle it down into something like (A) by providing for bad debts, faulty work, and so on.

If we spell out the requirements for (B), we find that they point to two things: liquidity and external transactions. Further, liquidity implies the arrival of cash (or 'near cash' such as debtors), and also the possibility of valuing these assets with some confidence. Again, 'external transaction' implies both a contract with an outsider and an earning process. ('Earning' is a surprisingly vague word, but it suggests activity and sacrifice that enable the firm to fulfil its side of the bargain; thus theatre tickets sold in advance contribute to profit only when the play is performed.) In all, therefore, full-blooded realisation implies four different attributes.

---

[1] For a full discussion, see B. Carsberg and C. Noke, Reporting of Profits and the Concept of Realisation, ICAEW, 1991.

1

'Realisation' and 'recognition' may seem to be much the same thing. But presumably realisation means that asset growth is acknowledged in the profit and loss account - and so raises the likelihood of cash distribution; whereas recognition means only that the growth is acknowledged somewhere or other (e.g. in 'reserves') and not necessarily in the profit and loss account.

Realisation and the law

In both Britain and USA, the courts have struggled to decide whether various forms of asset growth constitute profit. The realisation rule seems to be one possible test.

Thanks probably to the influence of Standards and the Second EC Directive, the realisation rule has been enshrined in UK company law: 'only profits realised at the balance sheet date shall be included in the profit and loss account.' (Companies Act 1985.) But nearby words show that this seemingly decisive rule is in fact very much the inferior partner in a team of three:

(1)   true and fair;
(2)   prudent, and
(3)   realised.

Moreover the lawyers pervert definition in a somewhat astonishing way: a further clause states that realised profits are such profits 'as fall to be treated as realised profits ... in accordance with principles generally accepted with respect to the determination for accounting purposes of realised profits'. (Sched. 4, para. 91.) In other words, we have a conceptual free-for-all; any definition is legitimate if it is employed widely enough.

Usefulness to investors

Some writers, in their quest for a sensible solution to the realisation problem, have appealed to the now popular idea that the prime purpose of accounts is to give information that will aid decision by investors, and have asked which definition best meets this end. But we are apt to forget how recently this idea became current. It was first promulgated in the (US) Trueblood Report of 1978. 'It seems barely credible now' Professor Solomons tells us 'that such a conclusion could ever have been considered controversial' yet a survey of reactions to the Report showed that 'only 37% of respondents then approved the "usefulness to investors" objective'.

I must admit that, had I been questioned for that survey, I should probably have joined the benighted 63%. The plain fact is that the usefulness-to-investors idea was hit on by recent committees bent on promulgating statements of principle for the benefit of the rest of us; the idea makes their job much simpler. It resembles the economists' helpful assumption that the firm's aim is profit maximisation. This too makes analysis much simpler; it too has some truth in it, but is not the whole truth (firms may aim also at e.g. social goals such as giving employment).

2

The rule's evolution

The idea is now acquiring status, but gets little support from accounting history. This suggests that originally the prime task of accounts was to keep track of debtors and creditors. It suggests too that the realisation rule must have emerged at a fairly late date. Accounting grew up in an economy in which cash was very scarce, and so book-keeping barter was usual. A merchant often sold to get a credit in another merchant's books, and not for cash; later the other sold him goods, or arranged for a credit transfer to him in a third merchant's books; his gain was never realised in our sense of the word. Possibly he could not calculate profit. He must have felt that he was prospering, not if he was becoming liquid, but if his accounts (for debtors, voyages, ventures, etc.) pointed to a growing ability to demand goods and services.

Barter still persists, and still makes realisation hard to define. Assets are exchanged for shares. Oil companies find convenience in swapping cargoes of oil in different parts of the world. During the 1930s, an oil company sent crude to its subsidiary in Nazi Germany, which lacked foreign exchange for payment. So the company ordered new tankers from German yards, and added these to its fleet. Was there here a realised gain despite the switch of assets from more to less liquid? By the information-to-investors rule, the answer must be yes; the company's wealth had grown in a way gratifying to investors. But (I shall presently venture to suggest) an older and wiser rule would let the company judge the matter for itself, in the light of its working procedures and over-all liquidity.

The historian tells us too that, after cash became plentiful and full double-entry more common, notions of recognition and realisation grew out of the procedures of simple book-keeping. The book-keeper spared himself labour by making no entries until his hand was forced by an external transaction (e.g. stocks into debtor). Then profit was automatically deemed to be realised - to make the books balance, and not from fine concepts or any wish to give information to outsiders. The accountant now added control of cash to control of debtors and creditors. These were the essential aims of accounting. They still are. The main reason for publication is to confirm that the books have been properly kept.

Liquidity

However, after the idea of realisation had evolved in this unforeseen way, some firms of merchants saw a great advantage in it. A profit figure gives rise to expectations of, and sometimes rights to, cash distributions; it provides ammunition to e.g. tax-gatherers, persons paid on commission, partners, and shareholders. The realisation rule strengthens the likelihood that these expectations will not be aroused till the firm has enough cash to meet them. If the rule is not applied (e.g. if profit is swollen with unrealised appreciation), payment from profit may leave the firm perilously short of liquid assets; moreover it will give the tax-gatherers, shareholders, etc., a privileged position, as they get income in a form that is better (more liquid) than that of the paying firm. The payments are both dangerous and unfair.

That surely is the case for the rule. Information is a good thing; avoidance of bankruptcy is a far better one.

3

Despite its merits, the rule (in its narrower forms) is disregarded so often that plainly it is not basic to revenue measurement. As a US committee has sensibly said 'the point at which income may be deemed realised ... is inevitably a matter of judgement'.

And we ought perhaps to feel uneasy about the rule on another score. An accounting theory is surely more entitled to respect if it applies to costs as well as revenues; it should be symmetrical. All forms of the rule fail here. When we charge depreciation, accrued expenses, bad debts, etc., and when we write down stocks to the lower of cost or market, we cannot seek justification in either liquidity growth or external transactions; we ignore the rule. Our procedure must be defended on grounds of prudence, not principle; as a judge has said, it makes 'good conservative accounting, but is quite illogical'. This inconsistency further shows the rule to be sadly lacking in conceptual strength.

So it seems that the rule should be regarded as no more than an optional aid to sound finance. It is no part of a general income concept. Firms should be allowed to judge for themselves whether - and in which of its forms - it suits them. Its more obvious forms are often not suitable. Any Procrustean standard that tried to impose uniformity would create untold confusion.

Accountancy, July, 1992.

4

EARLY CRITICS OF COSTING
LSE in the 1930s

Early Critics of Costing:
LSE in the 1930s

W.T. Baxter
London School of Economics
and Political Science (Emeritus)

Abstract: In the 1930s, an able group of young men at the London School of Economics, inspired by an outstanding teacher, set about applying the reasoning of economics to accounting and business. They concluded that if cost accounting is to help the businessman make decisions, it should look to opportunity cost theory, i.e., should compare the costs and revenues of alternative plans. A built-in system of cost bookkeeping is thus less useful than one-off budgets for each new problem: instead of recording past costs, the accountant should estimate the variations caused by each alternative plan. Costs that do not vary are irrelevant, and so allocation is indefensible.

INTRODUCTION:
BUSINESS ADMINISTRATION AT LSE

In what follows, I shall retell the history of some events of the 1930s, when young men at the London School of Economics—prompted by a notable teacher called Arnold Plant—published essays on cost theory. I shall try to summarize these and to estimate their effects.

LSE was founded in 1895. From its very start, it gave commercial courses "in order to prevent the English clerk from being ousted by his better educated German rival" [Caine, p. 41]. Accounting was introduced in 1902. The class was given in the evening, teacher and students both attending only part-time [Hayek, p. 1].

The first degree courses required continuous study of a common core of subjects, with much stress on economics. The subjects tended to merge with one another, and there were no formal teaching departments; indeed the word *department* was taboo (a happy state that pressure of numbers has since made impossible). Thus, Plant was at the same time able to study for two degrees. He won first-class honors in both.

PLANT'S KINDERGARTEN

Plant was born in 1898, and—like most British boys of those days—went straight from school to work. By the age of 21 he was manager of an engineering company. But he was also enrolled at LSE and won his degrees in 1922 and 1923.

138

When a Chair in Commerce was created at Cape Town, his tutor told him that he would be a fool not to apply. In those far-off days, a promising candidate had no need of a publications list, and he was duly appointed (age 25). Six years later, he was translated back to LSE [Coase, 1986, p. 81].

He found himself in a constellation of brilliant new recruits— Robbins, Hayek, Hicks, and others. None was over thirty. A student of those days tells us that Hayek played an important part "in encouraging rigor in our thinking and in enlarging our vision" [Coase, 1982, p. 33]. Robbins did most of the undergraduate teaching of economics and told his students to read Wicksteed's *Commonsense of Political Economy* and Knight's *Risk Uncertainty and Profit*. ("It was our close study of them which gave us such a firm hold on cost theory" [ibid.].)

Plant was remarkable in that he has had great influence on accounting theory and yet published nothing on this subject (and not much on any other). His ideas percolated indirectly, through his students. He was an inspiring teacher—tall, formidable, free alike with praise and rebuke. A student likened his lectures to the dissecting of a cadaver by a master surgeon. They roamed over wide areas, and he convinced his audience that economic principles have relevance far beyond the classroom door.

He was lucky in that he had talented disciples, notably Ronald Coase, Ronald Edwards, and Ronald Fowler. (The name Ronald seemed to guarantee excellence.) These men applied his ideas in their writings of the late 1930s, by which time he had recruited them to his staff.

THE SERIES IN *THE ACCOUNTANT*

Though the writing of Coase and Edwards has proved important, they did not regard it as "research"; its ideas were common property among their LSE colleagues. It was not published in learned journals, but in the weekly *Accountant*. This publication was devoted to technical matters, tax cases, etc. But it had a courageous editor (Miss Snelling) who in 1938 agreed to take a series of articles by Edwards and then another by Coase. The installments were written fast each Wednesday night and published on Saturday. It soon became clear that both series included attacks on many of accounting's most cherished ideas. Somewhat to the young authors' surprise, these attacks caused bewilderment and indignation.

The Coase series was called "Business Organization and the Accountant." It looks at cost from the standpoint of LSE economics. (Coase has had a distinguished career as an economist, ending as professor at the University of Chicago.) Edwards' series had the title "The Nature and Measurement of Income." It lays bare some flaws in the accountant's value and profit measures and advocates forward-looking (discounted cash flow) methods of appraising capital and its growth (income) as at least the conceptual ideal.[1] A senior colleague (a professional accountant) publicly denounced this concept as "dangerous nonsense . . . sheer insanity," and for good measure likened it to Dr. Johnson's leg of mutton: "ill bred, ill fed, ill killed, and ill dresst" [Rowland, 1938, p. 609]. (Since that time, the practical accountant's attitude toward academics has undergone a remarkable change. He now regards academic writings as worthy of respect, if incomprehensible.)

Edwards also dealt with cost theory in a public lecture entitled "The Rationale of Cost Accounting" [Edwards, 1973, pp. 71-92]. This lecture and the Coase series are discussed below. Coase gives the broader background of theory, and I therefore start with him.

COASE ON THE NATURE OF COST

OPPORTUNITY COST

The Coase article was an attempt to apply the marginalist thinking of economists to business problems. The cost notion he uses

> is that of "opportunity" or "alternative" cost. . . . When someone says that a particular course of action is "not worth the cost", he merely means that he prefers some other course . . . [Coase, 1973, p. 108].

Thus, when a businessman has decided on an activity, its cost (in the economist's sense) can be regarded as the net receipts that could have been obtained if he had not made that decision, i.e., is the net revenue forgone. And "to cover cost" and "to maximize profit" are two different ways of saying the same thing. Cost is an appendage of decision making and the study of alternatives.

VARIABLE VERSUS FIXED COST

It follows that, when the businessman is making a decision, he should concentrate on the *variations* in revenue and expense that it will cause. Unvaried (fixed) items are irrelevant.

It further follows that a traditional costing system does not give the data that are most helpful for decisions. It fails in several ways:
- its figures relate to past operations. The decision maker needs estimates of the future; there is no point in looking back at the past—save as an object lesson;
- its figures do not vary with the decision; instead,

---

[1] Edwards' article, revised and shortened, appears in Baxter and Davidson's *Studies in Accounting* [Edwards, 1977]; Coase's, in Buchanan and Thirlby's *L.S.E. Essays on Cost* [Coase, 1973]. Edwards also published an earlier article in which he criticized secret reserves on the grounds that they mislead investors and so impede the flow of investment to its best uses [1936, p. 683].

- its figures are often *average* and not *marginal* costs, i.e., they include arbitrary allocations of fixed cost;
- its figures cannot allow for the fact that this year's doings may affect those of next year.

To illustrate his argument, Coase gives numerical examples of the problem facing a businessman who has to find the optimum scale of output for one of his products (examples familiar in economics textbooks but—in those days at least—wholly alien to costing). He will wish to expand output so long as marginal revenue exceeds marginal cost. He must also be assured that total receipts cover total variable costs. A conventional cost system is unhelpful on both points.

NONMONETARY FACTORS, UNCERTAINTY, AND TIME

The usefulness of accounts (Coase continues) is limited in various other ways. Some costs and revenues cannot be expressed in monetary terms, because a course of action may have results that are nonmonetary. Thus, a businessman may be swayed by social or political considerations, e.g., he may think it antisocial to work with the armaments industry. (And, we can now add, he may be sensitive to Green issues.)

More importantly, the figures in an estimate are subject to uncertainty. Thus, they do not show the whole truth: there is the further question of how likely they are to be realized. And the most probable outcome does not always sway decisions; sometimes an unlikely possibility carries more weight, e.g., the buyer of a lottery ticket is not prompted by the most probable result. So, when a businessman has to decide between alternatives, his choice will partly depend on his attitude toward risk. And the correctness of his decision cannot be disproved by later events; when he makes it, he thinks that the chance of gain outweighs the risks, "and whether he ultimately succeeds or fails has no relevance to this preference" [Coase, 1973, p. 105].

Intriguing consequences stem from the notion that cost exists only in the mind of the businessman. He alone can measure it. And it is never realized since it is the rejected alternative.[2]

Coase also discusses timing, i.e., the need to transform scattered receipts and payments into their equivalents at one date (say, the present). Here he anticipates the writing by Joel Dean and others on discounted cash flows. But DCF budgets provide a further example of uncertainty; the businessman's attitude toward risk taking will qualify his faith in the future figures, and so influence his decisions. Accounting cannot disclose these since it cannot reproduce his mental processes.

---

[2]See the articles by G.F. Thirlby (another Plant disciple) in Buchanan and Thirlby [1973].

"OPPORTUNITY" OR "ALTERNATIVE"?

Coase next applies his theories to familiar cost problems. He thereby clarifies and strengthens his argument. If cost must be tied to decision (as he argues), then it can be found by comparing budgets for alternative plans. If these include revenues, then any "revenue forgone" will be obvious, and the phrase "opportunity cost" is readily understood. In some of the Coase examples, however, the plans do not at first glance include any revenue, and so the phrase may not seem apt. For that matter, at first glance the existence of alternative plans may not be evident. But Coase explains that displaced revenue, though not obvious, in a sense does feature in his examples; thus, if material is bought for a job, its price is a cost, and "this accords exactly with the 'opportunity' cost concept—since, if the materials were not purchased, that money would be available for the business" [Coase, 1973, p. 109].

In other words, Coase argues that the manager costs the materials by in effect making Plan A (material is used) and Plan B (material is not used) and then comparing these alternatives to see their effect on cash. His phrase "alternative cost" here seems more helpful than "opportunity cost." The following of his examples illustrate these matters.

DEPRECIATION

To use a machine on a job may involve two kinds of sacrifice: (1) another job may be squeezed out (the net revenue forgone can understandably be called either an opportunity or an alternative cost), and (2) the machine's life may be shortened by wear and tear. If the machine had been left idle, this "user depreciation" would have been avoided. ("Alternative" here seems apt, "opportunity" less so.) User depreciation can in principle be calculated by comparing the asset's values (found from DCF budgets of the asset's future relevant flows) if it is (a) used on the job and (b) left idle. In practice, the calculation must be highly speculative since "it turns upon estimates of the future yield of an asset in each period of its life" [Lewis, p. 233].

Coase elaborates by taking the case of a mine. Here user depreciation can readily be visualized as the "using up" of a mineral seam: an extra ton raised this year means a ton less in the final year. And a full statement of the alternatives must study the marginal ton's revenue and cost at the changed output levels of both years.

"Time depreciation" (i.e., the value loss caused by the passage of time rather than use) is not affected by the job and is so not part of its cost—even though, like user depreciation, it is a charge in income calculation.

Ronald Fowler (mentioned above as one of Plant's disciples) wrote a book on depreciation, in which he too stresses the irrelevance of time depreciation:

Once capital equipment has been installed, it has to earn
what it can. Its remuneration is a "quasi-rent". It will pay
both monopolists and competing producers, in the short
run, to produce at any price that covers prime costs
[Fowler, 1934, p. 3].

COST OF MATERIALS

Where materials are to be bought specially for a given job, there is
no problem about their cost: it is the estimated sum of money to be
spent on their purchase. But problems arise if they are already in stock.
Their "using up" on a job will then either force the firm to replace them
or deprive it of the chance to sell them. So the cost of use is, according
to circumstances, either replacement cost or net realizable value—and
not past payments, or payments fixed by past contracts.

The article elaborates on this by considering a firm that contracts to
buy a minimum annual supply of materials at a fixed price. Suppose
the price is £10 per ton and that the supply now exceeds current needs.
Here use of a ton on a job does not force the firm to pay an extra £10
for replacements; it instead stops the sale of surplus. So the cost of use
is the net sale proceeds forgone. And despite the fixing of purchase
price, cost still fluctuates with the current market.

INTEREST

Costing textbooks were in those days baffled by the problem of
whether or not interest should be included in costs. On balance, they
were hostile to it. They adduced several reasons:
- it might not be an actual money payment;
- it would not fit into double entry;
- it would raise closing inventory values and thus anticipate
  profit;
- it is complicated and would entail much clerical work;
- it is "entirely a matter of internal finance, and is in no way
  connected with the cost of manufacture" [Bigg, p. 83].

These are hardly compelling grounds for dismissing the cost.

Coase argues that interest must usually be paid whether or not a
machine is used on a job and so is not part of the job's cost. Talk of
interest distracts attention from the opportunity cost of use—the net
receipts that would be got if the machine worked instead on another job.

DEPARTMENT ACCOUNTS

Following sour criticism in *The Accountant*, Coase reinforced his
argument by discussing departmental accounting. He argues that
departmental profit figures may not show what is important for a
decision, namely, how much a department's existence adds to total
profit. This is particularly true where the accounts allocate general fixed
costs among departments.

Coase makes his point by revising the figures in an example to
show how (on reasonable assumptions) their sizes would change if a
given department were closed. The department's own sales and direct
expenses would then of course disappear. So might some of the general
overheads—almost certainly not by the allocated amount. Plans,
however, may here be interdependent: the closure of one department
would probably affect the others, e.g., by giving them more space, but
reducing the number of customers entering the building. The net effect
of these changes might well be very different from the department's
profit in the accounts. The same reasoning can then be applied in turn
to each of the other departments; closure of each would change profit to
an extent that differed from the accounting profit.

Special calculations are thus more useful than routine departmental
accounts for predicting the effect of important decisions (e.g., a seeming
loss maker may in fact be contributing a worthwhile surplus).

EDWARDS ON COSTING'S LIMITATIONS

Edwards' public lecture relied on much the same reasoning as the
Coase article. But he was an accountant, and he links theory more
closely to practice.

Cost accounting textbooks of that era (and long afterwards) were
not much more than dry descriptions of clerical routines; they showed
no awareness of economic theory; and they contained little discussion of
aims. Edwards thus strikes a new note when he starts by saying that
costing must produce figures that influence policy—a foretaste of the
modern emphasis on decision. Some people (he goes on) of course like
information merely to gratify their curiosity; there is nothing wrong
with this so long as they remember that it is a way of consuming
income, not producing it.

TYPES OF USEFUL INFORMATION

He then asks what information—out of the mass available in any
firm—justifies the cost of collection. He answers that worthwhile
information must throw light on two kinds of problems:

- entrepreneurial, i.e., how to find the size or rate of output
  that maximizes profit;
- technical; i.e., how to produce this output at the lowest
  cost.

COSTING AS AN AID TO EFFICIENCY

Unlike the textbooks, Edwards allots little space to the technical
problems. He concedes that cost records may reduce waste, but takes the
unexpected view that if

the rate of output is a settled question, then so long as the
relative prices of the factors of production remain

unchanged, the efficiency question is not one for the cost
department, it is just a matter of vigilance on the part of
the works manager [Edwards, 1973, p. 87].

But when those relative prices change, the cost department should find
whether the combination of resources could with advantage also be
changed. (Here is an example of his oft-repeated view that useful cost
statements must be one-off studies—and not part of continuous
bookkeeping, even though such a tied-in system is the "hallmark of
respectability" [ibid., p. 88].

ENTREPRENEURIAL DECISIONS
AND AVOIDABLE COST

Edwards starts his main section by clarifying terms. He prefers
"avoidable" to "direct" cost (because "the most important thing about
costs is the extent to which they change with output" [Edwards, 1973,
p. 76]). "Direct" covers the items that it is worthwhile to trace to jobs,
etc. It thus depends on routines and bookkeeping convenience rather
than cause-and-effect. "Avoidable" is more helpful for decisions: it
means costs that will not be incurred if the job is not undertaken. It
may or may not coincide with the traditional direct costs. Thus, direct
labor cost is not avoidable if the workers will be retained anyway. And
even some of the "fixed" costs will be avoided if the job is not done,
e.g., there may be savings of interest, and of wear and tear on machines.
When a firm takes on a job, continues a department, etc., extra cost
is incurred. To be worthwhile, the activity in question must contribute
at least enough extra revenue to outweigh that cost. So a manager
ought to know the latter's size. Routine budgets and cost accounts both
fail him here because their calculations consist of (a) direct costs, plus
(b) allocated fixed cost; thus, they do not concentrate on avoidable
items. As we have just seen (a) may not coincide with avoidable costs
and (b) certainly will not.

ENTREPRENEURIAL DECISIONS
ON PRICE AND OUTPUT

Edwards goes on to discuss demand and output in ways familiar in
textbooks on economics but at that date foreign to those on costing. As
the firm should try to equate marginal revenue with marginal cost
(neither of which fits into the ledger), the accountant ought to draft
comparative budgets to find optimum output. Here again, variability is
what matters; if, say, budgets compare cost at output of 100 units with
output of 101 units, they should ignore cost that will not be changed
by the one-unit increase. Thus, "fixed cost" should be omitted (unless
the changes are so great that it in fact ceases to be fixed).
Like Coase, Edwards illustrates his case by considering interest and
material costs. He argues that

- if the job, etc., will tie up capital that could earn interest elsewhere, this interest forgone is a cost. But capital that is sunk in fixed assets cannot be invested elsewhere, and so interest on it is not a cost.
- Accountants argue over the rival claims of FIFO, LIFO, average cost, etc. What matters is the extra cost imposed by use of the materials. Normally this is their replacement cost.

Job costing, too, should concentrate on avoidable cost. It is the minimum price at which the work should be accepted (though the actual quotation will depend on the state of the order book and the market). Any job that yields more than its avoidable cost adds to total revenue and is worth doing unless it squeezes out more profitable work. To put allocated overhead into the budget is to confuse this issue; the greater part of such a figure is in fact not caused by the job. The same applies to the *ex post* job account in the cost ledger; a total that includes overhead fails to tell the manager whether he was right to take the job.

The reasoning is extended to departments and by-products. The latter provide a good example of the joint cost that economics warns us not to split. If the proportions are fixed, the splitting of overhead tells nothing useful. If they are variable, what matters is the way in which changes in proportions would affect costs and revenues; this should be the concern of costing. "The expense of allocation is money wasted" [Edwards, 1973, p. 86].

COMMENT

DECISIONS, OPPORTUNITIES, AND ALTERNATIVES

I suggested above that Coase and Edwards could perhaps have made their case more palatable to accountants by stressing "alternative" rather than "opportunity." The opportunity cost concept has no doubt been invaluable in studies of an entire economy: since the prices paid for resources must be equal to, or (slightly) greater than, what they would yield in another use or to another user, cost (the price of the resources) *is* opportunity cost.[3] But the concept may seem less directly apt when applied to a firm for two reasons: (1) it is helpful to say that Plan A yields 9 and the alternative B yields 7; it is usually less helpful to say that A yields 2 after allowing for opportunity cost (though this is of course what we do when we discount), and (2) there is ambiguity if "cost" can mean either:

- net revenue of the rejected course, or
- expenses of the chosen one.

---

[3]Coase defends his earlier work in his 1990 article "Accounting and the Theory of the Firm," where he points out the importance of costing: its figures do within the firm what price does from outside.

The concept's corollary—that costs of inputs can be found by comparing alternative budgets—is much easier to grasp.

This idea lately received some support in the work of yet another LSE economist, Mr. J.R. Gould. He tells us that opportunity cost calculations should be regarded as no more than a method of approach, of little direct help to businessmen; these are better served with the view that economics tackles many problems as a choice between alternatives [Gould, p. 141].

"COST" OR "PRICE"

It can perhaps be argued that Coase and Edwards underrate the difficulties of pricing. A businessman may accept their views, yet find the task of pricing so burdensome that he feels forced to take refuge in the allocation ritual of "cost plus." Its figures can serve at least as a convenient base from which to test the market.

The danger here is that he will inadvertently treat a full cost figure as rigid minimum (i.e., will suppose that a lower price must bring loss). He could reduce this risk (and clarify his thought) by a change of words—by treating the overhead load not as "cost" but "price" [see Baxter and Oxenfeldt, 1969]. (Thus, a machine-hour rate would become the price for an hour's use of resource [cf. the hourly charges of an accounting firm].) He would have little hesitation about trimming a price to gain desirable work.

CONCLUSION

THE CONTINUITY OF LSE TEACHING

After World War II, Coase and Edwards worked for a time at LSE, but in fields other than accounting. Their views were, however, absorbed by the new staff of the accounting department and have ever since played a central role in its teaching. In time, many members of the staff left to set up departments at other universities (e.g., David Solomons), and this diaspora aided the spread of the Coase-Edwards thesis.

How far has it been accepted outside the universities? Sadly, the best answer perhaps is that many accountants are content to distinguish two areas of work, governed by inconsistent rules:
- decision making (here the Coase-Edwards approach has had some impact), and
- routine management accounting (here tradition still reigns, e.g., allocation is usual, although the partial use of so-called "marginal costing" betokens at least some change of heart).

THE LSE CONTRIBUTION

As I said near the start, Coase and Edwards were surprised at the hostility with which their work was received by accountants. But they have since been given bouquets as well as brickbats, and their articles have been widely reproduced. They received a particularly handsome bouquet from the Nobel laureate Professor J.M. Buchanan. He tells us that they made an important contribution not only to accounting but to economics. Their work

> demonstrates major flaws in the applications and extensions of economic theory. [Yet t]hey did not themselves fully appreciate the uniqueness and originality of their approach. To an extent they looked on themselves as writing down, in the context of practical-problem situations, what "everyone knew" about cost [Buchanan, pp. 13, 16].

REQUIEM

Edwards was a man of immense energy. Among his many other activities, he founded the Accounting Research Association, which published monographs and reviews until World War II caused its demise. One of the reviews was particularly useful in that it introduced British readers to *The Valuation of Property* by James Bonbright [1937] of Columbia University. This book did for asset valuation much what Edwards and Coase did for costing (in Britain at least, a prophet is never without honor . . .).

Edwards was later able to apply his theories as he himself became a businessman and achieved great success in practical affairs. He gave up a chair at LSE to become head of Britain's state-owned electricity industry and thereafter of Beecham. He held directorships in other large companies. He served on many government committees and was knighted. He died in 1976.

REFERENCES

Baxter, W.T., and A.F. Oxenfeldt. "Approaches to Pricing: Economist versus Accountant." In: B.V. Carsberg and H.C. Edey, eds., *Modern Financial Management*, Baltimore, Md.: Penguin Books, 1969, pp. 184-208.

Bigg, W.W. *Cost Accounts*. London: MacDonald and Evans, 1939.

Bonbright, J.C. *The Valuation of Property*. New York, N.Y.: McGraw-Hill, 1937.

Buchanan, J.M. "Introduction: L.S.E. Cost Theory in Retrospect." In: J.M. Buchanan and G.F. Thirlby, eds., *L.S.E. Essays on Cost*, London: London School of Economics and Political Science with Weidenfeld and Nicolson, 1973, pp. 1-16.

Caine, Sidney. *History of the Foundation of the London School of Economics and Political Science*. London: G. Bell and Sons, 1963.

Coase, R.H. "Business Organization and the Accountant." In: J.M. Buchanan and G.F. Thirlby, eds., *L.S.E. Essays on Cost*, London: London School of Economics and Political Science with Weidenfeld and Nicolson, 1973, pp. 95-132.

_____. "Economics at LSE in the 1930s." *Atlantic Economic Journal* (March 1982), pp. 31-4.

_____. "Professor Sir Arnold Plant: His Ideas & Influence." In: Martin Anderson, ed., *The Unfinished Agenda*, London: Institute of Economic Affairs, 1986, pp. 79-90.

_____. "Accounting and the Theory of the Firm." *Journal of Accounting and Economics* (January 1990), pp. 3-13.

Edwards, R.S. "Some Academic Doubts about Secret Reserves." *The Accountant* (May 1936), pp. 683-6.

_____. "The Rationale of Cost Accounting." In: J.M. Buchanan and G.F. Thirlby, eds., *L.S.E. Essays on Cost*, London: London School of Economics and Political Science with Weidenfeld and Nicolson, 1973, pp. 71-92.

_____. "The Nature and Measurement of Income." In: W.T. Baxter and Sidney Davidson, eds., *Studies in Accounting*, London: Institute of Chartered Accountants, 1977, pp. 96-140.

Fowler, R.F. *The Depreciation of Capital*. London: King, 1934.

Gould, J.R. "The Economist's Cost Concept and Business Problems." In: W.T. Baxter and Sidney Davidson, eds., *Studies in Accounting*, London: Institute of Chartered Accountants, 1977, pp. 141-55.

Hayek, F.A. "The London School of Economics, 1895–1945." *Economica* (February 1946), pp. 1-31.

Knight, F.H. *Risk Uncertainty and Profit*. Boston, Mass.: Houghton Mifflin, 1921.

Lewis, W.A. "Depreciation and Obsolescence as Factors in Costing." In: W.T. Baxter and Sidney Davidson, eds., *Studies in Accounting*, London: Institute of Chartered Accountants, 1977, pp. 210-33.

Rowland, S.W. "The Nature and Measurement of Income." *The Accountant* (October 1938), Correspondence, pp. 609-10.

Thirlby, G.F. "Economists' Cost Rules and Equilibrium Theory." In: J.M. Buchanan and G.F. Thirlby, eds., *L.S.E. Essays on Cost*, London: London School of Economics and Political Science with Weidenfeld and Nicolson, 1973, pp. 273-87.

_____. "The Economist's Description of Business Behaviour." In: J.M. Buchanan and G.F. Thirlby, eds., *L.S.E. Essays on Cost*, London: London School of Economics and Political Science with Weidenfeld and Nicolson, 1973, pp. 201-24.

_____. "The Ruler." In: J.M. Buchanan and G.F. Thirlby, eds., *L.S.E. Essays on Cost*, London: London School of Economics and Political Science with Weidenfeld and Nicolson, 1973, pp. 163-98.

_____. "The Subjective Theory of Value and Accounting." In: J.M. Buchanan and G.F. Thirlby, eds., *L.S.E. Essays on Cost*, London: London School of Economics and Political Science with Weidenfeld and Nicolson, 1973, pp. 135-61.

Wicksteed, P.H. *Commonsense of Political Economy*. London: Macmillan, 1910.

DEPRECIATING ASSETS

Contents

1

Preface

You will have noticed that depreciation often plays a big part in accounts. A balance sheet is likely to include machines, etc; it usually shows them at their cost when new, and then deducts the total depreciation that has been written off since their acquisition. And the income statement includes in its costs the current year's addition to that total.

Thus everyone who looks at accounts – investors, managers, bankers, students, and so on – should have some idea of how depreciation is calculated. What do the asset values and the costs mean? Depreciation measures can have a great effect on a company's results, yet they are chosen from a wide range of possible figures, by rules that are vague and little understood.

This monograph tries to explain the accountant's methods of dealing with depreciation and to suggest ways of testing these methods. But it is too short to cover all sides of its complex subject: you will have to read further to get a full view. You will gain much by so doing. For depreciation is beset by interesting problems, some of which are linked with lively controversies (*eg*, over inflation accounting). In what follows I must sometimes take sides in these controversies; however, when I do so, I try to point out that there are other views.

The monograph has five chapters. The first four sketch the framework, and attempt to establish logical rules for measuring depreciation in times when prices are stable. The fifth asks how these rules should be amended when prices change.

Earlier drafts have been read by the group that manages this series of publications for the Scottish Institute – Professors D. Flint and A.M. McCosh, Mr. P.N. McMonnies and Professor D.P. Tweedie; and also by Miss Winifred Elliott and Mrs Paula Walker. Their criticism was invaluable, and I am grateful.

2

1 The Problem

Final accounts usually cover a year. So they would be easy to draft if the firm's happenings all came to a neat full-stop by the year-end — in particular if the firm could get all its inputs (goods and services) in doses that were used up exactly by then.

But a firm in fact buys inputs in doses that straddle business years: at the year-end its wealth thus includes sources of future inputs, such as stores not yet consumed, rent prepaid and machines that will still give service. The accountant must value these assets in his balance sheet. Likewise he must value the part of each asset that became input during the year and include this cost in the income statement. You will face the same problem if you keep monthly accounts, and have three-month season tickets or three-weekly haircuts.

The accountant's task may not be hard where the number of remaining input units can be checked physically and where the value per unit can be readily found. Thus stores-on-hand can be listed as so many tons or gallons, each worth so much money; and prepaid rent can be valued at so much per remaining month. Minerals (gravel-pits, oil-wells, etc) are less easy: experts may, or may not, know how many physical units are left; unit-values may or may not be well known and should presumably be trimmed to allow for, *eg*, increasing extraction costs as veins peter out.

Assets such as machines are a much worse problem: It is hard enough to define their invisible service-units, let alone estimate the residual number. And how do we find the value of each unit, especially if the asset will in future years grow less useful and need more repairs? It is mainly these difficulties that distinguish depreciating assets from the others.

3

Depreciating assets viewed as stores bought in bulk

Despite the greater difficulty of measuring and valuing the service-units of depreciating assets, the relevant principles seem much the same as for other sources of input such as stocks and stores. (And it should not matter, surely, that the balance sheet classes machines as "fixed assets" and stocks as "current".)

Our understanding of depreciation will in fact be greatly helped if we look on a depreciating asset in this light. We can imagine a firm that decides to buy stores (say, oil for heating) in bulk, because bulk-buying gives a lower unit-price and extra security and convenience. The oil is then consumed during more than one year; and accounting has evolved fairly adequate rules for charging each year with its usage and for valuing the residue at each year-end. Likewise the firm may choose to buy a machine with a long life because it is a better source of inputs, rather than buy a series of second-hand machines with shorter remaining lives or rent a machine by the month. The analogy with stores is thus close and should help us to devise rules for measuring depreciation.

The problem in diagram form

You may find that Diagrams 1 and 2 help you to see the problem. They illustrate the twin aspects of the asset's life-story: Diagram 1 traces its dwindling value over its life-span, *ie*, its value "pattern" or "profile"; Diagram 2 shows the fall in value during each year, *ie*, the yearly depreciation cost.

1.   *Asset value patterns*

MC is the cost of acquiring the asset. KK′ is its final re-sale price ("salvage" or "scrap" value). MK is its life-span.

At the date of "birth", M, usually the only known figure is the price MC. The accountant can only guess how long the life MK will stretch and what the scrap proceeds KK′ will be (though past experience with like assets may help his guessing). And what sort of path does the value curve CK′ follow during the life?

The diagram suggests three of these possible value patterns between C and K′. They reflect three of the traditional accounting methods for writing off depreciation:

4

Diagram 1 **Asset Value Patterns**

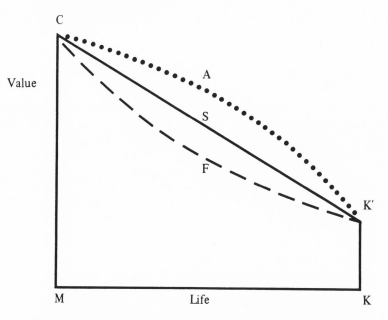

(1) CSK′ (unbroken line), found by *the straight line* method.

(2) CAK′ (dotted line), a "humped" curve, found by the *annuity* method (which allows for "interest" or "cost of capital").

(3) CFK′ (broken line) a "sagging" curve, found by the clumsily-named *fixed percentage of the diminishing balance* method. Most of the other popular methods also give sagging curves.[1]

The choice of curve can make a vast difference to the balance sheet figures, and to the value fall that must be written off each year.

2. *Yearly write-off patterns*

Diagram 2 shows three of the possible patterns of yearly write-offs (depreciation charges to successive income statements over the asset's life), namely

---

[1] The diagram suits an asset that, say, costs £1,300, lasts 16 years, and fetches £300 as scrap. The hump of CAK′ then accords with interest costs of 14% p.a. The fixed percentage here written off each year to produce CFK′ is about 8.75.

5

those reflecting the three value patterns of Diagram 1. (For clarity, the vertical scale of Diagram 2 is exaggerated.)

Diagram 2 **Yearly Depreciation Costs**

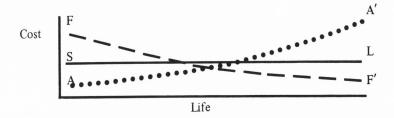

(1) The horizontal SL shows constant yearly costs (*ie*, the constant value falls of CSK′ above). It thus shows the depreciation charges of the straight-line method.

(2) The upward sloping AA′ shows costs that are low at the start but grow each year (*ie*, the increasing value falls of CAK′ above). It thus shows the net charges by the annuity method. This tilted pattern can be described as "low-high".

(3) The downward-sloping FF′ shows costs that are high at the start but shrink each year (*ie*, the diminishing value falls of CFK′ above). It thus shows the charges by the fixed percentage method. This pattern can be described as "high-low".

Our task is to ask ourselves which of the traditional book-keeping methods — the three illustrated above and some four others — best fits the circumstances of a given asset. And we may well ask, too, whether some quite different type of cost curve — say, one with much higher early charges — would not fit better; or whether we should not devise a special curve for each asset, instead of clinging to stereotypes.

Importance of using the best method

Even though the various methods all aim to write off the whole cost of an asset by the end of its life, the spread of this burden between years can be a matter of importance, particularly where depreciation is a big part of the firm's costs.

6

Profit figures are a useful guide to further investment. If the profits of a firm seem high, its owners will seek to expand it; and other firms will be attracted to the same field. Conversely, low figures discourage investment. Sound figures thus promote a healthy economy.

If then a firm chooses, say, a low-high depreciation pattern when a high-low one would suit the facts, the resulting tilt in the profit pattern will tend to attract too much investment at the start of life and too little at the end. The wrong choice of high-low rather than low-high may like-wise distort investment in the opposite way. Thus the methods play a part in our economy's resource allocation.

They may also affect a manager's decisions. But here we must think carefully. Once machines have been bought, their cost must often become "fixed" in the sense that it is not varied by activity. Thus a manager should look very sceptically at decision-budgets that contain depreciation; usually cash flows are a far more reliable guide to true cost.

7

2 Concepts and Definitions

Value decline *versus* matching

Chapter 1's approach to depreciation (you will recall) takes decline in asset values as the base of its logic; its argument starts with change in successive balance sheets, not with costs in income statements. It is thus somewhat at odds with the reasoning often followed elsewhere which explains depreciation in terms of, for instance, "matching costs with revenues".

As the balance sheet and income statement interlock, the two lines of reasoning should lead in the end to the same conclusions. But the approach *via* assets is in my view both simpler and safer. "Matching" suggests mere ledger technique, not observation of economic facts. Its advocates tell us that cost must be distributed over the years "in a systematic and equitable manner"; but what do these fine words mean if they are divorced from decline in wealth? And surely assets can still depreciate even if there is *no* revenue to match (*eg*, where an activity has come to a standstill).

Current *versus* historical values

Note, too, that my argument may seem to imply freedom to use values found in the current market. In fact, of course, accountants mainly use historical costs (though the arguments for current figures now win mounting support — see the 1980 Accounting Standards (SSAP 16) on current cost accounting; depreciating assets are normally valued at some fraction of their original price (plus installation costs, et.), and the yearly depreciation charges are slices of this historical sum.

In my view, argument built on current values is clearer and more reliable than argument built on historical cost. Dead figures may not reflect

8

today's realities; and they lack inherent logic. So current values are likely to point to the best depreciation methods.

But I do not think this conflict over theory need delay us. One can sensibly hold that methods found from current values, if adapted to historical data, will make the best of a bad job, *ie*, will yield the least indefensible historical measures. If this be true, the accountant should reason, when trying to choose a historical method, as if current and historical values will be identical, *ie*, he should assume that market values never change after the asset is bought. Here we shall start with this assumption (and so our discussion will help judgment of the historical methods); but later we shall relax it, and ask what should be done if assets are revalued to reflect current conditions.

Use-depreciation and time-depreciation

Some assets "die" when they are worn out by use. Others — perhaps most — die because of events that time brings anyway (regardless of use). For instance, machines may be scrapped because better models are invented; and a building lease runs out at a contracted date. It is thus convenient to talk of "use-assets" and "time assets".

The distinction is important when the accountant is picking a depreciation method. If the figures are to be helpful, a "cost" should be defined as sacrifice due to a given activity or event. So, with use-assets, a figure for depreciation cost should depend on extent of usage: it should be high in years of high use, low in years of low use. With time-assets, use costs nothing: value falls because the firm keeps the asset for another period; so the depreciation charges should here depend on passage of time. In other words, use-depreciation is a function of "service-units" such as miles run, whereas time-depreciation is a function of "time-units" such as the year.

Depreciation breeds "secondary assets"

Depreciation costs cut profit. Therefore, if owners take their income statement seriously, they will tend to pay out smaller dividends because of the depreciation entries. Then the firm will conserve cash. In time it may invest much of this cash (*eg*, in more stocks or even in other depreciating assets, or by repaying loan). Depreciation policy can thus help the firm to acquire a range of extra assets which in time improve the whole balance sheet. This helps to explain why it is economical for a new firm to start with few assets, and to expand later.

9

It is convenient to tack on the adjective "primary" to the depreciating asset whose pattern is our study, and "secondary" to the extra assets acquired thanks to the depreciation provisions.

Over the primary asset's life successive balance sheets will show a switch of values from primary to secondary. Thus, if a machine is bought for £1,200 at date 0, lasts for 3 years, and is written down by the straight-line method, the relevant bits of the balance sheets may run:

Table 1

Balance Sheets showing Primary and Secondary Assets

	Date: 0 £	1 £	2 £	3 £
Primary asset	1 200	1 200	1 200	1 200
Less Cumulative depreciation		400	800	1 200
Net value		800	400	–
Secondary assets:				
Bought with the year's depreciation quota		400	400	400
From earlier years			400	800
Cumulative		400	800	1 200
	1 200	1 200	1 200	1 200

This drift from primary to secondary can be illustrated also with diagrams. In Diagram 3, the vertical distance OC represents the owner's capital (= total assets), and OK shows the primary asset's life. CK – here, say, a straight line – traces the falling value. To maintain his capital despite this fall the owner must accumulate extra assets, shown by the triangle CC'K.

Depreciation policy can thus affect the growth and health of the whole asset structure. (Some critics ascribe the decrepit state of many industrial buildings in Britain to the fact that, until recently, British firms seldom wrote-down buildings.)

"Secondary earnings"

We now come to an important point that is usually missed. Though the balance sheet total may stay constant, the secondary assets swell the firm's

10

Diagram 3 **Depreciation and the asset structure**

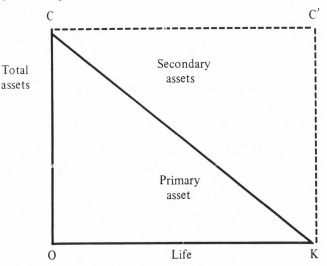

physical size. And, as the firm will not buy extra assets unless these yield benefits (more revenue or lower costs), total profit must tend to rise throughout the life of the primary asset. (In the Table 1 example, for instance, the £400 of secondary assets retained in year 1 will contribute to revenue in year 2). This is obvious where the secondary assets take the form of interest-bearing investments. These extra earnings, obtained thanks to the build-up of secondary assets, can conventionally be called "secondary earnings". They rise at a compound rate throughout the primary asset's life. When it dies, the cash outflow for its replacement tends to wipe out the secondary assets – and their earnings. The same cycle is repeated over the replacement's life.

Thus the preceding balance sheet and diagram, though good as a start to our studies, are rather naive – and so is much discussion of depreciation that ignores secondary assets and earnings. It is these that give the theoretical arguments for depreciation methods that allow for "interest".

Depreciation and replacement

You will sooner or later meet the view that the aim of depreciation policy is to save up the money needed to replace the asset after its death. Diagram 4 seems to lend colour to this view: the secondary assets KC′, particularly so

11

147

far as they are liquid, must indeed be a help with replacement.

A corollary of this view is that, if we are to abandon historical cost and turn to inflation accounting, the right depreciation charge for any year must be a function of replacement price.

Many authorities back this idea. But it seems to me to be only a part truth. For one thing, it assumes that replacement will in fact take place. But suppose the owner plans *not* to replace the asset (because, for example, he makes supplies for North Seal oil rigs and will switch to other activities after the oil gives out). Does the asset no longer depreciate? The answer surely must be that it does – probably in the sense that each year sees the owner left with a smaller store of potential future services. Again, awkward problems arise where "Old" will be replaced by a very different "New" – say, one whose physical traits are radically changed or whose cost is far above (or below) KC'. At best, the replacement criterion is incomplete as a generalisation.

You must therefore ask yourself whether a better criterion is not *maintenance of the owner's capital* (OC in Diagram 4). Should not the test of depreciation policy be that it leaves the owner as well off (so far as the given asset is concerned) at the end of the asset's life as at the start? Here, of course, the difficulty is to define "well off". To my mind, the owner stays as "well off" only if his future receipts will enable him to maintain the same standard of living. During inflation, historical capital is certainly no guide to a realistic answer: the best guide is historical capital adjusted to allow for the fall in the £'s value (so that the best depreciation charge is historical cost raised with an index of general purchasing power). But here we are on contentious ground, and should postpone fuller discussion until we have covered the main framework.

Depreciation and tax on income

Page 9 pointed out that depreciation charges may lessen dividends, and so breed secondary assets. But that may also lessen tax, with similar beneficent effects for the firm.

The depreciation rates of tax law may differ from the rates that the firm deems best for its own accounts (which is one reason why taxable profit often differs from the profit in the firm's accounts). In his computation the inspector adds back the firm's figure and then deducts the official "capital

12

allowances" instead. The official rules are far too complex for description here.

Governments often tamper with the tax rules in the hope of encouraging firms to invest more. In the mid-1970s business suffered from a liquidity crisis, probably aggravated by the failure of accounts to allow for inflation. The Labour Chancellor thereupon made new rules to ease the tax burden on firms hit by higher replacement costs of stocks and plant. The concession for depreciation is astonishingly generous: in many cases, the whole cost of a new asset can be charged in the first year. This allows effectively for inflation. But the two patterns of yearly charges (for tax and for accounts) are forced wide apart.

Obsolescence

This word has no very precise meaning, but we tend to use it when an asset's value falls for economic reasons that are not accompanied by physical decline. Thus a machine may be "as good as new" and yet lose some or all of its value because a better machine is invented or its products no longer sell well.

In accounts there is seldom point in distinguishing obsolescence from depreciation. At the start of a time-asset's life, when the accountant is deciding how fast to write it down, he tends to shorten his estimate of life if obsolescence is likely; then depreciation charges automatically include obsolescence cost. Only if value falls unexpectedly at some later date is a special obsolescence write-off needed.

Types of current value

Earlier paragraphs contrasted historical cost with "current value". These two words sound straightforward enough, but in fact they can mean several things, notably:

1. "Economic value" (EV)

We buy things because we rate them more highly than the cash that we pay as price. Thus, when a firm is deciding whether or not to buy a machine, it will – if it deems a sophisticated study worthwhile – draft a "capital budget" that sums the machine's benefits (perhaps wage savings and final scrap proceeds, less repair costs) all discounted to purchase date. These "discounted

13

cash flows" (DCF) show the machine's economic value at the start of its life and can be compared with the purchase price.

(This use of the phrase "economic value" was popularised by the Sandilands Report.[1] You may well feel it to be unfortunate, since the other current values are just as "economic".)

2. "Market values"

(a) Replacement cost (RC)
This may be the current buying price. But sometimes other figures must also be allowed for. Thus, if I can replace an existing machine (call it Old) for £1,000, but an improved alternative model (call it New) will yield maintenance savings whose DCF is £200, the true replacement cost is only £800.

(b) Net realisable value (NRV).
This is selling price less any costs (such as agent's commission) still needed to effect the sale.

3. Deprival value (DV)

Since inflation accounting became topical, many British accountants have come to see that the most logical current value is *selective, ie,* found by choosing, according to the actual circumstances of each asset, one of the above three types of current value — EV, RC, NRV. This selective value[2] is sometimes called "value to the business" but that phrase seems vague, and (as the concept hinges on how much poorer the owner would be without the asset) I use "deprival value" instead. The "lower of cost or market" rule for current assets is a more familiar — but less rational — example of a selective value.

Deprival value is thus concerned with the worsening of cash flows that would follow the asset's loss. It can be defined as the lower of the asset's replacement cost and its expected direct contribution to cash flows. An undeprived owner will deal with the asset in the way that brings the highest contribution, either keeping or selling it; so "expected direct contribution"

[1] Report of the Inflation Accounting Committee, Cmnd 6225.
[2] The logic of such a value was first argued in J.C. Bonbright, *The Valuation of Property*, McGraw-Hill, New York, 1937, reprinted in 1965 by Michie Company, Charlottesville, Virginia. The first hundred pages or so of this classic should be compulsory reading for every young accountant.

14

(sometimes called "recoverable cost") means either economic value (*eg*, service in use) or net realisable value, whichever is bigger.

Thus the formula is:

DV = lower of

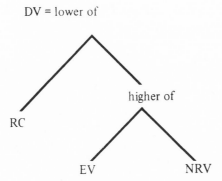

RC

higher of

EV   NRV

The reasoning behind the formula runs thus. Suppose a manager is deciding whether a proposed job is worth doing. His calculations must allow for the using-up of inputs (already owned), *eg*, stores issued for the job. To cost such stores, he must compare budgets of the future cash flows if he:

(*a*)   uses up the stores on the job; or

(*b*)   does not use them on the job, but retains them and then deals with them in the best remaining way.

The difference between (*a*) and (*b*) is the benefit of owning, that is, deprival value.

If he uses up the stores, normally he will replace them. Then budget (*a*) is at once burdened with their replacement cost; (*b*) is not; later cash flows are the same in both, as the replacements will yield the same contributions as the original stores and so these flows do not affect value. Thus, if the manager must buy replacements (for £70) because he will need such stores for a later job yielding £100, his budgets run:

15

151

	(a)	(b)
If stores are	*Used now*	*Not used now*
Then:		
cash outflow (replacement cost) is:	(70)	
cash inflow (future contribution) is:	100	100
	30	100

The £70 difference btween (a) and (b) is obviously due to replacement cost. This cost is here the deprival value of the stores; they are worth £70 to the business.

But sometimes the manager will not replace the stores, because *eg*, they have become dear or unsuitable. Then replacement cost drops out of the budgets. The difference between (a) and (b) is now the loss of the asset's future contribution – either NRV or EV: DV is the higher of these two.[1]

Current value patterns over whole life of a depreciating asset

For depreciating assets, the figures of each kind of current value will change as the asset grows older. Thus we must envisage a life series of, for instance, EV figures: the series starts high at acquisition date and sinks as the stock of services is consumed. Likewise NRV and RC values constitute series of diminishing figures.

Moreover "replacement cost" can mean two different sets of diminishing values:

(1) buying prices in the second-hand market (*eg*, a series of worn car prices, falling with age); and

(2) fractions of whatever cost the owner will in fact incur at replacement date. This series starts with, for example, the price of a brand-new car; subsequent values are geared to this initial cost. (Remember what page 4 said about viewing a machine as a store of inputs, bought in bulk at the cheapest rate per unit.)

So, when we are speaking of replacement values, clarity often demands that we add words to show exactly what we mean, *eg*, "replacement cost (new)"

I illustrate the budgets and give the reasoning more fully in chapter 12 of *Accounting Values and Inflation*, McGraw-Hill, London, 1975.

16

and "replacement cost in the second-hand market".

It is helpful to trace all the current values over the whole life of a depreciating asset:

Diagram 4 **Various value patterns of a depreciating asset**

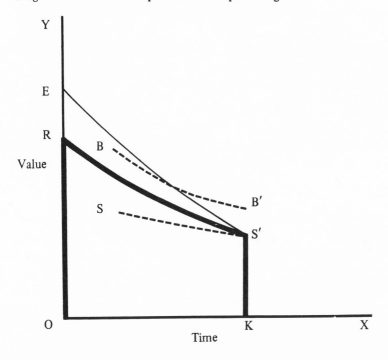

The value curves over the life are:

(1) RS′: the deprival value. Here it happens to sag, like CFK′ in Diagram 1. One sometimes hears it said that depreciated values are meaningless. But deprival value has a meaning: RS′ traces the replacement cost of the dwindling stock of input units (assuming a deprived owner would replace them by buying in bulk at the cheapest total cost, OR).

(2) BB″: the buying prices of similar worn assets (*ie*, replacement costs in the second-hand market). BB′ must lie above RS′, since the latter shows the cheapest source of inputs.

17

(3) SS': the net realisable value of a similar worn asset. SS' must lie below RS' so long as the asset is worth keeping. Otherwise the owner would gain by selling — as he does at K, where KS' is the scrap value.

(4) ES': the DCF values of future services (plus scrap value KS').

If you look back to page 15, you will see how its DV formula fits Diagram 4. Economic value ES' is higher than sale value SS' (otherwise the asset is not worth keeping), *ie*, ES' shows the direct contribution; and so long as replacement cost RS' is below contribution, it shows deprival value. At date K, both ES' and RS' are about to sink below SS'; sale price will soon be deprival value; the best plan is to sell the asset at once.

18

3 Choosing Optimum Life

Before he can decide on the depreciation charges for a newly acquired asset, the accountant must predict how long it will last (*ie*, the length of OK in our diagrams). Our textbooks are surprisingly reticent on how he does so.

"Life" is a matter of owner's choice

Unfortunately many kinds of assets do not "die" in a clear-cut way. Most assets have elastic lives: if the owner cares to spend more on repairs, new parts, etc, their life-spans can be stretched. Even where the asset is a living creature, its owner can often lengthen the span by spending more on diet and health care; when in the early nineteenth century the British navy cracked down on the slave trade, prices of American slaves rose — and they lived longer.

So an asset's life is best thought of in terms of the owner's cash flows. He is torn between two conflicting forces. On the one hand, he wants to put off replacement outlay by stretching the life. On the other, ageing assets suffer from various economic ailments — mounting repair costs, breakdowns, obsolescence, etc. The owner must try to find the best compromise between these forces, *ie*, the life-span that minimises his sacrifices.

Comparative budgets for various life-spans

He can find this compromise by putting the relevant cash flows into comparative budgets. Suppose for instance that the likely lives are in the range of 4 to 7 years. He must list the flows — initial price, repairs, etc, and scrap proceeds — for a life of 4 years, of 5 years, and so on.

19

155

But now he meets an unwelcome snag. He must not just compare, say, the 5-year total with the 4-year total (a process that would inevitably suggest the 4-year life to be the less costly). For, if he scraps Old at the end of year 4, normally he must at once pay for a New. To make comparison with the 5-year life, he must expand the budget of the 4-year life so that it not only includes Old's outlays in the years 0 − 4, but also allows somehow for the sacrifice of owning a New during year 5. Similarly all his other budgets must allow for overlapping lives.

The full solution is to extend his vision until it covers a very long series of 4-year lives, of 5-year lives, of 6-year lives, etc. This could be done by drafting a table of DCF budgets, embracing all years from now to his time horizon, to show which life-rhythm minimises the present value of future flows.

However, though logic demands this grandiose approach when conditions are complex (*eg*, if the costs of future News will change), happily there are ways of doing the calculations more simply if conditions are straightforward. The following example shows a crude but often sensible method.

Example

A firm buys a machine at year 0 for £130. The other cash flows for this type of asset are:

Year		£
1 − 3	(no repairs, etc.)	—
4	Repairs	10
5	do	15
6	do	25
7	do	44

After year 7, repairs will be so high that a longer life is out of the question. Scrap value will be *nil* for all lives.

The optimum life can be found by drafting budgets (the vertical columns in Table 2) for each of the likely life-spans and then working out *the average cost per year* of each, as in the row marked C.

The lowest average cost is the £30 in the 6-year column; so the optimum life is 6 years.

20

156

Table 2

Comparative budgets to show optimum life

Year	4 £	5 £	6 £	7 £
A. *Old's cash flow in year*	10	15	25	44
B. *New's cumulative flows* over various potential life-spans:				
At purchase, year 0	130	130	130	130
In 1st, 2nd, & 3rd years	–	–	–	–
In 4th year	10	10	10	10
In 5th year		15	15	15
In 6th year			25	25
In 7th year				44
Totals for each life-span	140	155	180	224
C. *New's average* per year of life	35	31	. 30	32

Old dies when New becomes cheaper

It is important to understand the reasoning behind Table 2.

A firm scraps assets at the point of time when it benefits by doing so. Normally this means that Old is scrapped in the year when New becomes superior in terms of cash flows. The test, by this marginal approach, is that Old's pending flows for repairs, etc, will surpass a figure that measures – in constant yearly terms – the sacrifice of buying and maintaining New.

Averaging, as in row C, is a way of reducing New's cumulative flows to a constant annual figure. Thus the table's logic is as follows. Row A shows Old's remaining flows at any date. Rows B and C show New's flows, and point to their minimum average cost of £30. When Old's flows rise past £30, it should be scrapped. Columns 6 and 7, row A, show Old's flows rising from £25 to £44; so Old should give way to New soon after the end of year 6.

This simple arithmetic is defensible only where the first asset and its successor are expected to have the same flows (or perhaps where the future is so uncertain that the successor's flows just cannot be foreseen). If changed flows can be predicted for the successor, rows B and C must be altered accordingly.

21

Average yearly cost = notional rent

We should think twice before accepting the above average cost as a reliable figure.

There are cases in plenty where average (or "allocated") cost is meaningless or downright harmful. In the context of depreciation it can, however, correspond to a genuine economic quantity — a market price. An asset's services can be acquired by paying either one sum at the start (purchase) or a series of periodic sums (rental). The averages of our calculations are meaningful to the extent that they convert the totals of a purchase budget — such as a column in section B — into a constant yearly equivalent ie, a rent. So, to be realistic, the rent figure must suppose the lessor to bear the budget's repair costs, etc, and to receive the scrap proceeds; it would improve, too, if it were raised to allow for his interest costs.

Largely for tax reasons, many firms are nowadays tending to lease assets instead of buying them. So we are not being fanciful if we imagine an owner saying: "I shall scrap this asset when its upkeep grows to more than the rent of a replacement".

This analogy with rent can be useful over and over again when one is reasoning about depreciation. One may view the firm as if it were split into separate sections for (a) administration, and (b) operation. Then section (a) can be deemed to buy the asset and lease it to (b) at an imputed rent that just covers the net cash flows. This notional rent charge is an excellent guide when we are seeking for the right depreciation pattern.

Discounting

Many depreciation calculations can be made in either a crude or refined form. Refinement allows in particular for "cost-of-capital" or "interest". There are strong grounds in theory for such an approach: economic sophistication insists that £1 in year n is of less concern than £1 at an earlier date.

Accuracy must therefore fall if one relies on the crude form. Whether the error is big enough to worry about depends on the rate of interest and the length of the period.

It is reasonable to hold that the crude calculation of Table 2 is sufficiently accurate for the facts envisaged (especially as the data must in practice

22

be subject to uncertainty). But a refined version[1] would tend to put optimum life at *more* than 6 years: and the higher the interest rate, the longer the life. "I use a high interest rate" is elegant for "I am hard-up"; and, for instance, the car owner who is hard-up (*ie*, short of ready cash, but perhaps wealthy otherwise) is apt to prefer costly repairs to the even higher cost of replacement.

Uncertainty

Figures such as those in Table 2 may suggest that the accountant can accurately foretell the future. Plainly that is not so. Most of his budgets are a kind of soothsaying. His firm may indeed be better off with such budgets than without them, but he must be ready for surprises and willing to revise his figures as time shows them to be wrong.

Optimum life budgets would seem particularly prone to error. Thus the Old in our example may turn out to be badly made, so that the repairs in fact rise faster than expected in the original row A, and bring death before year 6. Or, when year 6 comes, New's price may soar to a height that justifies extra years for Old.

Clearly, a firm with many similar assets can compile data that may lessen such uncertainties. You might suppose, too, that tables of asset lives (like the mortality tables of life insurance) would be available. But in fact they are hard to find. Even if such data existed, they would not help much (save where the firm owns enough similar assets to treat them as a group): if the actuaries' table for human lives put an age-group's average expectancy at n years, a given member may well die much sooner or later than n. In the same way, if tables of asset lives put the average at ten periods, individual lives will spread to either side. And in fact this spread seems to be remarkably wide. With some kinds of assets, less than 8% dutifully die in period 10; a few succumb in infancy, a few pass 20, and the majority lie scattered between these limits.

However, a study of depreciation (such as this) must for simplicity start by assuming the future to be predictable; otherwise it will get nowhere. And an accountant also, faced with a vast range of possibilities, is justified in working on this assumption when he picks a depreciation method. But surely he should later stand ready to modify his patterns if, as is probable, events give the lie to his first guesses.

[1]   Shown in my book *Depreciation*, Sweet and Maxwell, London, 1971, p. 15.

23

The relevant cash flows for the comparative budgets

The phrase "relevant cash flows" crops up often in the above description of optimum life budgets. But by what tests do we decide which flows are relevant to those budgets — or indeed to any other budgets whose task is to aid decision?

The answer becomes clearer when we adopt the economist's "what difference does it make?" attitude. Let us suppose that we are deciding between two alternative lines of action, X and Y. We therefore draft a cash budget for X and another for Y to see which has the balance of advantage. These budgets should concern themselves only with flows that are a consequence of X and Y. Every flow (receipt or payment) caused by X should go into the X budget. Every flow caused by Y should go into the Y budget. But many of the firm's flows will occur no matter how it decides as between X and Y. These flows might go into both budgets; but then they would not affect the balance; and therefore logic as well as economy tell us to omit them completely.

Thus a flow is relevant only if it points the contrast between competing flows.

Where the decision concerns optimum life, in theory we contrast totals of future flows of rival series of say 4-year lives, 5-year lives, and so on. Differences between totals will depend on how often the replacement price will be paid and the scrap proceeds received; also on repair outlays of each year, so far as these change as the asset ages. These flows certainly are relevant.

With some assets, other flows are relevant too. Thus an asset may work less accurately in old age; the accountant should then try to put a cash value on, for example, the cost of its spoilt work. Again, age may sometimes lead to change in revenue; thus, if an elderly asset's breakdowns will cut output, the accountant must try to allow for the fall in receipts. One may, however, doubt whether the ordinary firm (with some spare capacity, and ability to get replacements fast) will let the aging of one asset have much effect on revenue; repair bills seem more likely to typify the ills of aging. We shall therefore in future pages tend to use the shorthand "repairs" for all the changes in an aging asset's yearly flows.

To illustrate. If the yearly wages of a repair team will be the same for this asset and its successor, they are irrelevant for optimum age budgets. But if the wages must rise because of aging, the increase is a relevant flow.

24

4 Patterns of Value and Cost

We now come to our central chapter. It looks critically at possible patterns of value and cost over the asset's whole life. It does so in four stages:

(A)   This describes — in case you do not know them — the methods that accounting has traditionally used to write off depreciation. The methods are simple and convenient, but rough-and-ready. Different methods may yield very different costs. We must ask how the accountant should choose between them and, indeed, how far any of them reflect economic reality.

(B)   This explains the patterns of deprival value for depreciating assets.

(C)   This uses the patterns of deprival value to test traditional methods.

(D)   This brings cost-of-capital into the discussion.

(A) THE TRADITIONAL METHODS

To set out the traditional formulae shortly, let us call the asset's original cost C, its scrap proceeds S, and its life n years.

In arithmetical examples let us say the asset's cost (C) is £1,250, and its scrap value (S) is £50 after a life (n) of 3 years.

The normal bookkeeping (illustrated below in the section on the straight-line method) uses three accounts. One is for the asset; it is debited with the asset's cost at the start of life and stays unchanged (unless the asset

25

is revalued) till the final tidyings-up at death, The second, Cumulative Depreciation Account, is credited with the asset's depreciation charges year-by-year; its balance thus goes on growing till the end of the life, when its total is carried to the asset account. (The asset's value pattern is therefore the net balance of these two accounts). The third, Depreciation Cost, merely gathers together each year's charges for all depreciating assets as a preliminary to debiting total depreciation cost of the year to the income statement.

Straight-line

The yearly charge is $\frac{1}{n}(C-S)$ in all years.

In our example, it is thus $^1/_3$ (1250-50) = 400. The value pattern runs 1250, 850, 450, 50.

Diagram 5   **Straight-line method**

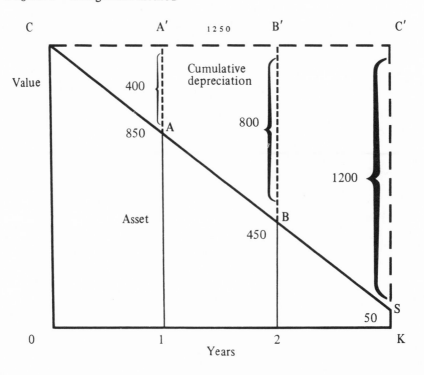

Diagram 5 may make the patterns more vivid. OCSK traces the (primary) asset's value. CC'S show how cumulative depreciation (= secondary assets) grows over the years – to AA' (400), then BB' (800), and finally SC' (1200).

In the ledger, the same facts are shown thus:

Machine Account

		£				£
Year 0			*Year 3*			
Dec 31	Cash	1250	Dec 31	Cum. depreciation	1200
				Cash	50
		1250			1250

Cumulative Depreciation Account

		£				£
			Year 1			
			Dec 31	Depreciation cost	400
			Year 2		
			Dec 31	do	400
					800
Year 3			*Year 3*		
Dec 31	Machine	1200	Dec 31	do	400
		1200			1200

In practice, the scap proceeds are unlikely to be exactly £50, and so may prove too high or low to balance off the machine account. The difference is then taken to the current income statement (*eg*, if the proceeds are too low, the shortfall may be written off as extra depreciation of year 3).

Fixed percentage of the diminishing balance

Here the diminishing net value is each year written down by a constant percentage, so that the charges have a high-low pattern and the value curve sags.

27

163

In practice, some firms apply the method less primly than your textbooks suggest. They may for instance choose one plausible rate and apply it slap-dash to a composite total value for many assets, with scant regard to whether these have similar lives or indeed still exist. Thus the method has been called "the lazy accountant's friend". Where he is not lazy, he must keep a separate account for each asset, and find the rate r — a fraction of 1 — from:

$$S = C (1-r)^n$$

or $\quad n \log (1-r) = \log S - \log C.$

An awkward feature of these formulae is their sensitivity to the size of S — normally an uncertain and perhaps insignificant quantity. If S is small, and also if life is short, the first-year's write-off tends to be very big. Thus r is .658 in our example and the write-off pattern is 822, 282, and 96. Value drops steeply (to only 428) in the first year: the extent of the drop can be seen by contrasting CABS in Diagram 6 with the (broken) line CS, showing the straight-line pattern.

Diagram 6   **Fixed percentage of diminishing balance**

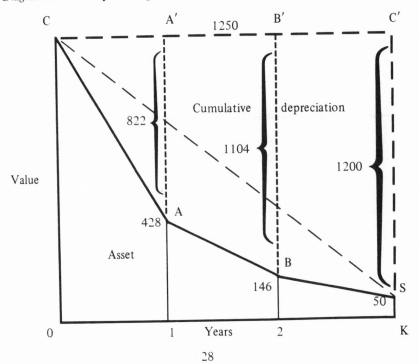

Sum-of-the-years'-digits

This method is popular in America. It, too, gives a sagging value curve; but the curve tends to be gentle and the arithmetic is fairly painless.

A decreasing fraction is applied each year. Its denominator is in all years the sum of the years' digits — in our example, $1+2+3 = 6$. Its numerators are the digits in reverse order.

Thus, in our example, the fractions are:

Year 1 $\qquad \dfrac{3}{1+2+3} = \dfrac{1}{2}$

Year 2 $\qquad \dfrac{2}{1+2+3} = \dfrac{1}{3}$

Year 3 $\qquad \dfrac{1}{1+2+3} = \dfrac{1}{6}$

The resulting charges are 600, 400, and 200. The book-values are 1250, 650, 250, 50. Diagram 7 traces these as the curve CABS - fairly near the straight-line values (broken line CS).

Double-declining balance

This, too, is used in America, to get a markedly sagging curve. The arithmetic is light-hearted: a fixed percentage is applied to the diminishing balance; this percentage is double that of the straight-line method where S is ignored. In our example, such a straight-line percentage would be $33^1/_3$; so the double-declining percentage is $66^2/_3$.

The resulting patterns are:

Year	Opening value £	Rate		Write-off £	End value £
1	1250	x $66^2/_3\%$	=	833	417
2	417	x $66^2/_3\%$	=	278	139
3	139	x $66^2/_3\%$	=	92	47
				1203	
Balance (roughly scrap value)				47	
				1250	

29

Diagram 7   **Sum-of-the-digits method**

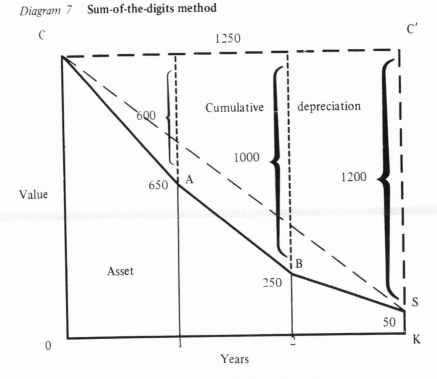

Fixed yearly charge to cover both depreciation and repairs

The above methods confine themselves to only two cash flows, *C* and *S*. It is arguable that we could with advantage widen their scope to include the flows for repairs.

The reasons are:

(1)   Economic logic tells us that repairs — and sometimes certain other flows — are just as relevant to value calculations as *C* or *S*. Accounting treats the latter (as "capital" items) differently from repairs ("revenue" items); the distinction makes for easy book-keeping, but does not always have economic significance. Chapter II showed that repairs are part of the relevant flows for calculation of optimum life. Equally, they affect value. Suppose a firm has two middle-aged assets, A & B, identical save that B will need

30

166

costly repairs when it gets older; plainly this pending burden makes it less valuable than A.

(2)   Methods that ignore repairs do not allow automatically for the asset's current state of repair. Suppose Asset C has just been given a major overhaul, whereas its twin D is in sore need of one; if the balance sheet shows both C and D at the same value, it gives a false view. Again, the income statement is open to criticism if it fails to allow for the high cost of pending repairs.

It is not hard to devise a formula that makes approximate allowance for repairs.

Let R = estimated total repairs during life. The yearly charge is then $\frac{1}{n} (C-S + R)$. This is a constant, and higher than straight-line charges; however, repair outlays are here not charged against profit but added to the asset's value.

Let us amplify our example by bringing in repairs of, say, £200 in year 2 and £400 in year 3. The yearly charge rises to $\frac{1}{3} (1250 - 50 + 200+400) = 600$. The value pattern now runs:

Year	Opening value £	Write- off £	Repairs capitalized £	End value £
1	1250	(600)	–	650
2	650	(600)	200	250
3	250	(600)	400	50

Diagram 8 shows this pattern. Realism and aesthetics both suggest that the £200 and £400 should be totals of smaller outlays, made every few months and growing as the asset ages. Then the value curve will be jagged, with teeth becoming more prominent over time. Moreover it sags below the straight-line pattern CS. It will always do so where the repairs increase with time.

Comparing Diagrams 7 and 8, one sees that both show the same values at the year-ends: 650, 250, 50. But in practice the two methods are likely to yield somewhat different values. To make them equal we have here chosen a repair pattern (0, 200, 400) that exactly complements the 600, 400, 200 depreciation pattern of the sum-of-the-digits method (ie, raises the total to 600 in each year). As later pages will explain, this choice of figures illustrates an important point.

31

Diagram 8   **Fixed charge to cover depreciation and repairs**

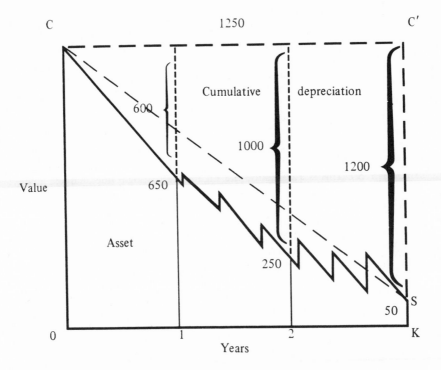

Service-unit

All the above methods are firmly linked to *n*, and thus assume that value drops because of time. They therefore seem suitable for time-assets. The service-unit method (and one or two slight variants, such as the depletion method for minerals) is linked instead to units that reflect activity, such as miles run or products made. It thus assumes the activity to cause the fall in value, and is suitable for use-assets.

In our example suppose the asset is expected to yield 100,000 service-units during its 3-year life. $(C-S) \div 100,000$ gives the unit-cost of £.012. The write-offs of each year depend on the service-units "consumed" during that year, say:

32

Year	Service Units		Unit Cost £		Write-off £	End value £
1	25,000	x	.012	=	300	950
2	60,000	x	.012	=	720	230
3	15,000	x	.012	=	180	50
					1200	

Here the asset is mainly used in year 2 and, accordingly, value drops sharply in that year.

(B) DEPRIVAL VALUE AND DEPRECIATION

Our next task is to find how depreciation is calculated when DV is guide.

The HAVE and HAVE NOT budgets

As page 14 explained, DV equals the decline in wealth that an owner would suffer if he were deprived of the asset. So DV is found by comparing his cash budgets for two alternative scenarios, namely if he (1) retains the asset (call this the HAVE budget); or (2) loses it (call this the HAVE NOT budget).

With depreciating assets, the future flows are likely to be exceedingly complex; but we can reduce them to manageable size in two ways. First, we assume (at least at the start of our studies) that a deprived owner would buy a New, and a New with the same pattern of flows. Second, we rely on the idea that New's flows can be turned into a constant yearly equivalent (the notional rent of page 22) without violence to economic logic.

So the two budgets are likely to contain:

(1) HAVE

   Old's flows over the rest of its life — namely "repairs" (in the broad sense that includes any flow changes due to aging), and final scrap proceeds.

(2) HAVE NOT

   New's notional rent over the same period.

33

Note that the asset's contributions (cost savings or revenue) might not be lost at deprival; often New would yield them thereafter. Then they are common to both scenarios, and both budgets can omit them.

Layout of the budget

A convenient form for calculating DV (where this is as usual based on replacement cost) is a table with columns for each year of life, and rows for:

i.   Old's cash flows (the HAVE budget).
ii. New's cash flows, converted into a constant notional rent (the HAVE NOT budget). Where New's flows are the same as Old's, the rent is the average of the figures in row *i*.
iii. The excess of *ii* over *i*, i.e. the net benefit of ownership during each year.
iv. The total net benefits still to be received at each year-end, i.e. the sum of the *iii* figures in the columns further to the right.

Thus *iv* gives the DVs (the replacement costs of remaining input units) for consecutive balance sheets, and *iii* gives each year's write-off.

Example

Let us put the *C* and *S* of our staple example into such a table. It then looks like this:

Table 3   *Deprival value of a depreciating asset (no repairs, etc.)*

Year of Life	0	1	2	3	3´
	£	£	£	£	£
i HAVE budget					
Old's cash outflow	1250				
Old's cash inflow					(50)
	£				
Net total	1200				
average p.a.	400				
ii HAVE NOT budget					
New's notional rent		400	400	400	
iii Benefit of owning for					
year (*ie* write-off at year end)		400	400	400	50
iv Deprival value					
(= future years' benefits per *iii*)	1250	850	450	50	-

34

(C) TESTING THE TRADITIONAL METHODS

Straight-line

The figures in rows *iii* and *iv* of Table 3 turn out to be the very same as those of page 26, illustrating the straight-line method. Thus the DV approach triumphantly confirms that this popular method has validity — always provided actual conditions match Table 3's assumptions, namely:

(1) the asset is a time-asset; and

(2) repairs (and other yearly flows) are constant over life; and

(3) cost-of-capital can be ignored; and

(4) all prices are constant.

Sagging curves

Where, instead, the flows get worse over the years, DV no longer sinks in a straight line.

Suppose again there are repairs of £200 in year 2, and £400 in year 3. Now the budgets change to the figures of Table 4, page 36.

Here the write-offs follow a high-low pattern; the value curve drops steeply at first and gently later. So a traditional method that produces a sagging curve may meet our needs.

In fact, because we have here used repair figures (0, 200, 400) that complement the write-offs of our sum-of-the-digits example (page 29), the two sets of values are the same. Given this repair pattern, the sum-of-the-digits method is a short-cut to DV values. With other repair patterns, it might not be so suitable; the fixed-percentage methods might (or might not) fit better.

Fixed charge for depreciation and repairs

DV'S yearly write-offs, as shown in row *iii* of Table 4, complement each year's repairs, etc. to produce a constant total charge for the two costs. This is logical where the repairs are debited to the income statement as

35

171

Table 4

Deprival value of a depreciating asset (with repairs)

Year of life	0	1	2	3	3′
	£	£	£	£	£
i HAVE budget					
Old's cash outflows	1250		200	400	
Old's cash inflow					(50)

	£
Net total	1800
Average p.a.	600

	0	1	2	3	3′
ii HAVE NOT budget					
New's notional rent		600	600	600	
iii Net benefit of owning for year (*i.e.* write-off at year-end)		600	400	200	50
iv Deprival value (= future years' benefits per *iii*)	1250	650	250	50	-

a separate item (the usual bookkeeping). But, particularly where repairs are pending at the year-end, a still better course would be to debit the full rent of row *ii* to the income statement, and the repair outlays to the enlarged cumulative depreciation allowance.

But this is precisely what the fixed-charge-for-depreciation-and-repairs method does; the diagram that illustrates it (page 31) could equally well be used for Table 4's DV figures. So this method wins high marks by the DV test. Unfortunately it is less popular than the other methods, presumably because the unpredictability of repairs lessens the chance of neat end-figures at the asset's demise.

Service-unit methods

Obviously any "consumption" of a use-asset during a year must lessen the owner's loss if he is deprived at the year-end. Therefore DV must respond

36

to such consumption.

DV figures for a use-asset can be found by changing the rents in row *ii* of the tables: instead of the constant for each year, we put in a charge per use-unit, multiplied by the year's number of units. Given the facts assumed by the example on page 32, the DV values will be the same as those of that example.

However, a more realistic example would include repairs also. DV tables would here end with more sensitive values, influenced by both use and repairs. This suggests that accounting should combine two methods, *ie*, service-unit and fixed-charge-for-depreciation-and-repairs.

Summary

To re-cap. By recording declines in asset value, accounts create charges in income statements. These charges should represent a constant cost per unit of fixed asset "consumed" by use or passage of time (*cf*. charges for stores). A depreciation method meets this test if it charges the income statement with either:

(1)   a cost that complements other relevant flows charged in the given year, so ensuring a constant total charge per unit; or

(2)   a constant cost that is high enough to cover not only convention-al depreciation but also the other relevant flows, which must here be capitalised.

With such a method, asset values become sensitive to the remedial effects of overhaul, etc, and then may have a somewhat saw-like pattern.

Where a traditional method comes close to meeting this test, then its use is justified. Where none of the traditional methods answer, then surely the accountant should devise a special method, with the help of DV analysis.

(D) INTEREST

Asset value can be approached in two different ways (which, under ideal conditions, yield the same figure): (1) forward-looking; and (2) backward-looking. Thus, to find a mid-life value of a depreciating asset we can either (1) look back to original cost and other relevant past flows, and write off

37

173

depreciation; or (2) look forward to future flows, as in a table of HAVE and HAVE NOT budgets.

Both methods grow in accuracy if they allow for interest. In (1), interest on the investment is as truly a cost as outlays on *eg*, installation or foundations. In (2), discounting makes for realism (indeed, long-range calculation becomes senseless without it): capital budgets and DV budgets both gain if they treat the firm's cost-of-capital as an ingredient.

Thus it seems sad that we make so little use of methods that allow for interest. There are plenty of reasons for our neglect, such as: (1) the methods are not simple; (2) interest cost on a given asset is inconspicuous — a concealed part of the firm's total cost-of-capital (which itself is apt to be inconspicuous); (3) humped value curves seem at odds with conservatism; (4) accountants are bad at compound interest.

Methods that allow for interest

Our textbooks usually extend their list of traditional methods by adding the annuity method and the sinking fund method. The distinction between these two seems to relate less to principle than to type of secondary assets (with sinking funds, usually external investments such as government stocks).

It is, however, helpful to regard an "interest method" not as an addition to the usual list but rather as an improved version of a method that ignores interest. Thus the straight-line method burgeons into the annuity method when interest is recognised. And all other methods could likewise, with a little ingenuity, be spruced up to allow for interest.

Annuity method

The "annuity" in question is in fact DV's notional rent series, increased by interest. Suppose the only cash flow of an asset with a 3-year life is its price of £1,000, and the firm's cost-of-capital rate is 10%. Interest tables show that, at 10%, 2.487 buys a 3-year annuity of 1; therefore 1,000 buys one of 1000 ÷ 2.487 = 402. The latter figure is the annual charge by the annuity method.

The cash flow of our usual example includes the £50 received in year 3. To find the yearly rent, U, we must allow not only for the price of £1250 but also for present value of £50. If the cost-of-capital rate is 10%, then tables

38

put the present value of 1 due in 3 years at .751, and U is found from:

$$1250 = 2.487\,U + 50 \times .751$$
$$\therefore U = 487.54$$

Backward-looking approach

The easiest way to show the method's mechanics is *via* the backward-looking approach of the historical cost ledger, with one combined account for the asset and depreciation. Each year this account is debited with interest on the opening balance, *ie*, the depreciated value is raised by this cost; the credit is put into (say) the finance section of the income statement, probably as an offset to interest paid. The asset account is credited with the full depreciation charge; the debit goes eventually to the income statement, *eg*, as a manufacturing cost.

An example of the asset account follows:

Machine account

	£		£
Year 1		*Year 1*	
Jan. Cash	1250.00	Dec. Manufacturing a/c	
Dec. Interest	125.00	(depreciation charge)	487.54
		Balance c/d	887.46
	1,375.00		1,375.00
Year 2		*Year 2*	
Jan. Balance b/d	887.46	Dec. Manufacturing a/c	
Dec. Interest	88.75	(depreciation charge)	487.54
		Balance c/d	488.67
	976.21		976.21
Year 3		*Year 3*	
Jan. Balance b/d	488.67	Dec. Manufacturing a/c	
Dec. Interest	48.87	(depreciation charge)	487.54
		Cash	50.00
	537.54		537.54

39

175

Forward-looking approach

The forward-looking approach of DV budgets yields the same values. The HAVE budget must include interest as a cost, and the HAVE NOT budget must use the high rent of £487.54 (which, adopting the actuaries' wording in loan repayment tables, can be called the "full service charge"). Table 5 shows the calculation:

Table 5

Deprival value.of a depreciating asset
(interest recognised)

Year of life	0	1	2	3	3'
	£	£	£	£	£
i HAVE budget					
Old's price	1250				
Interest on balance per *iv*		125	88.75	48.87	
Scrap proceeds					(50)
ii HAVE NOT budget					
New's full service charge		487.54	487.54	487.54	
iii Benefit of owning for year					
(*ie*, net write-off at year-end)		362.54	398.79	438.67	50
iv Deprival value (=Future					
years' benefits per *iii*)	1250	887.46	488.67	50	

These values follow a humped course (somewhat like CAK' in the diagram on page 5).

Where the HAVE budget includes rising repairs, these will tend to offset interest's effect on the value pattern: sagging force now conflicts with humping force. The resulting pattern may approximate to a straight line. Perhaps this is a justification for use of the straight-line method.

Final accounts for each year of life

A table of final accounts, covering the whole life, gives satisfying proof of the annuity method's logic.

Suppose that the asset in our example earns about £738 a year (after all the costs except depreciation) throughout its life; that secondary assets earn 10% and that the owner withdraws all profit. Table 6 shows the full story.

40

Table 6

Annuity method in a complete set of final accounts, over whole life

Year	1	2	3
	£	£	£
Balance sheet			
Primary asset			
Balance brought forward	1250	887	488
Add 10% cost-of-capital	125	89	49
	1375	976	537
Less Depreciation	488	488	487
Net value	887	488	50
Secondary assets	363	762	1200
Total (= capital)	1250	1250	1250
Income statement			
Operations			
Revenue	738	738	737
Less depreciation	488	488	487
	250	250	250
General			
Secondary earnings		36	76
Cost-of-capital added to primary asset	125	89	49
Total	125	125	125
Total profit (= dividend)	375	375	375
Rate of return on £1250 investment	30%	30%	30%
N.B. Depreciation can be analysed as:	£	£	£
Net value write-off	363	399	438
Cost-of-capital	125	89	49
Full service charge	488	488	487

41

177

The humping produced by interest can be seen by comparing the pattern of net values (887, 488, 50) with the straight-line values (800, 400, 50).

Note the following:

(1)   We must be careful to distinguish between *gross* and *net* depreciation (see analysis at the foot of the table). The gross (= full service) charge is constant over the years. But, because high-low interest costs are added to the asset balances, the net write-offs are less than the full charge, and are tilted low-high.

(2)   Thus net charges against revenue rise each year. But so do secondary earnings — to exactly the same extent, thanks to our use of the secondary earnings rate of 10% in the calculation of the charges.

(3)   Therefore profit is constant over the 3 years — and also over later 3-year cycles if these are repeated. The rate of return on the £1250 investment (30%) is constant too. These constant figures seem the best guide to users of the accounts, given our assumption of stable revenue, etc. If you re-write the table with a method that ignores interest, you will get tilted figures.

Full and net cost curves

Diagram 9 shows the various cost curves that result from recognition of interest. AA' traces the full service charge, *ie*, the constant gross figure. DD' traces the net charge. The vertical distance in any year between these curves represents the cost-of-capital.

For comparison, the diagram shows too the straight-line charges, SL. The positions of the other curves imply a high rate of cost-of-capital and a long life; otherwise these curves would lie closer to SL.

The full service charge would seem a useful tool for management control. Because it includes imputed interest, it is better than, say, the straight-line method for showing the whole sacrifice caused by asset ownership. Manufacturing accounts with such high charges would tell everyone how much the works manager's equipment really costs the firm, and perhaps make him more cautious in his requests for fresh investment.

42

Diagram 9 **Net and gross charges where interest is recognised**

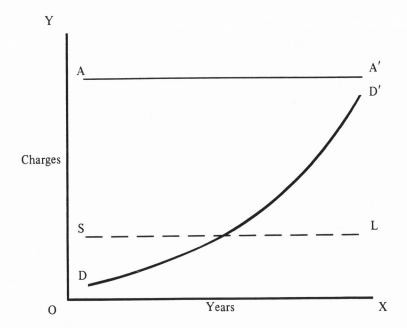

43

179

5 Revaluation

Up to this point we have for simplicity assumed that prices, etc, remain stable. We must now abandon this assumption, and deal with changing conditions and their effects on value patterns.

So long as accounting uses historical costs, changing conditions will affect its value patterns to only a very limited extent (as where obsolescence causes a faster write-off).

If, however, a firm relaxes its adherence to historical cost, revaluation may often be necessary. Then the attitude and techniques of deprival value become exceedingly helpful. Tables of HAVE and HAVE NOT budgets, such as that on page 36, again meet our needs; but they must be amended, at the date of change, to make their later figures match the new conditions. In particular, New's notional rent must be updated. Then the revised depreciation and value patterns emerge automatically.

We can best deal with our topic under the heads of (*A*) general price-change (since 1939, inflation); (*B*) price-change specific to the given asset; and (*C*) combination of both general and specific change. Understanding is easier if we suppose the change to be abrupt, *ie*, confined to one year; and if we overlook the refinement of discounting.

(A) INFLATION

Common sense suggests that, if the general index goes up by, say, 40%, revaluation must lift the historical cost patterns of later times by 40% too. But common sense is right only if the price-change is indeed general, affecting *all* the relevant flows to an equal degree.

44

180

Asset values

Suppose, in the example on page 36, that the 40% rise occurs at the end of year 2 (and after the £200 repair of that year). If we do a formal calculation, we must redraft Table 4, splitting its year-2 column into pre-change and post-change parts. Table 7 is the result. After the rise, all the figures go up by 40%, *eg*, New's rent jumps to £840.

Table 7

Revaluation after inflation

Year of life	0	1	2 Pre-	Post-	3	3
	£	£	£	£	£	£
i HAVE budget						
Old's Cash flows	1250		200		560	(70)
ii HAVE NOT budget						
New's notional rent		600	600		840	
iii Net benefit of owning						
for year		600	400		280	70
iv Deprival value – future years' benefits, as foreseen:						
Prior to inflation (line *iii*, page 36)	1250	650	250			
After inflation (per *iii* above)				350	70	

Thus row *iv* confirms what one would expect: value rises 40% at the time of price-change – from £250 to £350.

Diagram 10 illustrates the change of pattern. It assumes repair costs (*eg*, the £200 of year 2) to consist of many small payments, so that we are justified in smoothing the value curve. Over the whole life, value follows the pattern CFHSK, instead of the original prediction of CFK'.

It is important to recognise how limited is inflation's impact on these patterns. (It can elsewhere have great effect, *eg*, by reducing the purchasing power of cash and other assets whose values are tied to the £.) All that our calculations do is to re-state the post-change facts in a money-unit of lower worth, much as if the ledger was switched from £s to $s. The facts themselves

45

181

Diagram 10   **Asset revaluation because of inflation**

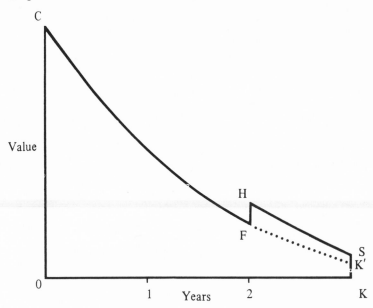

do not change; for instance, an optimum life table for New (on the lines of the table on page 21) would show that New's life neither grows nor shrinks. If the vertical axis of Diagram 10 measured value in units of constant purchasing power, the value curve would retain its original pattern.

The revised balance sheet

If the revised net value of the depreciating asset is to go into the balance sheet, other figures must change also. To be consistent with the normal layout, we must show the asset's gross value and cumulative depreciation; so, in our example, both of these must be raised by 40%. The secondary assets will presumably be revalued also (so far as they are not monetary items). The equity must then go up, to maintain balance: theory bids us raise the capital, but in fact the needed increase is likely to be shown separately, with some such name as "inflation allowance".

For our page 45 example, the balance sheet at the end of year 2 must thus be revamped as in Table 8.

46

Table 8

Balance sheet, end of year 2, revalued after inflation

	(1) Pre-revaluation	(2) Post-revaluation
	£	£
Primary asset (cost, new)	1250	1750
less Cumulative depreciation	1000	1400
Net value (worn)	250	350
Secondary assets	1000	1400
	1250	1750
Capital	1250	1250
– inflation allowance:		
primary asset		100
secondary assets		400
		500
	1250	1750

Annual charges

In the years after the price rise, the annual write-offs should, if the owner is to maintain his real capital, be higher than historical cost charges – *ie*, should be the historical figures raised with a general index factor. Revaluation yields these higher figures automatically. In our example, the year 3 charge is put up by 40% and becomes £280 instead of £200; and so the owner will end up with his real capital unimpaired (*ie*, with 1750 of the end-£s, equivalent in his eyes to 1250 of the beginning-£s).

The backlog bogie

Some people argue that, after each price change, the next income statement must be charged not only with a revised depreciation cost of the current year, but also with "backlog" depreciation to boost the contributions of earlier years. Thus, in the example, they would have us charge an extra £400 to top up the historical depreciation of column (1) from £1,000 to £1,400.

This is yet another instance of how historical figures can confuse. If

47

183

the balance sheet is corrected to current £s, it shows that inflation in fact brings no need for backlog charges: in column (2), depreciation is re-stated at the proper figure of £1,400 without any boosting. And, if there is further inflation in future years, depreciation will go on rising automatically in corrected accounts.

But, you may argue, the post-revaluation figures of Table 8 are so healthy only because the secondary assets appreciate there by 40%; and they will fail to do so if they include net monetary assets (since the face value of such assets does not change). True: but then the failure is due to liquidity policy, not depreciation; the accounts mislead if they blame the shortfall on "backlog depreciation" instead of "loss on holding money".

(B) SPECIFIC PRICE CHANGE

In this section, we assume one or more of the relevant flows to change during a period when general prices remain tolerably constant. So here we are dealing with *relative* change — something that is likely to have economic consequences of importance; any rise or fall in value is now "real", as distinct from the "nominal" or "fictitious" movements of inflation.

Revised figure of optimum life

Let us suppose that the 40% rise in our example is confined to New's price (*ie*, repairs and scrap value stay unchanged). This shift makes replacement more disagreeable, and so tends to lengthen life (put at 3 years on earlier pages). To find what happens, we must look at the flows of years 4 and 5; let us say the repairs will be £700 in 4 and £1300 in 5. The optimum life calculation (explained on page 20) becomes (see Table 9; page 49).

Thus New's optimum life rises to 4 years (instead of 3), and its notional rent to £750 (instead of the £600 on page 36). What about Old's life? If Old is kept during year 4, its net flow will then be £700 less scrap £50, *ie*, £650 — less than New's rent. If Old is kept during year 5, its net flow will be £1,300 less £50, *ie*, £1,250 — more than New's rent. So Old should now be kept till the end of year 4 (instead of 3).

48

Table 9

Comparative budgets to show optimum life

	Year	3	4	5
		£	£	£
A. *Old's flow in year*		400	700	1300
B. *New's cumulative flow* over various potential life-spans:				
At purchase		1750	1750	1750
In 1st year		—	—	—
In 2nd year		200	200	200
In 3rd year		400	400	400
In 4th year			700	700
In 5th year				1300
Scrap receipts		(50)	(50)	(50)
Totals for each life-span		2300	3000	4300
C. *New's average per year* of life				
(= notional rent)		767	750	860

Revised asset values

Old's owner must feel pleased that he bought when he did. Ownership now confers enhanced benefits, in the sense of obviating need to pay the extra for a dearer New.

"Every valuation is a comparison"; the gratifying contrast with New raises Old's deprival value. The original and revised values can be shown in diagram form.

Life is here extended from OK to OM. The value pattern, originally expected to be CK'K, is revised at E (end of year 2) and becomes CFHM'M.

The value can be found with HAVE and HAVE NOT budgets, as in Table 10 below. Their figures are the same as in Table 4 till the price rise late in year 2. The post-change columns, on the right, thereafter put New's rent

49

Diagram 11   **Revaluation after specific price-change**

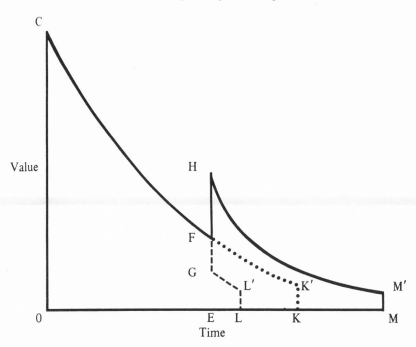

at its increased level of £750. Thus they lift the yearly benefits of ownership in line *iii*, and the values in line *iv* (*eg*, at the end of year 2, future yearly benefits will be £(350 + 50 + 50) = £450, and so value jumps from £250 to £450).

"Replacement cost" is not "replacement price"

Comparison of Tables 7 and 10 (pages 45 and 51) shows that specific price-change upsets value patterns more than does general change. Not only has specific change stretched Old's life, but it has (partly because of this extra spell of service) raised Old's value disproportionately: the price jump of 40% has raised value by 80% (from £250 to £450 — see page 51, last line of table, year 2 values). Remember that the HAVE and HAVE NOT budgets must allow for the new life and repair figures as well as the new price, and so the final line may well change more or less than price. As page 14 pointed out, "replacement cost" covers more than "replacement price".

50

186

Table 10

Revaluation after specific price-change

Year of life	0	1	2 Pre-	Post-	3	4	4
	£	£	£	£	£	£	£
HAVE budget Old's cash flows	1250		200		400	700	(50)
HAVE NOT budget New's notional rent		600	600		750	750	
Net benefit of owning for year		600	400		350	50	50
Deprival value							

−future years'
    benefits, as
    foreseen:
      Prior to
      inflation (line iii,
      page 36)
	1250	650	250				

After inflation (line iii, above)				450	100	50	

An unfortunate and little recognised consequence is that the short-cut of revaluation with a specific index may yield inaccurate results. Published indices presumably reflect the prices of brand-new assets. The accountant needs other indices as well, to reflect values of worn assets.

The revised balance sheet after specific change

In the balance sheet, the primary asset's gross and net values must be raised as in Table 11, which shows the figures for our example at the end of year 2. The price of a new asset is £1,750; Table 10 puts current value (worn) at £450: so depreciation must be the difference of £1,300. The net increase of £200 is reflected in the equity.

If (as is probable) the secondary assets are unlike the primary asset, they may not appreciate at the same pace. Then they will no longer match cumulative depreciation. A shortfall will clearly create problems if the asset is to be replaced at the end of its life.

51

Table 11

Balance sheet, end of year 2, revalued after specific price-change

	(1) Pre-revaluation £	(2) Post-revaluation £
Primary asset (new)	1250	1750
less Cumulative depreciation	1000	1300
Net value (worn)	250	450
Secondary assets	1000	1000
	1250	1450
Capital	1250	1250
Revaluation surplus		
Primary asset		200
	1250	1450

Annual charges

Specific price-change alters depreciation charges of later years. For instance, Tables 4 and 10 show them going up to £350 (from £200) in year 3, and to £50 (from nil) in year 4. In the end, the cumulative total will mount (see line *iii* of Table 10) to £600 + £400 + £350 + £50 + £50 = £1450. This is more than the original investment (£1250), but less than replacement price (£1750).

So should the later charges to the income statement be less than depreciation cost, or equal to it, or (backlog again) more than it? Your answer to this question depends (see page 12) on how you define the owner's "well-offness", *ie*, on what sort of capital is to be maintained.

The capital maintenance test

You must choose between three possibilities:

(1)   Money capital.

(2)   Real capital.

In the absence of general price-change, (1) and (2) are the same.

52

If the owner ends up with assets worth £1,250, he is as well-off as when he started — in the important sense of still being able to buy much the same basket of goods-in-general and so keep up his living standard.

(3)   Physical capital (or "operating capacity")

If the owner ends up with less than £1750, he is less well-off in the sense of ability to replace the given asset.

You therefore face the difficult choice between real and physical capital. Accountants are split on the question. I favour real capital[1] because (*a*) the main reason for measuring income is to give the owner a guide to his consumption plans; (*b*) the calculations can go wildly astray if they hinge on physical rather than economic characteristics; and (*c*) replacements can be quite different from the first asset, because of technical improvements, etc.

Entries in the income statement

If *real* capital is chosen as yardstick, the depreciation provisions must maintain the owner's command over goods-in-general, not ability to replace the given asset. The low charges of the original estimate remain correct for the whole life, since they here keep the owner's wealth at its starting level. Thus, in our example, the year 3 charge is still only £200 (as on page 36); if revenue is say £800, profit is £600, as in column (1) of Table 12.

But the same profit can be reached by a route that is more informative, and fits in with current values in the balance sheet. Column (2) shows this alternative. It charges the current (*ie*, higher) depreciation (here £350 — see page 51); but then it credits the appreciation on the slice of asset realised in the year (£150 — the difference between the current and historical charges of £350 and £200). Profit is again £600.

If the firm wants to maintain its assets at their expanded level of £1750, it may finance this £500 addition by for instance making voluntary appropriations of profit, say at £250 each year (see the foot of columns (1) and (2)).

1   I argue the case more fully in *Accounting Values and Inflation* (McGraw-Hill, London 1975), chapter 8.

53

Table 12

Alternative forms of income statement, for year 3,
after specific price change

Type of capital to be maintained	(1) *Real* £	(2) *Real* £	(3) *Physical* £
Revenue			
Trading	800	800	800
Realised appreciation (current less historical depreciation, as below)		150	
		950	
Less Depreciation			
Historical cost (page 36)	200		
Current cost (page 51)		350	350
Backlog (see below)			300
			650
Profit	600	600	150
Less Appropriation for increase in specific cost, say	250	250	
	350	350	

If the vote goes to *physical* capital, then the higher depreciation figures of the post-change estimate (page 51) are again charged, as in column (3), but the income statement fails to recognise the appreciation. And, to make good the seeming under-provision at revaluation date, backlog depreciation may be charged too (in our example, say £300 in year 3). One can imagine cases in which this double burden would be intolerable.

Fall in value

In the absence of general price change, the values of depreciating assets are perhaps more likely to need downward than upward revaluation. There are depressing forces in plenty, *eg*, accidents and unexpected physical faults, or economic change such as drop in demand for the asset's product or the invention of a better model.

These forces will tend to lessen Old's life as well as its value. The figures can be found from tables analogous to 9 and 10. The value curve may take a

54

new shape such as CFGL'L in Diagram 11 (*ie*, the asset will be scrapped at L instead of K); or, if the depressing forces are strong enough, value will plunge vertically to the scrap figure, and the asset will be sold at E.

(C) COMBINED GENERAL AND SPECIFIC PRICE-CHANGE

Now that we have seen how general and specific changes affect accounting when they come separately, we can more readily understand what happens when — as is usual — they come hand-in-hand.

A table of HAVE and HAVE NOT budgets, on the same lines as earlier tables, will show the new patterns of value and depreciation cost. The asset's optimum life may change, thanks to the specific ingredient.

Real *versus* physical capacity

Once again one must choose between the three concepts of capital maintenance (page 52). A switch to almost any form of inflation accounting means rejection of money capital. To my mind, real capital still commands respect, while the faults of physical capital become even more plain.

Apart from its other virtues, the real capital concept turns a spotlight onto an important quantity — *real gain or loss* (*ie*, the surplus or shortfall between a specific value and what the value would have been if it had moved like prices-in-general). Suppose an asset cost £100 when the general and specific indices stood at 100; if thereafter they rise to 140 and 150 respectively, the owner has made a real gain ("real holding gain" or "real appreciation") of £10. This figure seems an eminently sensible measure of his increase in "well-offness".

The "Inflation Accounting Standard"

Despite the arguments for real capital, SSAP 16 (the Standard dealing with inflation accounting, issued in 1980) opts for "Current Cost Accounting", *ie*, the physical basis. Thus it prescribes a CCA income statement that includes an adjustment to raise historical depreciation to the level of current replacement cost.

Admittedly the physical concept is often the easier to apply. Its entries

55

are the crude ones described in section B above. Its advocates argue that, if the owner is enabled to replace his physical capital, he can turn a blind eye to inflation: specific prices are a good enough surrogate for costs raised with the general index, so there is no call for further refinement. This is sensible where specific and general prices move in close step, but can have bad results when they diverge. Suppose new inventions make a firm's machinery almost worthless; current cost depreciation will then dive, leaving profit at a cheerful figure that fails to reflect the disaster; historical charges, raised with the general index, yield a profit that here is vastly more prudent.

The "ideal" system

If accounting is to be reformed thoroughly, there are strong grounds for measuring income by the test of real capital. But there are also strong grounds for using current values for assets and costs. The advocate of real capital can get the best of both worlds by blending the two concepts, ie, by using the so-called "ideal" (or hybrid) system.[1]

This values assets at current levels. But it analyses their appreciation into its two components:

(a)   Fictitious, ie, inflation induced. This part is found by applying a general index factor to historical cost.

(b)   Real, ie, the residue (sometimes negative).

It shows the two figures separately in the equity. (a) is given some such name as "inflation allowance" and is left permanently (unless the general index moves down again). (b) is called "unrealised real appreciation"; later, if it is realised, it is credited to income (following the same logic as column (2) on page 54). The final income figures is thus geared to real capital.

Example

Illustrative figures may be helpful. Suppose a firm starts the year with £1,000 in cash, and at once invests this in a machine — when both general and special indices stand at 100. Very soon after, the indices jump to 140 and 150 respectively, and then stay steady.

[1]   The name was given on page 45 of the *Background Papers* to Exposure Draft 18, Current Cost Accounting, published in 1976 by the Accounting Standards Committee.

56

At the time of this price change, reformed accounts will write up the asset from £1,000 to £1,500, and add the £500 appreciation to equity. The ideal system unravels the components of the £500; the fictional gain of £400 ($= \frac{40}{50}$ x £500), duly ascribed to inflation; and the £100 residue − real appreciation, classed as a type of profit. So the balance sheet shows equity as:

	£
Capital	1 000
Capital − inflation adjustment	400
Unrealised real appreciation	100
	1 500

Suppose next that the machine is thereafter hired out for a yearly rent of £350; and that historical depreciation cost per year is one-fifth of the asset's price, *ie*, £200. In the ordinary accounts − see column (1) of table 13 − profit for the ensuing year is thus £350 − £200 = £150.

It is less, as inflation accounting demands, in the two brands of reformed statements illustrated in columns (2) and (3). These raise depreciation to current cost: one-fifth of the asset's new value of £1,500 is £300, so the charge goes up to this realistic figure. By the physical test of column (3), profit is cut to only £50.

But the ideal system does not overlook the £100 of real gain shown above. It now deems one-fifth of this gain ($\frac{1}{5}$ x £100 = £20) to have been realised by the year's operation, and transfers this £20 to revenue as in column (2). The resulting profit is £70. It meets the test of real capital maintenance: £350, less the £200 historical depreciation raised with the general index to £280, is likewise £70.

Thus the ideal system gives up-to-date values and charges, but also a profit that satisfies the logic of real capital maintenance.

Unfortunately, none of the proposed reform methods will be easy to explain to laymen. Inflation's effects are not simple: and, if accounts are to respond adequately, they cannot be simple either.

57

193

Table 13

Final accounts – alternative versions after revaluation

Type of capital to be maintained	1 Money £	2 Real ("ideal system") £	3 Physical £
Income statement			
Revenue			
Rent	350	350	350
Realised appreciation		20	
		370	
Less Depreciation			
Historical	200		
Current cost		300	300
Profit	150	70	50
Balance sheet			
Fixed asset (new)	1000	1500	
Less Depreciation	200	300	as (2)
	800	1200	
Secondary assets	350	350	
	1150	1550	
Capital	1000	1000	1000
Inflation adjustment		400	
Revaluation surplus			500
Unrealised real appreciation			
(100–20)		80	
Profit	150	70	50
	1150	1550	1550

Conclusion

These five chapters have tried to spell out the life story of a depreciating asset. They have shown how a wide set of cash flows controls optimum life and asset value. They have argued that we should deem asset values to govern depreciation charges (and not the other way round). They have described the traditional methods of depreciation as handy but crude, and explained how to test their adequacy in a given case with the budgets of deprival value. These budgets enable us also to evolve more sensitive methods that will

58

allow — where the need arises — for complex cash patterns, cost-of-capital, inflation, and current values.

The next few years will see great changes in accounting. We must hope that depreciation methods can develop in ways that satisfy both reason and practical needs.

59

DEPRECIATION, REPLACEMENT PRICE, AND COST OF CAPITAL*

* Baxter, W.T., and N.H. Carrier. "Depreciation, Replacement Price, and Cost of Capitol." *Journal of Accounting Research* 9, no. 2 (Autumn 1971), pp. 189–214.
© Institute of Professional Accounting, 1972. Reprinted with permission.

Depreciation, Replacement Price, and Cost of Capital

W. T. BAXTER AND N. H. CARRIER*

The Problem

It is generally accepted that, when prices change, the costs charged in ordinary accounts (being historical) tend to lag behind current costs and revenue, with various ill results. The operating costs most subject to the time lag are those for materials and depreciation.

Reformers say this error can be corrected by adjusting historical charges to current levels, either by direct revaluation or by use of a suitable price index. The aim of our paper is not to challenge the logic and desirability of reform—far from it—but to examine the values at stake and to ask how far its arithmetic is right.

In a sense, the answer to our question is plain enough. If, when assets subject to the time lag are consumed, their replacements are in fact bought at current price, the proposed correction achieves its aim. If however the replacement is not bought at the current level but later, as is usual with depreciating assets, the correction is not obviously adequate. We shall try to analyze this possible shortfall. To do so, we must distinguish between various types of account, of asset, and of price change.

COST IN BUDGETS AND IN INCOME STATEMENTS

Cost measurement is likely to be important in two contexts. First, the cost of inputs may be wanted for budgets to aid management decision—for instance, to find whether the cost of a job is likely to be less than its revenue. It may be wanted too for post mortem accounts to test whether the decision to do the job was justified.

* Professor and Reader, London School of Economics and Political Science. The authors wish to thank Mrs. S. Dev and Professor J. Flower for their helpful criticisms.

Second, the firm's costs for the year are needed for the income statement. But these costs need not agree with those of the decision budget (e.g., such a budget should confine itself to the marginal cost of the given job, whereas the income statement must include also costs that are fixed so far as each job goes).

"USE DEPRECIATION" AND "TIME DEPRECIATION"

When the asset in question consists of direct materials, its conversion into input causes a physical shrinkage. So there is here a cause-and-effect link between using up and the need for the replacement outlay, and the latter is clearly an avoidable sacrifice of the job.

With some depreciating assets, an analogous process seems to exist: the asset's life will end only when a certain amount of physical use has taken place. So its use on a job normally entails an avoidable replacement cost; and such use depreciation is a cost for purposes alike of decision and income measurement.

With other depreciating assets, however, use has no effect on the date of the replacement outlay, as this is governed by factors such as obsolescence, a contract, etc. Therefore the use of such assets on a job causes no sacrifice, and depreciation should be left out of the job's budget. But the passage of time does bring the outlays nearer, and so time-depreciation is a proper charge in income statements.

No doubt many depreciating assets have both a use and a time component in their yearly cost.

GENERAL VERSUS SPECIAL PRICE-INDEX ADJUSTMENT

Price change may be either general (affecting a wide range of commodities and services, as during inflation), special (peculiar to the given asset) or, more usually, a mixture of both. Advocates of reform in accounts differ in their stress on the two forms of change, and thus divide into two camps. Though both reject the conventional view that income is the excess after money capital has been maintained, they dispute over the alternative definitions of capital. One group argues for the maintenance of real capital (usually defined in terms of the owner's standard of living), the other for the maintenance of physical capital. Their tools for correcting cost and income are therefore respectively the general index and the special index.

General index. The "general index man" holds that where inputs are kept long enough for their price to change, their historical costs in the income statement should be updated with a suitable index of general purchasing power, so that they will be expressed in $s of the same value as the revenue $s.

Special index. The "special index man" aims to adjust the inputs' historical cost to their current market value (on the grounds that the latter is also replacement cost, and income is the surplus after providing for this cost).[1] He finds current value by adjusting historical cost with a special index for the particular type of asset, or by direct revaluation.

NATURE OF COST

When anything more than a record of stewardship is wanted, cost measurement should be forward-looking. Just as value is a matter of expected future benefits, so too cost is a matter of future sacrifices. The cost to a firm of a given job is the job's effect in worsening the future cash flow. Thus, when the firm turns an existing asset into input for the job, typically the adverse consequence is that the firm will pay cash to replace the asset; so the cost of using up this asset is its replacement price. (There are some exceptions to this rule, but they need not concern us here.)

Moreover, the obvious costs of acquiring inputs (purchase price, freight, etc.) may need to be augmented. When the asset is bought ahead of needs, ownership involves also less obvious (but no less real) sacrifices such as storage of the assets and cost of capital on the sum invested. With cheap assets and a quick turnover, these unobtrusive costs may well be trivial, and they are seldom added to the asset's book value. But cost of capital must play an essential part in discussions of principle since one cannot compare outlays of different dates without discounting. In what follows, we have no option but to accord more weight to depreciation methods that allow for "interest" (e.g. the annuity method) than their use in practice warrants. It is a pity that practice neglects them so; particularly when rates are high, cost of capital must have a marked effect on depreciation cost and the values of depreciating assets.

Stable Prices

CURRENT AND REMOTE REPLACEMENT COST

Replacement cost is easy to measure if inputs are replaced promptly and in lots whose physical size can vary with needs. These conditions are often met when the input consists of materials. Thus the decision to use up x lbs. of stores may well lead to the outlay of the current replacement cost of x lbs.

Measurement becomes less easy, even with stable prices, where inputs are not replaced within the accounting period, e.g., where they are bought in lots whose size exceeds the needs of a given job, etc. This situation is not unusual; for instance, there may be a saving in buying materials in large lots. Depreciating assets would seem, from the standpoint of the economic realities, to be merely large lots of input bought ahead of needs.

---

[1] The issues are described, and case for the special index approach put, by R. S. Gynther, *Accounting for Price-Level Changes* (Oxford: Pergamon Press, 1966).

DEPRECIATION AS THE WORSENING OF CASH PROSPECTS

Where input is bought in large lots, the use of part of the lot will affect the date of a future replacement; indeed, if the using-up of one lot is always the signal for buying another, it will affect the whole chain of future replacements. So today's cost, and the value of the remaining asset, depend on a change in budget prospects. Suppose, for instance, that the firm buys stores in 100 ton lots, ahead of needs, and normally uses 25 tons a year. It buys a lot at the close of 1970. If it happens to use no stores in 1971, the replacement dates will be 1975, 1979, and so on; if it duly uses 25 tons, the dates will be 1974, 1978, etc. The cost of using the 25 tons in 1971 is this shift in the chain—the worsening of the cash prospect. It can be found by comparing the present values of the two chains of future payments; presumably, in the absence of special circumstances, these stretch to a far-off time horizon and so are best treated as perpetuities.

It may be objected that this view must be nonsense because the inherent uncertainties of remote prediction make accurate measurement impossible. The answer surely is that the cost is real enough even though its dimensions are not precisely known. One must accept the use of estimates or else abandon reason. And here, as in many other situations, a careful analysis of uncertain forces may often help sound judgment even though the sensible man will sometimes decide in the end to cut the corners by working on very simple assumptions.

VALUE AS THE POTENTIAL WORSENING OF CASH PROSPECT BY DEPRIVAL

For most accounting purposes, value too can perhaps be defined most serviceably as the gap between two prospects—those facing an owner and a deprived owner. In other words, it is the compensation that should in normal circumstances be paid to a deprived owner to make good his loss. It can be found by comparing the future outlays in what may be called the "Have" and "Have-not" budgets. A deprived owner would have to pay for a new asset forthwith, for a replacement at the end of that asset's life, and so on, i.e., he would be faced with the immediate burden of a perpetuity-due of replacement payments. An undeprived owner need not make a replacement payment till his asset reaches the end of its life; then he too will face the burden of a perpetuity-due. The difference between these two budget prospects is the benefit of ownership, i.e., "deprival value," or "opportunity value."

Prices in the second-hand market will not affect deprival value except when the asset is on the point of being scrapped; if the firm always buys an input in large lots, the price of small lots is irrelevant. Thus the firm may prefer new to second-hand trucks, i.e., may think that ton-miles come cheaper in large lots (in some broad sense that covers not only price but

factors such as availability and reliability). Then depreciation has nothing
to do with the buying prices of second-hand trucks; it has everything to do
with unit costs derived from the outlays on a new truck. Replacement cost
here has a specialized meaning that does not match everyday speech.

DIAGRAMMATIC TREATMENT OF LONG-RUN REPLACEMENT COST

In Figure 1, OX shows time, and $Y'OY$ value. As the main cash flows in
question constitute a burden rather than a benefit, values are shown below
OX. OP is the present value of the perpetuity-due of replacement payments
at date O; and, with stable prices, a horizontal line PQ traces the burden
that faces a would-be owner at any later date, e.g., KK' at time K'.

Suppose the owner buys the asset at time M' and it lasts till K'. Ownership at once makes his long-term burden less onerous, reducing it to CM',
the present value of KK'. But the relief evaporates as the years pass and
replacement looms nearer; by time D', for instance, the present value of

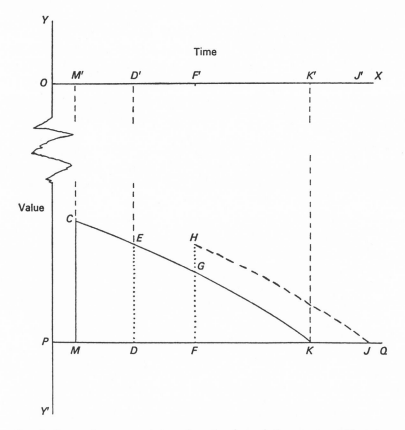

FIG. 1. Perpetuity approach to value of a depreciating asset—stable prices.

KK' has grown to *ED'*. The pattern of burden over the asset's life is the falling line *CK*.

CK thus traces the values found in Have budgets and *MK* those in Have-not budgets. The vertical distances between them give the deprival values at different dates; *MC*, for instance, is the value at acquisition (equal to initial price), and *DE* at *D'*. Thus *MCK* is the asset's value curve. It here assumes that the cash flow does not include uneven outlays for repairs, etc., or a final receipt for scrap. For instance, between the two dates *D'* and *F'* the asset's value sinks from *DE* to *FG*; depreciation is *GH*. A backward-looking approach tries to describe *GH* in terms of fall in the original cost *MC* and is hard put to justify its size. Our forward-looking approach regards *DE* and *FG* as contrasts between budgets, and depreciation as the worsening of these contrasts. With stable conditions, one can say that the value of the asset's future services would, but for the lapse of the period or use during it, still be the same at *F* as at *D*; replacement would thus be postponed from *K* to *J*, and at date *F* the Have curve would be *HJ* instead of *GK*: so use etc., causes a fall in value of *FH-FG*, i.e., *GH*. Here the forward-looking and the historical approaches both lead to the same answer, but they might not do so if prices changed.

The area *MCK* can be lifted from the perpetuity framework and shown as *OCK* in the simpler and more familiar style of Figure 2. Again *OY* shows value and *OX* time; *CK* is the value curve, and *GH* is the fall in value between *D* and *F*. But, whether they are made explicit, the perpetuities give the logical basis for the simpler figure.

COMPARISON WITH THE ANNUITY METHOD

With stable prices, the asset values of the figures agree with those found by the annuity method of depreciation. But though this method yields the

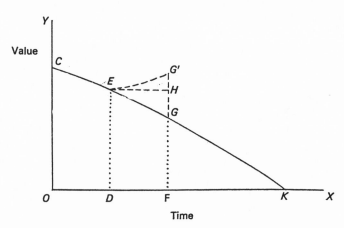

FIG. 2. Value curve of a depreciating asset—stable prices.

same net annual charge as the figures, it throws in extra information by:
- (a) charging operations with the whole cost of ownership for the year—what we call the "full servicing charge" for the investment in the asset. This has two components:
    - (1) the forward-looking cost already considered (e.g., *GH* in the figure) which might be labelled the "replacement charge" or "net depreciation"; and
    - (2) imputed interest (which we prefer to call "cost of capital") for the year on the opening value.
- (b) crediting (2) to another section of the income statement (say, that for interest charges).

Profit is the same whether the gross or the net cost is charged in the income statement (since, if the gross sum (a) is debited, the imputed interest (b) must be credited, as in the example below). But the gross figure shows the full annual sacrifice caused by the decision to own and employ the asset. It may be likened to a notional rent charged by the firm, as a test of efficiency, to the department using the asset.

CONFLICTING PULLS: DEPRECIATION VERSUS APPRECIATION DUE TO
COST OF CAPITAL

The two steps of the annuity method serve to show that there are two conflicting pulls on a depreciating asset's value. On the one hand, cost of capital tends to raise the value; if discounting makes a remote benefit less valuable, then the obverse is that the benefit must appreciate as time brings it closer. On the other hand, the asset's conversion into input must more than offset this appreciation. The rival pulls can be illustrated diagrammatically if the input is assumed to be left undisturbed till near the end of each year. Thus Figure 2 shows them for the year between *D* and *F*. Value first appreciates at the cost-of-capital rate (the addition of "interest" by the annuity method) from *E* to *G'*. At year-end, when the input is taken, value falls abruptly. With a time-asset, this fall is from *G'* to *G*. With a use-asset, the fall is also from *G'* to *G* if the planned amount of input is duly consumed, but is only to *H* if some hitch postpones using up the input till next year. The full servicing charge of the annuity method is *GG'*, while the replacement charge is *GH*.

Even with use-assets, the cost-of-capital part of the full service charge (*HG'*) would seem to be an unavoidable cost of jobs. If the job is not done, the value curve of Figure 1 becomes *HJ*, and nothing higher; value must in Figure 2 drop from *G'* to *H*. Undesired delay can hardly raise value. So the cost-of-capital ingredient is a fixed cost of the period; as long as one is measuring cost for job budgets, not income statements, this appreciation within each year should be omitted. To make the point, the income statement might be drafted along these lines.

Section for operating department

Depreciation:		
Avoidable cost:		
Replacement charge for use-assets...............................		$50
Fixed cost:		
Replacement charge for time-assets...........................	$50	
Cost of capital on both types of asset.........................	20	70
Full servicing charge..		$120

Section for interest charges

Deduct:	
Cost of capital charged to operations...............................	$20
Net writedown in value..	$100

SECONDARY ASSETS, COST OF CAPITAL, AND EVENTUAL REPLACEMENT COST

The long-run cost of capital has important effects on the value pattern, producing the curvature of CK in the diagrams. Thus it also affects the replacement charge pattern.

Suppose a man at the end of year 1 holds stores whose price is $100, and that if he used them on a job now, he would have to buy another batch for $100 at the end of year 2. The sacrifice caused by the job in year 1 would not be $100 but only the present value of the future payment of $100; use-cost is here replacement price reduced by cost of capital. The same answer can be reached by saying that the man will maintain his capital if, on doing the job in year 1, he sets aside enough "secondary assets" to make good the "primary asset" in 12 months' time; as these secondary assets will themselves add to earnings, they can start at below $100.

The primary asset is the depreciating asset that is being measured. The secondary assets are the additional assets that the firm acquires as a result of providing for the depreciation of the primary asset. These additions may at first take the form of cash. But later the cash will probably be put to some fruitful use. Thus it may be used to repay loan and so reduce cost of capital, or to buy all manner of other assets, perhaps including other depreciating assets. In one shape or another, these additions will in time cut costs or swell revenues or appreciate. Thus the depreciation provisions engender a stream of extra benefits. These change the replacement charges in the way described in the preceding paragraph, i.e., they are just as relevant to the value of the primary asset as, say, its repairs.

The further away the replacement date and the higher the secondary earnings, the less the depreciation cost during the early years of life. High secondary earnings make for late depreciation cost; it is these earnings that impart the curvature to a depreciating asset's value pattern and which justify the annuity method's addition of imputed interest. To be pedantically precise, one should talk about the rate of secondary earnings rather than of interest or cost of capital.

ARITHMETIC OF DEPRECIATING ASSETS

Despite our liking for the annuity method, we propose not to use its formulas; their algebra may deal well enough with the stable prices but does not generalize readily for other situations. We shall use instead formulas that link with the burden of perpetual ownership. This approach generalizes well, as it covers the otherwise troublesome problems of dealing with a decision's future repercussions (possibly after prices have changed). Admittedly the notion of perpetual ownership is unfamiliar; but, just as the common way of getting an asset's services (purchase of one asset for an initial price) is sometimes replaced by hire at an annual rent, so too it might—in theory at least—be replaced by purchase now of the whole succession of assets for a bigger initial sum. This sum would be the present value of a perpetuity of yearly rents and also of a perpetuity-due of prices for successive assets.

Operations are deemed to start with the buying of an asset, or the perpetual use of an asset, at time $t = 0$.

A' = outlay on the asset. With materials, A' is the asset's price. With depreciating assets, there may be many relevant outlays (e.g., price and varying annual repairs), while final scrap proceeds constitute a negative outlay; then A' must be interpreted as the present value, at the start of life, of a complete set of the relevant outlays over a life. In the following formulas, A' for simplicity assumes initial price to be the only outlay.

P = present value of A' in perpetuity, just before the first payment (in advance).

k = the asset's life span, from purchase to scrapping. The possibility of k being changed by technology, etc., is excluded.

i = the earnings rate on the secondary assets.

v = $1/(1 + i)$, the discounting factor.

Transactions take place at time t (when the asset has a remaining life of m), and accounts are then drawn up for the preceding 12 months, i.e., for the period since $t - 1$, when the asset had a life of $m + 1$.

The perpetuity. Let P = the present-value of the burden of perpetual ownership. Using the above terms, one can by definition obtain it as:

$$P = A' + A'v^k + A'v^{2k} + \cdots$$
$$= A'/(1 - v^k). \tag{1}$$

Asset value. $V(m, t)$ is the deprival value of an asset at time t, when the remaining life is expected to be m years. Without the asset, a firm wanting perpetual use of an asset must immediately incur a burden of P (traced over time by PQ in Figure 1). But if at time t it already owns an asset with m more years of life, the burden is deferred for m years and has a present value of $v^m P$ (in the figure, ED' at D'). The balance, namely $P - v^m P$, is the value of the partially worn asset (DE in the figure).[2]

Thus

$$V(m, t) = P(1 - v^m). \qquad (2)$$

Replacement charge. If at date t the owner works a use-asset to the planned extent, he is left with a burden whose present value is Pv^m. Without use, the burden would be only Pv^{m+1}. The cost of use (or, with time-assets, of the passage of the year) is the difference. Thus:

$$\text{Replacement charge} = P(1 - v)v^m \qquad (3)$$

or this may be expressed as $V(m + 1, t) - V(m, t)$, or as $A'(1 - v)v^m/(1 - v^k)$.

(3) contains only one term that depends on m, namely v^m. At the end of the first year, remaining life will be 1 less than a complete life, i.e., $m = k - 1$. A year later, remaining life will have fallen to $k - 2$. Thus the expressions for the replacement charges for successive years will contain factors v^{k-1}, v^{k-2}, $\cdots$, v^2, v and 1. Since v is less than unity, these form an increasing series, i.e., the charge (in the absence of disturbing forces such as rising repairs) grows as the asset ages. In the figure, this is reflected by CK's increasing rate of fall.

Full servicing charge. This is the yearly cost of the decision to acquire the asset. Suppose the firm has a capital P which it will use to buy the perpetual use of an asset at either time $t - 1$ or t. If it opts for t, the capital can continue to earn in some secondary use and so grows to $(1 + i)P$; if it opts for $t - 1$, it loses these earnings. Thus the cost of ownership for the year is $(1 + i)P - P$, i.e.,

$$\text{Full servicing charge} = iP. \qquad (4)$$

The argument remains valid for all the years of life. If ownership is deferred from time 0 to any time $t - 1$, the saving at $t - 1$ is $P[(1 + i)^{t-1} - 1]$; if it is deferred from 0 to t, the saving at time t rises to $P[(1 + i)^t - 1]$. The difference is the cost of the tth year of ownership; valued at time t, it is:

$$P[(1 + i)^t - 1] - (1 + i)P[(1 + i)^{t-1} - 1] = iP,$$

as before. This fits in with everyday experience of a rent being constant.

---

[2] Where the asset's varying annual outlays and scrap value are big enough to merit consideration, they will change P and formula (2). At t, let the present values of the remaining outlays and scrap value be $O(m)$ and Sv^m respectively. Formula (2) then becomes:

$$V(m, t) = P(1 - v^m) - O(m) + Sv^m.$$

An analogous formula is developed in A. J. Merrett and Allen Sykes, *The Finance and Analysis of Capital Projects* (London: Longmans, 1962), p. 470.

Components of full servicing charge. Figure 1 shows how the burden of ownership can be treated as a whole or as two parts: thus, at date D' the whole burden is DD', which is made up of ED' and DE—respectively the amount needed to earn future replacements and the asset's value.

The yearly equivalent of the burden can likewise be treated as a whole (the full servicing charge, the constant iP), or as two parts:

Replacement charge (with stable real prices, the same thing as *net write-down in the asset's value*). Formula (3) in effect expresses this in terms of i and the part of P needed to provide replacements.

Cost-of-capital charge. This can be expressed[3] as $iP(1 - v^{m+1})$, i.e., as cost of capital on the asset's opening value for the year.

Thus all three quantities can be expressed in terms of i and P or its components.

Since the full charge is constant and net cost of use rises over the years, cost of capital must be a falling charge.

An arithmetical example that illustrates the use of the formulas is given in Appendix 2.

General Price Change

We must now consider what happens when prices change before replacement. Let us first suppose that the change is general and affects the money values of all the firm's assets at the same rate—which implies that the yearly depreciation provisions of our model are never left as money assets, but are promptly invested in secondary assets whose money values can go up and down. In these convenient circumstances (it is reasonable to suspect), change in money values cannot by itself change real values one whit: the owner is no better or worse off than if prices had stayed stable.

It is necessary to choose an income concept on which to base the new formulas. We assume that income statements are drafted largely with the aim of helping the collective owners with their consumption decisions. If the income figure is to have meaning, the charges for wealth lost as input should be measured in the same \$s as wealth gained as revenue, and (in view of the statement's aim) this equivalence is probably best defined in

---

[3] From formulas (3) and (2), the replacement charge plus cost of capital on opening value can be written:

$$P(1 - v)v^m + iP(1 - v^{m+1})$$
$$= P[v^m - v^{m+1} + i - iv^{m+1}]$$
$$= P[i + v^m - v^{m+1}(1 + i)]$$
$$= P[i + v^m - v^m]$$
$$= iP$$
$$= \text{full servicing charge by formula (4).}$$

terms of the owners' purchasing power. So cost subject to a time-lag should be updated with the general index.

ASSUMPTION OF CONSTANT RATE OF PRICE-CHANGE

One can simplify a first approach to the problem in a way that perhaps is in the long run not too unrealistic by assuming that the price change occurs at a steady rate, g. As A' is the price of an asset at the time 0, $A'(1 + g)$ will be the price at 1, $A'(1 + g)^2$ at 2, and so on. g may be positive (where prices rise) or negative (where they fall).

REVISED FIGURE FOR PERPETUITY APPROACH

Figure 1 changes under the influence of g, and Figure 3 shows the revised curves. PQ, the burden of deciding to own an asset in perpetuity, is no longer a horizontal straight line but becomes concave to Y'; here it has been given a downward slope, implying that prices are assumed to be rising, i.e., that g is positive. If g were negative, PQ would slope upward but would still be concave.

MC is again the initial price. CK again assumes the particular asset to have no varying cash flow (on repairs etc.) during its life; any point on CK can be found by discounting the full burden at K back to the given date. Vertical distances between MK and CK measure the benefit of ownership and hence value, e.g., DE and FG are values at dates D and F.

MODIFICATION OF ALGEBRA FOR CHANGING PRICES

To deal with changing prices, the algebra must be modified.

$A'(t) =$ the price of the asset at time t. For brevity, the price of the first asset [$A'(0)$] will be written simply A'.

$P(t) =$ the cost of the perpetual use of the asset at time t. The cost at 0 will be written P.

Real and illusory cost-of-capital rates. With general price change, the secondary earnings rate, i, will probably seem to change. During inflation, for instance, these secondary assets will appreciate; if i was .1 p.a. in a stable preliminary period, and then prices rise at the rate of .06 p.a., an equity investment of \$1 will in one year grow to \$1.166, so that the growth rate may loosely be described as .166, whereas (as the capital of 1 opening \$ is equivalent to 1.06 of the depreciated closing \$s) the real rate is still [(1.166/1.06) − 1] = .1.

One must thus distinguish two versions of the rate. We shall use i for the illusory rate (.166 in the example) found from \$s of different values. Where the real rate is relevant, we shall use i^* instead; $i^* = (1 + i)/(1 + g) - 1 = (i - g)/(1 + g)$. This rate is not altered by general price change and so in the example stays at .1.

The formulas of earlier pages use i, and so their v is here based on the illusory rate. Where a real discount rate is more convenient, we shall now use q instead of v; that is:

$$q = v(1 + g).$$

The formulas can be adapted to general price change as follows. The perpetuity [see formula (1)]

$$P = A' + A'(1 + g)^k v^k + A'(1 + g)^{2k} v^{2k} \cdots$$

$$= A'/1 - q^k. \tag{5}$$

As q is the unchanging real discount rate, based on i^*, the burden is the same whether or not general prices will change; the owner of nonmoney assets is indifferent to such change. In Figure 3, OP is the same whether PQ is horizontal or curves.

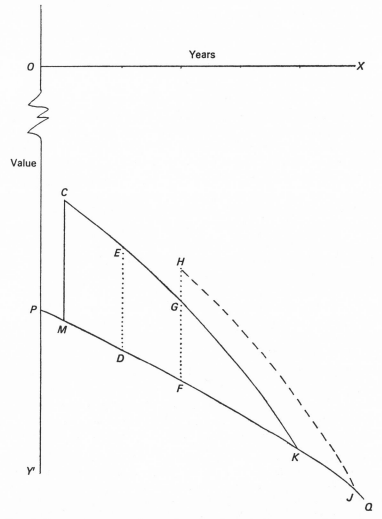

FIG. 3. Perpetuity approach to value of a depreciating asset—rising prices.

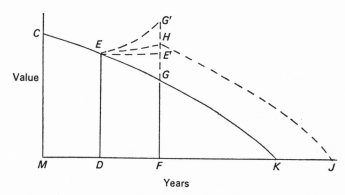

FIG. 4. Annual movements in the value of a depreciating asset—rising prices.

Asset value. The argument of formula (2) can be adapted to show that

$$V(m, t) = P(t) - P(t + m)v^m$$
$$= P(1 + g)^t(1 - q^m). \tag{6}$$

Formula (6) enables one to measure how far the current value has departed from historical book value.

The whole value pattern can be derived from Figure 3 by measuring vertical distances between MK and CK. Figure 4 shows this pattern as MCK. A comparison of such patterns with those for like assets under stable prices (e.g., OCK in Figure 2) would reveal that a positive rate of g leads to a higher hump in the curve[4] (just as if, with stable prices, the rate i increased). The rising cost of future replacements causes growth in the deprival value of a partly worn asset.

Replacement charge. Adapting formula (3), one finds the charge for the year to (and in the money of) t becomes

$$P(1 + g)^t(1 - q)q^m \tag{7}$$

or

$$A'(1 + g)^t(1 - q)q^m/(1 - q^k).$$

Thus in current money terms the charge grows proportionately to the price change.

The same thing can be explained from the figures. In Figures 1 and 2, the omission to employ a use-asset at time F shifted the Have curve CK to the right; value, instead of falling from DE to FG, stayed at FH; thus, use

---

[1] To establish this, it has to be shown that $(1 + g)^{k-m}(1 - q^m)/(1 - q^k)$ is an increasing function in g, with $m < k$ and $q < 1$. Taking logarithms and differentiating, after some algebraic manipulation it is found necessary to show that $k/(1 - q^k) - m/(1 - q^m)$ is positive, i.e., that $x/(1 - q^x)$ is an increasing function in x for positive x. This can be shown by differentiating, putting $1 - y$ for q^x and expanding the logarithm of $(1 - y)$, for $0 < y < 1$.

causes a replacement charge of *GH* for the period. In Figures 3 and 4, similarly, the charge is *GH*. In Figure 3, however, the vertical distances between *HJ* and *FJ* are greater[5] than in 1. Thus *GH* is greater than when prices are constant; the replacement charge goes up because of the remote future rise in prices.

This is perhaps merely saying that when he perceived that prices are likely to rise, the man who has already bought a stock of scarce[6] inputs will congratulate himself on the acquisition. They appreciate at his moment of perception. But if he now decides to use some of them, the sacrifice is correspondingly greater.

Full servicing charge (GG' in Figure 4). This can still be simply expressed as $i^*P(t)$. Or one can substitute

$$P(1 + g)^t(1 - q)/q. \tag{8}$$

THE ADEQUACY OF GENERAL INDEX REFORM

The replacement charge in stable times [formula (3)] is $A'(1 - v)v^m/(1 - v^k)$. If, when prices begin to change, the accountant still uses historical costs, he is in effect rewriting the formula as $A'(1 - q)q^m/(1 - q^k)$, i.e., he retains the real[7] cost-of-capital rate i^*. The general index man corrects this in year t to $A'(1 + g)^t(1 - q)q^m/(1 - q^k)$. But the latter is precisely the desired charge of formula (7); his reform is vindicated triumphantly.

Moreover, the correction satisfies a further test. Thanks to the appreciation of the secondary assets each year at the rate g, the cumulative provisions will mount up over the life to exactly the replacement cost; there is no need to burden the later years with supplements to the charges of earlier years.

All of this strengthens the view that general price change is a mere effervescence that will (other things being equal) leave real wealth untouched. Accounts ought to show this underlying reality, and simple adjustment enables them to do so.

ARTIFICIALITY OF GENERAL PRICE-CHANGE ASSUMPTIONS

But the notion of a completely general price change plainly is artificial in the extreme. In real life, the prices of all the assets in a business are unlikely to move precisely in step with a general index; the cost-of-capital rate is also unlikely, for reasons both internal and external to the firm, to change precisely as a textbook demands. So the question is whether general

---

[5] This follows from the argument developed in the preceding footnote.

[6] Figure 3 assumes scarcity in the sense that loss of input at date *D* cannot be made good till *K* at earliest. This is realistic enough of many depreciating assets whose owners will not stock up with replacements ahead of needs because of storage difficulties and the risk of deterioration and obsolescence.

[7] If he instead uses the changing illusory rate, correction tends to overcompensate for the price change.

index reform still works well when the change in the future replacement price of the primary asset will diverge from the change in general prices.

Special Price Change

The simplest plan is to concentrate on the divergence, i.e., on the real change. This can best be done by assuming in the first instance that general prices remain constant. Therefore, in this section a firm is envisaged whose assets, except for the depreciating asset, have stable values throughout.

Reform can be concerned with several things—asset values, costs for decision budgets, and income measurement. We are at one with the special index man in holding that special prices govern asset values and decision costs; our arithmetic may improve his measurement of these where replacement is remote. But we are skeptical of his approach to income, sometimes shown by endorsement of LIFO as well as special index depreciation. We venture to suggest that when the general index is stable, historical cost depreciation is better; and our formulas are based on this view.

A cost budget is concerned with two alternative courses that face the planner at a given date; the cost of using an asset is the difference between two prospects at that moment, i.e., is swayed by the special replacement price of the asset. The income statement tries to measure change in the net assets between two different dates. We think it helpful to the owners to treat real holding gain on the inputs as part of this change. But the special index man, because of concern to protect the firm's level of physical activity, does not treat holding gains on input as revenue, though he includes them in the charges.

THE SPECIAL INDEX VIEW OF INCOME

In essence, the problem here is whether a $100 appreciation in asset A should, when A becomes input and needs to be replaced, seem a lesser sacrifice to the owner than a $100 gain in the shape of a physically separate asset B. We can discern little difference. And if the owner decides to maintain the business thereafter at its new level, we think that he is in both cases financing expansion (in the economic sense) by voluntarily ploughing back $100 of earnings; whereas the special index man (judging by his physical yardstick) thinks in the case of A that there is no expansion and that the owner is merely maintaining his original capital. We agree that replacement will demand extra resources but hold that the treasurer's problem here is the one that arises when any form of economic expansion is to be paid for, i.e., it is one of future finance but not of current income measurement.

COMBINING SPECIAL INDEX COST WITH HISTORICAL INCOME

It may be objected that if special index correction gives the best asset values and decision costs, there are grounds of convenience for showing special costs in the income statement: they would tie in better than historical costs with a revalued balance sheet and would be better guides to the costs of rival firms with new assets, etc.

Though this argument is entirely sound, it is not conclusive for income measurement. One can indeed charge special index cost in the income statement and yet, by also crediting the holding gain (i.e., the appreciation on assets while waiting to become input) end up with an unchanged profit.[8] This procedure has the further advantage of analyzing the components of income.

As an example, suppose a use-asset to be bought for $100 and to have a 2-year life, and that i is .1. With stable prices, for year 1 the replacement charge is about $47.6 and the full servicing charge $57.6. With price rising at a rate of .03, the year 1 net charge (based on future replacement prices) rises to about $49.81; and so jobs should not be accepted unless their margin exceeds this. The operating department is presumably responsible too for the fixed cost of "interest," still $10. On the other hand, its investment has earned a holding gain of $3. So the statement might run:

Section for operating department

Depreciation:	
Avoidable cost of use (replacement charge)	$49.81
Fixed cost of capital	10.00
Total	59.81
Less: Holding gain	3.00
Full servicing charge	$56.81

Section for finance

Interest charges:	
Deduction for charge to operations	$10.00
Net write-off from asset's value	$46.81

Note that the replacement charge and the net write-off in the asset's value are no longer the same thing. Therefore it is necessary to distinguish between a full charge that includes holding gain ($59.81 here) and one that excludes such gain ($56.81 here).

Holding gain may of course be negative (and where assets are subject to technological improvement, loss may well be more usual than gain). The above form of statement implies that loss such as obsolescence is charged against the department that invested in the asset.

MEASUREMENT

We shall use s for the rate of special price change and again assume change to be constant. Where A' covers not merely price but also present values of

---

[8] Our argument clearly owes much to E. Edwards and P. Bell, *The Theory and Measurement of Business Income* (Berkeley: University of California Press, 1961).

varying repairs, etc., s must be a composite for the cash flows of the whole life of each successive vintage of assets. s must in our calculations be less than i; if it exceeds i, the perpetuity arithmetic gives infinite or negative present values and so becomes futile.

Discounting. When present values are calculated, the growth due to s must partly offset the discounting due to i. The net discount factor is called p ($= v(1 + s)$).

The perpetuity. Figure 3 still gives a picture of the perpetuity curve. And, using the earlier reasoning, one finds

$$P = A'/(1 - p^k). \tag{9}$$

Value. This can again be described as in Figure 3. The formula becomes

$$V(m, t) = P(1 + s)^t(1 - p^m). \tag{10}$$

Holding gain. Figure 4 shows a year's gain as $E'H$, which is $sV(m + 1, t - 1)$.

Cost of capital. Figure 4 shows a year's cost as HG', which is $iV(m + 1, t - 1)$.

Replacement charge. This is GH in Figure 4. It can be calculated as:

$$P(1 + s)^t(1 - p)p^m \tag{11}$$

or as

$$A'(1 + s)^t(1 - p)p^m/(1 - p^k).$$

Full servicing charge. This is shown as GG' in Figure 4, i.e.:

$$(1 + i)V(m + 1, t - 1) - V(m, t) \tag{12}$$

and reduces to $(i - s)P(t - 1)$.

RESULTS OF ADAPTING TO SPECIAL CHANGE

Examples may help to show the effects of these formulas. One should compare the Appendix 2 figures for stable prices with those for special change (with falling prices), or the curves in Figure 5 (rising prices).

The values, etc., found by the forward-looking formulas (9)–(11) vary in all years from those of stable prices, i.e., the annuity figures. Thus the formulas yield suitable replacement charges for decisions. But as their income concept aims only to maintain the initial investment, over the whole life the sum of their value write-offs is still A'. In other words, if the income statement uses forward-looking replacement cost but credits holding gain, the net effect over the whole life is *nil*, and the extra cost of replacement is *not* set aside. Even if the holding gains are voluntarily accumulated as a replacement allowance, they will not match the extra cost. (To reach this figure, the accumulations would have to be topped up with sums found by calculating how much the secondary assets would appreciate if the special index applied to them.)

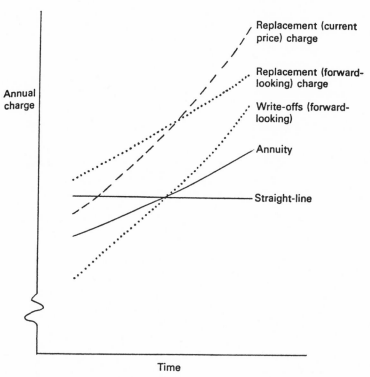

Fɪɢ. 5. Depreciation charges by various methods (with special change).

THE INADEQUACY OF SPECIAL INDEX REFORM

Formula (11), second version, puts the forward-looking replacement charge at $A'(1 + s)^t(1 - p)p^m/(1 - p^k)$. The special index man would instead adjust the annuity charge (3) with the current special index to $A'(1 + s)^t(1 - v)v^m/(1 - v^k)$.

The two patterns are by no means the same. They start and end very differently: the current charges understate the effects of change in the early years, and overstate them towards the end. The two curves intersect near mid-life, and so (given normal rates of s and i) their life totals may come quite close.

The cumulative provision of the special index man fails in the end to equal replacement price;[9] it will be less when prices rise and more when they fall. To achieve equality, he must each year adjust the charges of earlier years. With rising prices, this task may prove beyond the firm's means.

---

[9] If the firm has a stable group of like assets and replaces the same number of assets each year, the yearly replacement outlay equals the year's total of the special index man's charges for the individual assets. Some large and stable firms may come near to this theoretical model: their group of assets resembles the promptly replaced materials (page 191) rather than a single asset with a remote replacement date.

POLICY IMPLICATIONS

Where depreciation is a big part of a firm's costs, special price change can affect total cost and profit in ways that may seem rather odd. Thus a negative s (as with creeping obsolescence) means that firms which buy the expensive assets of an early date may face price cutting when other firms buy cheap assets later. Our formulas deal with this situation: their treatment of holding loss somewhat shifts the weight of the full servicing charge and net writedown to the start of life. Presumably a public utility could justly tilt its pattern of charges to consumers in the same way, though its spokesman might have some little trouble in explaining why the hope of cheaper assets in the future results in higher prices now.[10] Conversely, the prospect of rising replacement prices should tilt a public utility's charges in favor of today's consumers.

Mixture of General and Special Change

Lastly comes the realistic situation that combines both general and special change. Here again it is necessary to choose an income concept on which to base new formulas. The reasoning of the previous two sections suggests that asset values and decision costs should be updated with the special index, but that income should be measured by the general index approach. In other words, the way to unravel the new figures is to adjust the assets with the special index, and the owner's capital, etc., with the general index. The difference (real holding gain) is in our view a form of profit.

MEASUREMENT

Let the separate general and real (special) forces produce, when both are active, a total price change at the steady rate of c per annum; thus $(1 + c) = (1 + s)(1 + g)$. For discounting, let $(1 + c)/(1 + i) = r$, where i is the illusory rate produced by general appreciation.[11]

The perpetuity:

$$P = A'/(1 - r^k). \tag{13}$$

Value:

$$V(m, t) = P(t)(1 - r^m). \tag{14}$$

Replacement charge:

$$V(m + 1, t) - V(m, t). \tag{15}$$

---

[10] See Ralph Turvey, *Optimal Pricing and Investment in Electricity Supply* (London: Allen & Unwin, 1968), p. 56, and James C. Bonbright, *Principles of Public Utility Rates* (New York: Columbia University Press, 1961), p. 213.

[11] See M. Bromwich, "Inflation and the Capital Budgeting Process," *Journal of Business Finance*, Autumn, 1969, p. 39.

Full servicing charge:

$$(1 + i)V(m + 1, t - 1) - V(m, t). \tag{16}$$

RESULTS

These formulas, like (9)–(12), yield informative values and decision costs. But their net charges in the income statement are content to service the initial real capital: the cumulative write-offs mount up to the initial capital adjusted with the general index (and not to the special replacement price). Specimen figures, for rising general prices but falling real prices, are given at the end of Appendix 2. The relationship between our replacement charges and those of the special index man stays much as in the previous section. The special charges are inadequate for their task and do not in the end match replacement price.

If the income statement charges special cost, real holding gain should be credited, as in the example on page 205. Then the balance is still that of the general index concept.

In practice, there may well be real holding gains on *secondary* assets too. But such gains are analogous to the general index gains (see p. 203), in that they change the cost-of-capital rate and so do not upset the formulas. The firm may of course set the gains aside to help with final replacement; on our assumptions, they then constitute retained earnings and do not change income.

Conclusions

Our analysis suggests that reform will not be as facile as one could wish. Where the asset is not replaced till after the accounting date, charges should depend on prices that will be paid at a long series of future dates. Guesswork about the future is needed for finding values and use-costs; if rule-of-thumb procedures seem to avoid such guesswork, they must in fact rely on implicit assumptions that may be doubly dangerous because they are not recognized. One can derive workable expressions by assuming constant rates of price change where the rates are not expected to be constant, or results may still suggest the wisest strategy.

Our results confirm that inflation does nothing fundamental to non-money wealth. The obvious solution is here the right one: errors can be corrected by working in real terms. This vindicates the general index reformer who is in effect doing just that.

When there is change in the asset's real cost, reform is not obvious. The special index man's faith in current cost has not led him wildly astray in the measurement of avoidable cost, but has done so elsewhere. For income statements, if maintenance of the owner's purchasing power is the proper criterion, general index correction of historical cost will serve much better. With a little ingenuity, the accountant can draft an income statement that will both adjust cost with special indexes and end with the income figure of the general index.

Derivation of Algebraic Expressions

Introduction

It is necessary to establish solutions only for the general case combining general and special price change. The particular cases of stable prices, or of general or special change alone, may then be derived by setting the rates of change of irrelevant prices at zero. However, the algebra of the particular cases can usually be simplified by working from first principles.

Notation

The notation of the text is used. If $g = 0$, i becomes a real rate, as does c.

Assumptions

The vital assumptions are the constancy of the rates of interest and price change.

Preliminary Equations

From fundamental principles

$$(1 + i^*)(1 + g) = (1 + i) \tag{A1}$$

$$(1 + s)(1 + g) = (1 + c) \tag{A2}$$

from which expressions for i^* in terms of i, and s in terms of c, or vice versa, may readily be derived.

Basic Equations

$$A'(t) = A'(1 + c)^t \tag{A3}$$
$$P(t) = A'(t) + v^k A'(t + k) + v^{2k} A'(t + 2k) + \cdots$$
$$= A'(t)/(1 - r^k).$$

Hence

$$P = A'/(1 - r^k) \tag{A4}$$

and

$$P(t) = P(1 + c)^t \tag{A5}$$
$$V(m, t) = P(t) - v^m P(t + m)$$
$$= P(t)(1 - r^m). \tag{A6}$$

Charges for the period $t - 1$ to t (evaluated at time t)

The full service charge is $(1 + i)P(t - 1) - P(t)$, which is easily reduced

to $(i - c)P(t - 1)$. $\qquad$ (A7)

It is sometimes convenient to use the form

$$(1 + i)V(m + 1, t - 1) - V(m, t). \qquad (A8)$$

This is easily shown to be the same as (A7) by replacing the V-values, using (6).

Real cost-of-capital charge is $i^*V(m + 1, t - 1)$, measured in the currency of time $t - 1$, and thus

$$i^*(1 + g)V(m + 1, t - 1) \qquad \text{in the currency of time } t. \qquad (A9)$$

Value at the beginning of the year at time $t - 1$ is $(1 + g)V(m + 1, t - 1)$ measured in the currency of time t; and hence the value to be written off, in the currency of time, t, is

$$(1 + g)V(m + 1, t - 1) - V(m, t). \qquad (A10)$$

If the cost of capital and writedown in value are added together, and $(1 + i^*)(1 + g)$ is replaced by $(1 + i)$, the expression is seen to be the same as the full service charge in form (A9). Holding gain, like cost of capital, is first expressed in terms of $t - 1$ currency and, after conversion to t currency, is

$$s(1 + g)V(m + 1, t - 1). \qquad (A11)$$

Replacement charge is

$$V(m + 1, t) - V(m, t). \qquad (A12)$$

This readily reduces to

$$P(t)(1 - r)r^m. \qquad (A13)$$

A convenient way of evaluating the replacement charge may sometimes be to add the holding gain to the amount available to write value down. Adding them together [from (A10) and (A11)] gives

$$s(1 + g)V(m + 1, t - 1) + (1 + g)V(m + 1, t - 1) - V(m, t)$$

and, replacing $(1 + s)(1 + g)$ by $(1 + c)$, gives

$$(1 + c)V(m + 1, t - 1) - V(m, t).$$

Using (A6), one sees this to be the same as (A12).

The arithmetic can be made simple, as in Appendix 2. But the algebraic derivation of the expressions is necessary to justify the arithmetic.

APPENDIX 2

Arithmetical Example

Stable Prices

$$A' = 100; k = 6; i = 0.1; v = 1/(1 + i) = 0.909,091; v^6 = 0.564,473;$$
$$1 - v^6 = 0.435,527; P = A'/(1 - v^6) = 229.607; iP = 22.961.$$

Year	Value of asset at beginning of year (1)	Full service charge (2)	Cost of capital (3)	Replacement charge (= value write-off) (4)	Value of asset at end of year (5)
1	100.000	22.961	10.000	12.961	87.039
2	87.039	22.961	8.704	14.257	72.782
3	72.782	22.961	7.278	15.683	57.099
4	57.099	22.961	5.710	17.251	39.848
5	39.848	22.961	3.985	18.976	20.872
6	20.872	22.961	2.087	20.874	−0.002

Derivation

Column (1) first row: given

               remaining rows: column (5) of row before

      (2) initial calculation (values here all the same, but not in other cases)

      (3) column (1) $\times$ i

      (4) column (2) − column (3)

      (5) column (1) − column (4).

General Price Change Only

$$A' = 100; k = 6; i = 0.155; g = 0.05; i^* = (i - g)/(1 + g) = 0.1;$$
$$q = (1 + g)/(1 + i) = 0.909,091; q^6 = 0.564,473; 1 - q^6 = 0.435,527;$$
$$P = A'/(1 - q^6) = 229.607.$$

Full service charge for first year $= (i - g)P = 24.109.$

Year	Value of asset at beginning of year in currency of — beg. year (1)	Value of asset at beginning of year in currency of — end year (2)	Full service charge (3)	Cost of capital (4)	Replacement charge (= value write-off) (5)	Value of asset at end of year, in end of year currency (6)
1	100.000	105.000	24.109	10.500	13.609	91.391
2	91.391	95.961	25.314	9.596	15.718	80.243
3	80.243	84.255	26.580	8.425	18.155	66.100
4	66.100	69.405	27.909	6.940	20.969	48.436
5	48.436	50.858	29.304	5.086	24.218	26.640
6	26.640	27.972	30.769	2.797	27.972	0

Derivation

Column (1) first row: given

               remaining rows: column (6) of row before

      (2) column (1) $\times$ $(1 + g)$

      (3) first row: initial calculation

               remaining rows: row before $\times$ $(1 + g)$

(4) column (2) $\times$ i^*
(5) column (3) $-$ column (4)
(6) column (2) $-$ column (5).

Special Price Change Only

$A' = 100; k = 6; i = 0.1; s = -0.04; p = (1 + s)/(1 + i) = 0.872,727;$
$p^6 = 0.441,845; 1 - p^6 = 0.558,155; P = A'/(1 - p^6) = 179.162.$
Full service charge for first year $= (i - s)P = 25.083.$

Year	Value of asset at beginning of year (1)	Full service charge (2)	Cost of capital (3)	Value write-off (4)	Holding loss (5)	Replacement charge (6)	Value of asset at end of year (7)
1	100.000	25.083	10.000	15.083	4.000	11.083	84.917
2	84.917	24.080	8.492	15.588	3.397	12.191	69.329
3	69.329	23.117	6.933	16.184	2.773	13.411	53.145
4	53.145	22.192	5.314	16.878	2.126	14.752	36.267
5	36.267	21.304	3.627	17.677	1.451	16.226	18.590
6	18.590	20.452	1.859	18.593	0.744	17.849	−0.003

Derivation

Column (1) first row: given
 remaining rows: column (7) of row before
 (2) first row: initial calculation
 remaining rows: row before $\times$ $(1 + s)$
 (3) column (1) $\times$ i
 (4) column (2) $-$ column (3)
 (5) column (1) $\times$ s (gain if s positive, loss if negative)
 (6) column (4) $+$ column (5) if gain, $-$ column (5) if loss
 (7) column (1) $-$ column (4).

General and Special Price Changes

$A' = 100; k = 6; i = 0.155; g = 0.05; c = 0.008; i^* = (i - g)/(1 + g)$
$= 0.1; s = (c - g)/(1 + g) = -0.04; r = (1 + c)/(1 + i) = 0.872,727;$
$r^6 = 0.441,845; 1 - r^6 = 0.558,155; P = A'/(1 - r^6) = 179.162.$
Full service charge for first year $= (i - c)P = 26.337.$

Year	Value of asset at beginning of year in currency of		Full service charge (3)	Cost of capital (4)	Value write-off (5)	Holding loss (6)	Replacement charge (7)	Value of asset at end of year, in end of year currency (8)
	beg. year (1)	end year (2)						
1	100.000	105.000	26.337	10.500	15.837	4.200	11.637	89.163
2	89.163	93.621	26.548	9.362	17.186	3.745	13.441	76.435
3	76.435	80.257	26.760	8.026	18.734	3.210	15.524	61.523
4	61.523	64.599	26.974	6.460	20.514	2.584	17.930	44.085
5	44.085	46.289	27.190	4.629	22.561	1.852	20.709	23.728
6	23.728	24.914	27.408	2.491	24.917	0.997	23.920	−0.003

Derivation

Column (1) first row: given

remaining rows: column (8) of row before

(2) column (1) $\times$ (1 + g)

(3) First row: initial calculation

remaining rows: row before $\times$ (1 + c)

(4) column (2) $\times$ i^*

(5) column (3) $-$ column (4)

(6) column (2) $\times$ s (gain if s positive, loss if negative)

(7) column (5) + column (6) if gain, $-$ column (6) if loss

(8) column (2) $-$ column (5).

DEPRECIATION AND PROBABILITY

Depreciation and Probability

PETER WATSON AND WILLIAM T. BAXTER*

*Professors, University of Buckingham and London School of Economics

Usual methods of writing off depreciation assume the asset to have a known life of so many years. Accountants are well aware that such a figure is merely a handy approximation — that assets, like humans, have uncertain lives, and will probably die sooner or later than a predicted date. But our training gives us scant idea of the extent of this uncertainty, and still less what to do about it.

The short-comings of life estimates   At least one writer, Edwin B. Kurtz, has tried to assemble statistics on asset lives.[1] He starts by pointing out that our usual estimates, sometimes despite firm belief to the contrary, cannot be based on adequate data. He quotes an expert on public utility assets as saying that so-called life tables for such assets are unreliable, and tend to represent judgement and memory rather than actual experience:

> They are not based on the average experience with hundreds of items . . . such tables are entitled to consideration as being conscientiously made, but at best they are wholly improper for general use.[2]

Another expert stresses that estimated lives remain mere matters of opinion even when the estimates of different appraisers agree closely:

> The fact that they coincide within certain limits only goes to show that later guessers did not differ very greatly from their predecessors on a subject concerning which there was very little to be found to support an argument one way or another.[3]

MORTALITY TABLES

Kurtz tried to remedy matters by compiling mortality tables like those of life insurance offices. He distinguished 65 types of assets; for each type, he studied a population that might be as high as several thousands.

---

[1] *The Science of Valuation and Depreciation*, (Ronald Press, New York, 1937).
[2] *ibid*. p. 21.
[3] *ibid*. p. 20.

123

Kurtz wrote in 1937, so his figures may well be dated. But there seems no reason to quarrel with their import. They prove the range of possible lives to be surprisingly broad (though of course the tables do not tell us how far this is a matter of the owner's choice, i.e., how far he can govern life by varying maintenance and use).

The wide spread of possible lives The tables show what percentage of a given type dies in each period of life (a period being one-tenth of the average life). Deaths of some types bunch fairly closely around the average, period 10; thus the wooden ties on railways have a marked cluster, and steam locomotives and pumping engines follow closely. Even with these conformist assets, however, deaths already become noticeable by period 7, while some lives stretch to period 13 or beyond; only about one-third of the assets dutifully die in period 10.

At the other extreme, many kinds of assets have slight cluster. Submarine cables, manure spreaders, and the early telephone switchboards are examples. Here a few assets die in infancy, and a few linger on past period 20; less than 8 per cent die in period 10.

"Average life" In passing, one should perhaps recall the different versions of "average life". The *mode* is the year during which the largest number of assets die; and so it is likely to attract the observer's notice, and to be used in his calculations. But it can be wide of the *median* and *arithmetic mean*, which tend to lie close to one another. The last accords best with the aims of depreciation methods. So, with a large population of like assets, their average should be calculated thus:

$$\text{average life in years} = \frac{\text{total asset-years}}{\text{total assets that start life}}$$

Probability accounting If then the time of an assets' death seldom falls in the predicted year, and may fall much sooner or later, plainly our depreciation methods are unrealistic. The question is what (if anything) we should do about the matter.

One possibility is to switch from our average life (AL) methods to probability accounting (PA) i.e. to bring probabilities into our depreciation formulae. This would seem particularly sensible where the firm owns a large population of like assets, and can treat them as a group. Would it be sensible where it owns only one or a few assets of a given type?

It seems wise to approach this problem in a pessimistic spirit. Even if we had up-to-date and comprehensive mortality tables for every type of asset, prediction would still be treacherous (save perhaps for firms with big populations of like assets). We have excellent tables for human life, but these do not enable us to value one man's insurance policies in ways that mean much. The accountant has no choice but to predict value patterns for depreciating assets; yet in doing so he is flying in the face of logic.

HISTORICAL COST AND PROBABILITY

Let us first decide how we might recast familiar historical costs in a way that tries to weigh probabilities.

Simple example   Consider an asset that costs £1,200, and "has a 3-year life" (and no scrap value); maintenance expenses and physical performance are constant. Conventional wisdom tells us that the straight-line depreciation method is here suitable, and so the value pattern over years 0–3 is £1,200, £800, £400, and £0; depreciation cost is £400 in all years.

Suppose the owner has had experience with three similar machines, A, B, and C. A died in year 2, B in year 3, and C in year 4. (This symmetric pattern gives some justification to the statement that the new asset "has a 3-year life".)

If the firm were now starting afresh with a team of three such assets, instead of one, it would plan to write off depreciation for the combined team as follows:

TABLE 1
PA historical cost charges, 3 assets

	Year	1 £	2 £	3 £	4 £
Yearly charges:	A	600	600		
	B	400	400	400	
	C	300	300	300	300
Total charges for group:		1,300	1,300	700	300

With only one asset (the argument runs), the pattern should be proportionate to the above totals.[4] (If we like, we can look on the one machine

---

[4] "The depreciation rates are calculated for each possible service life of the asset and then the weighted average is computed using the service life probabilities as weights".
— Yuji Ijiri and Robert S. Kaplan, "Sequential Models in Probabilistic Depreciation", *Journal of Accounting Research*, Spring 1970, p. 35.

as a team of 3 little machines with 2-, 3-, and 4-year lives.) So the forecast patterns for the asset can be found:

TABLE 2
PA historical cost charges, 1 asset

Year	0 £	1 £	2 £	3 £	4 £
Charge for 3 assets		1,300	1,300	700	300
Charge for 1 asset		433	433	234	100
Value of asset	1,200	767	334	100	

The value at any date is the sum of the future amounts still to be written off (e.g. at the end of year 2, future charges as shown in line 2 are $234 + 100 = 334$).

Figure 1 compares the AL and PA values. The AL values are shown by the unbroken straight line, and the PA values by the broken curved line.

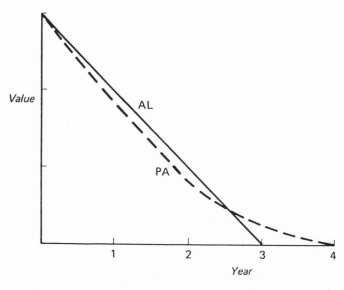

FIGURE 1
AL and PA historical cost values
(predicted at date 0)

PA yields lower values during the asset's youth; the possibility of early death lowers the predicted values of years 1 and 2. But the possibility that life will stretch to year 4 gives some value to the end of year 3.

Both the AL and the PA curves (it is important to bear in mind) show value as predicted at date 0, i.e. use tentative budgets at acquisition date.

It is feasible to elaborate the PA arithmetic to cover extra uncertainties, such as a range of possible scrap proceeds in any given year of death.[5]

PA's lower values, and therefore higher depreciation charges, in the early years of Table 1 are not just a fluke dependent on our choice of figures. With suitable mathematics, one can show the pattern to be general for a single asset: PA charges more than AL in the early years.[6] For a group of like assets, the difference may well be insignificant; it becomes zero for a static group (since here a year's charges — whatever the method — equal the replacement cost).

Possible advantages of allowing for probability Should accountants switch from AL to PA? Let us re-state the advantages of sound depreciation figures in annual accounts, and consider what PA could contribute.

Balance Sheet

In the balance sheet, sound figures help with the vague but nevertheless important task of showing the "size" of the firm's resources. In particular, they give some idea of the health and future prospects of the depreciating assets — plainly a matter of probabilities. So it seems eminently reasonable to hold that PA would be an improvement.

Income Statement

Here accuracy is important chiefly because faulty profit figures can give misleading impressions of investment prospects and management skill; and faulty cost figures may lead to mistaken pricing policies. If PA raises the charges of early years, the resulting low profits may be a useful warning of the risks and lags attending further investment — and thus also show management's tactics in a clearer light.

THE FAULTS OF PA

On the other hand, PA has certain faults:

1. It calls for harder work than AL at the start of life — and, further, for frequent revisions during life. Yet

---

[5] D. D. Martin, "Justification for Probability Depreciation", *Journal of Business Finance and Accounting*, Spring 1977, p. 83, gives an example.

[6] Ijiri and Kaplan, *idem*, p. 41. See also their "Probabilistic Depreciation and its Implications for Group Depreciation," *Accounting Review*, October 1969, p. 743.

2. The resulting figures may differ very little from those of AL. And
3. Applied to historical costs, PA pays more regard to arithmetic than to reality. It is thus cost allocation at its worst.

Let us consider these faults in turn.

The hard work of calculating PA   So far we have concentrated on PA's preliminary calculation — i.e. the estimated values and charges as foreseen at year 0. At this point, PA obviously demands more spade-work than traditional methods. But, if it then predicts better figures than do those methods, will it not in some way facilitate and lighten the accountant's later work at each year-end?

The answer is alas a resounding "no". Probability logic demands surely that, as the asset's life progresses and the future grows clearer, the figures must be revised — more often, and with more toil, than under traditional rules. If an asset survives years where death is possible, the future probabilities change; to be consistent, the accountant must each year use new factors to reshape his value-pattern. His task is not unlike that of the actuary of a life assurance company, who must regularly revalue the company's liabilities in the light of the ages in fact attained by surviving policy-holders.

Recasting — the traditional method   Obviously, even the traditional AL method pans out neatly only if the preliminary estimate of life is right. Thus, in our example, the estimate of £1,200, £800, £400 proves suitable if the asset obligingly dies in year 3. If instead it dies say in 2, the actual figures in successive balance sheets work out at £1,200, £800, £0; the accountant must in year 2's income statement get rid of £800 instead of his forecast charge of £400. And if the asset is still going strong at the end of 3, he faces the familiar problem of whether to write the asset down to *nil*, or (more logically) to revise his original year 3 estimate; if he opts for the latter course, presumably he spreads the residual £400 cost equally over years 3 and 4, so that the value pattern ends as £1,200, £800, £400, £200, £0. Thus the original set of possible patterns could be shown in the form of a branching tree:

TABLE 3
Possible AL patterns

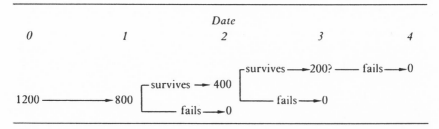

Recasting — the PA method If this asset's PA value must still hinge on historical cost, the accountant should review his figures as follows.[7]

Death in year 2 brings an immediate write-off to zero (as with the traditional method).

If however the asset survives the hazards of year 2, its forecast probabilities change: it now has equal chances of death in 3 and in 4. So we must re-vamp our earlier values. The first step is to envisage a team of only 2 assets at date 0 — namely B (with a 3-year life) and C (with a 4-year life); then, as before, we boil down their charges to suit the single asset:

TABLE 4
PA historical cost values, revised at date 2

Year	0	1	2	3	4
	£	£	£	£	£
Yearly charges for 2 assets:					
B		400	400	400	
C		300	300	300	300
Total for 2 assets		700	700	700	300
Charge for 1 asset		350	350	350	150
Revised value pattern	1,200	850	500	150	0

That is, the original value estimates of Table 2 (£767, £334, £100, £0) have proved too cautious: the date 2 balance sheet should show the asset at £500 instead of the original guess of £334, and the depreciation charge shrinks correspondingly.

At the end of year 3, likewise, either survival is certain, and cautious earlier guesses at value are replaced by £1,200 ÷ 4 = £300; or the asset is dead, and the write-off is £500 (instead of the projected £350).

The tree for the whole life is as shown in Table 5.

In short, PA's initial budgets — despite their more defensible figures — *never* prove right (whereas AL budgets are right at least occasionally); they must each year be rehashed in the light of actual experience. Such gymnastics are not likely to attract accountants, or to be understood by anyone else.

PA results may be close to AL results Our example deals with a type of asset that has a short life and slight cluster. These are conditions that accentuate

[7] See discussion in Frank C. Jen and Ronald J. Huefner, "Depreciation by Probability-Life", *Accounting Review*, April 1970, p. 290.

TABLE 5
Possible PA values

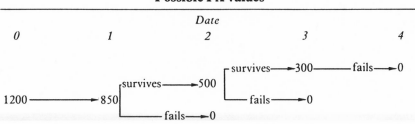

the difference between PA and AL patterns. Longer life and marked cluster lessen the difference, which thus may often be trifling.

Do PA historical costs match reality?   The aim of a depreciation method is to yield values that match economic reality — admittedly in rough-and-ready style. A good method throws up patterns fairly close to those that an appraiser, familiar with the market, should produce: the depreciated values should reflect the net cost of the asset's remaining service-units.[8] Values that respond to unfolding probabilities meet this test better than rigid patterns; so, even when they are fractions of original cost, PA values seem more defensible than those of AL. However, a method that abandons allocations (however sophisticated) of historical cost in favour of current market values should be better still — whether or not general and specific prices change. (And, if the accountant is unable to abandon historical cost, study of current value should at least help him to select the most inoffensive historical method.) How does probability affect current value?

PA AND CURRENT VALUES

Risk must obviously affect the price that buyers are willing to pay for an asset. If, as in our example, they pay £1,200 for an asset with a probable 3-year life, presumably they would pay only about £800 for an otherwise similar asset that is sure to last exactly 2 years, and about £1,600 for one sure to last exactly 4 years. (Time–discount would tend to taper the prices for the longer lives — a justification for the annuity system of depreciation. But here for simplicity we assume cost-of-capital to be negligible and investors to be risk-neutral, just as we assume the quality of each year's services to be constant. So we have reason to look on each year's sure services as having a market value of £400. Thus the yearly rent for hiring such an asset would, under our laboratory conditions, be a constant £400 per year of survival.

Current values foreseen at date 0   We can bring in uncertainty by applying probability factors to the £400 costs of each service-unit or yearly rent. If we buy a £1,200 asset that is subject to the uncertainty envisaged on page 129, we assume a $\frac{2}{3}$ chance of life exceeding 2 years, and a $\frac{1}{3}$ chance of life exceeding 3 years. The units can be evaluated thus at date 0:

TABLE 6
Value of service units foreseen at date 0

Date	Rent for 4-year asset	Probability	Cost (uncertain life)
0			
1	400	1	400
2	400	1	400
3	400	$\frac{2}{3}$	267
4	400	$\frac{1}{3}$	133
	Value (date 0) of uncertain life asset		1,200

At date 0, it is not possible to foresee the values of the asset at all future dates; however, because the asset is certain to survive for at least two years, the value at date 1 is known: £400 + £267 + £133 = £800. Thus depreciation over the first year is £400, which weakens the suggestion that normal methods do not allow enough depreciation in earlier years.

Recasting the budgets Current values, like their historical counterparts, will need to be recast as time alters probabilities.

At date 2, there are two possibilities. First, the asset may have survived. If so, year 3's services are assured, but there is a 50% chance that the asset will fail at the end of the year. Its value will therefore be £400 + $\frac{1}{2}$ × £400 = £600. Second, the asset may have failed, and its value is zero.

At date 3, either the value is raised by survival to one year's rent of £400, or it is written down to zero.

The values could be shown as the familiar branching tree. But, as clear figures for the ups-or-downs will help the argument, the tree has been elaborated slightly in Figure 2.

The main advantage of the revaluations at dates 2 and 3 is that the balance sheet figures are also those of capital budgets which allow for circumstances and probabilities. They are thus consistent with deprival values. They may not differ much from second-hand market values, which obviously slump if a machine dies young, and stay buoyant if it survives. In our examples, simplifying assumptions have been made about discounting for

[8] For a more adequate statement, see W. T. Baxter, *Depreciation* (London, Sweet and Maxwell, 1971) p. 34.

EFR-J

risk and time, and price level changes are excluded; but, in principle, there should be no difficulty about incorporating such factors.

VALUE CHANGE VIEWED AS HOLDING GAIN

Change in probabilities brings value changes that seem analogous to ordinary holding gain and loss. We therefore propose that, where full analysis is feasible, value change of each year should be shown to have two components: that part equivalent to the use of service-units during the year (in the example, £400) which we see as the proper charge for "depreciation" in the profit and loss account; and that part resulting from the uncertain knowledge about the asset's life.

With this system, the year 2 account would include £400 depreciation, and (with failure) a £400 holding loss, or (with survival) a £200 holding gain. The year 3 account would likewise include £400 depreciation and £200 of either holding loss or gain. The full figures are shown in Figure 2.

Thus the scheme differs from normal methods in that, as information about likely survival of the asset becomes clearer, it records unrealised holding gain or realised holding loss. Further, a constant depreciation charge is made in every year during which the asset is used, whereas the normal methods may make no charge for an asset that has exceeded its expected life. These seem considerable benefits.

CURRENT VALUES OF A GROUP

Because current value recognises the holding gain on survivors, the total value for a group of machines tends to be higher with current value than with historical cost. Let us elaborate our example by considering nine of its machines, in a steady state with three of its machines being replaced each year. The comparison is shown in Table 7.

TABLE 7
Current versus historical values for a group

Age	Number	Revaluation		Historical cost	
		Value per machine	Total	Value per machine	Total
0	3	1,200	3,600	1,200	3,600
1	3	800	2,400	800	2,400
2	2	600	1,200	400	800
3	1	400	400	200	200?
			7,600		7,000?

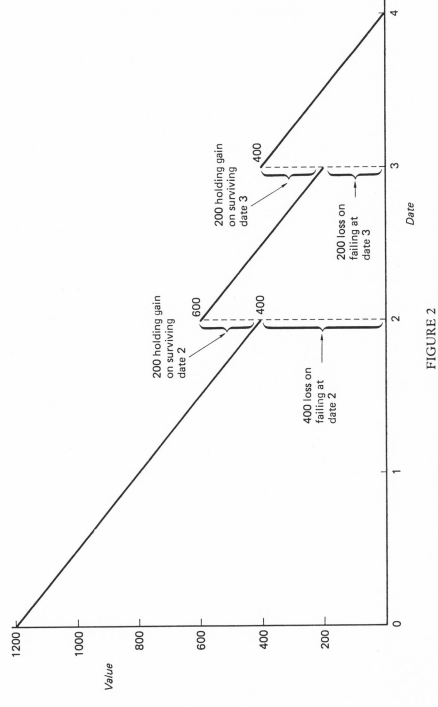

FIGURE 2

Possible value patterns depending on survival of asset

Correspondingly, the depreciation charges for a firm that is building up its stock of machines would tend to be higher with historical cost methods (a corollary of the lower values of the steady state). As noted earlier, however, once the steady state is reached the gross depreciation charge must be the same under the two methods (provided the historical cost method treats loss on disposal as depreciation).

CONCLUSION

PA, though slightly superior to the usual historical methods, does not stand up to serious analysis. Current values seem far sounder. These can adjust for information on survival without any conceptual troubles. However, in view of the many more pressing problems that revaluation poses, a theorist must sadly conclude that early use of probability refinements is unlikely.

DISCOUNT AND BUDGETS

With Constant Prices and Inflation

INTRODUCTION

There are lots of excellent books (some of which are listed on the last page) that deal with budgets and discounting at a fairly advanced level. To do this properly, they must go into detail, and must assume the reader to feel at home with a fair amount of economic theory and mathematics. Oddly enough, they tend to put little stress on inflation.

Anyone who wants to master budgeting must sooner or later get his teeth into such books. But a long spell of teaching has shown me that students often learn best if they are first taken over a new subject at a simple level. Such an approach may cut corners and hide intellectual pitfalls. But surely it is justified if it arouses the reader's interest, shows him the wood as well as the trees, and smoothes his way to more advanced study.

What follows is meant as such a simple introduction. I hope it will help students of business and accounting to see both the merits and limitations of budgets and discounting.

There are various ways of approaching these topics. However a main concern of economics is choice between alternatives; and businessmen use budgets largely as a help in choosing between different plans. So there are strong grounds for recognizing explicitly that discounting is in fact a way of comparing alternatives. This is what the following pages try to do.

W.T. Baxter.
London School of Economics.

9

I   TIME AND VALUE

Most of us can apply interest formulae without undue pains. If asked for the present value of £130 due a year hence, given an interest rate of 20%, we whip out our calculators and readily pronounce the answer to be £108. But perhaps the arithmetic comes more easily than full understanding. How does one in practice come to choose 20%? What exactly does our present value of £108 mean? And what indeed is the justification for the discounting process?

A bird in the hand . . .

The old proverb is a good starting place for a discussion of discounting. For it says in effect that we mentally equate some given quantity of wealth now *(x)* with some bigger quantity of future wealth *(y)*. The difference, $y - x$, could be called a discount.

And the proverb rings true for three reasons:

a We may fail to catch the bird-in-the-bush (i.e. risk).

b We may want to eat bird today rather than later (i.e. consumption *time preference*, perhaps irrational); or

c A bird-in-the-hand may help the hunter to gain future wealth. Thus it may as food give him extra energy; or, if he keeps it alive, it may have chicks, so that – by the time two birds-in-the-bush could be caught – he will have more than two home-bred birds.

All three reasons are important. But *a* and *b* are clearly subjective, and may vary from person to person. Reason *c* is somewhat less subjective and is simpler to quantify; so it is more likely to dominate any discussion of discount arithmetic.

To satisfy a pedant, the proverb would have to be expanded so as to allow for *time* as well as number. All three reasons suggest that, before we can equate one bird-in-hand with more birds-in-bush, we must have some idea of the time between now and the likely date of capture. Thus reason *c* gains in strength where there is enough time for our asset to breed plentifully.

The £ in the hand . . .

The argument still holds if we endow the birds with money values, or substitute cash for birds. Reasons *a*, *b*, and *c* all dispose us to regard a £ today
10

as more attractive than a £ due a year hence. But a big enough future sum – say £1.20 – would just turn the scales.

It follows that we may be willing to pay a price to someone who gives us spot cash in return for our right to future cash. In the above example, the price (or discount) is 20p. In formal terms:

$$\left.\begin{array}{l}\text{Face value of}\\\text{future sum less}\\\text{discount}\end{array}\right\} = \left\{\begin{array}{l}\text{present value of}\\\text{future sum.}\end{array}\right.$$

What applies to my assets applies to my liabilities too. A £ that I must pay at a future date seems less oppressive than a £ due now. But I may be willing to pay now in return for a suitable inducement; and reason c will play a big part in my decision on whether this discount is sufficiently tempting.

Budgets for projects

Since about (say) 1950, theorists and managers have grown more and more interested in the budgets that a firm should draft as aids to its decisions – especially its "capital budgets" for testing whether a proposed project is worth-while.

The budgets can take various forms. The best-known are:

(1) Payback period

Here the budgeter finds how long it will take before the future net receipts add up to the starting investment. Suppose projects A and B each cost £100 to start. A earns £50 a year, B £33 a year. Thus A has a 2-year payback period, and so may be deemed better than B with its 3-year period.

The trouble with this method is that it fails to allow for events beyond the payback period. For instance, B may have a long and fruitful life after the 3 years, and A only a short and barren life after the 2 years.

However, the method is popular, probably because it is simple, and because it stresses the near future (relatively safe and predictable) rather than the less-near (risky and dimly seen).

11

(2) Rate of return on capital employed (ROCE)

Here the estimated future figures are slotted into some such formula as:

$$\text{Average rate of return} = \frac{\text{Average yearly net cash flows} - \text{average depreciation}}{\text{Average investment during life}}$$

A project with a high rate is deemed better than one with a low rate.

This method does cover the whole life of the project. But it too ignores the *timing* of receipts and payments (cash flows), i.e. fails to recognize the superiority of early rather than late flows. One should regard this year's £ and a £ of each later year as different animals. A helpful budget must recognize their differences; it sins against logic if it adds or subtracts units of such unlike present worth.

Because of their failure on this point, methods (1) and (2) are both flawed in comparison with (3) and (4) below, which use *discounted cash flows* (DCF) and so are able to recognize the "time value of money".

(3) Internal rate of return (IRR)

This method discounts future £s with a factor reflecting the project's own rate of growth. It will be described later.

(4) Net present value (NPV)

This discounts future £s with a rate external to the project. There are strong theoretical arguments in its favour, and it is the main concern of later pages.

Extent of use of budgets

Important projects (as the marriage service warns us) are "not to be enterprized nor taken in hand inadvisedly, lightly . . .". But how far are any of these budget methods used in practice? If an accurate survey could be made, it would probably show that a good many managers still prefer hunch to arithmetic (and may even justify this stance as the essence of entre-preneurship). Of the rest, probably a majority content themselves with methods (1) or (2) (arguing that (3) and (4) are too complex, or rely too much on figures that are necessarily vague and uncertain). But the use of (3) and (4) – DCF budgets – seems to be growing, especially in big companies and for big projects. A well-educated manager should surely understand them, and at least use them in suitable circumstances.

12

Somewhat similar DCF budgets – perhaps under another name such as "cost-benefit analysis" – are useful also for decisions on wider social problems (e.g. road *versus* rail). Soviet planners went badly astray when, to preserve ideological purity, they ignored interest. They have since improved by using figures that look remarkably like interest, but are given such diplomatic labels as "capital productivity factor".

Interest and discount

A preliminary point – perhaps obvious – must be made. In loose talk, we may find it rather hard not to use "interest rate" and "discount rate" as if they are the same thing. But when £100 grows to £120 in a year, the growth rate ("interest") is 20%; when the £120 is given a present value of £100, the shrinkage rate ("discount") is

$$\frac{120-100}{120} \times 100 = 16.6\%$$

Strictly, we should use ponderous phrasing to spell out that our discount rate, based on a 20% interest rate, is only 16.6%

Discount in financial markets

Originally "discount" had the wide meaning of any deduction or counter-claim ("my prayers and penance shall discount for thy sins" says Dryden's virtuous maiden). Later its meaning narrowed to "interest discounted". It then was used, in particular, in bill of exchange dealings: thus where debtor A had promised (by signing a bill) to pay creditor B £1000 in three months, B might discount the bill at his bank for (say) £980 of ready money.

Because the words "discount" and "interest" are so prominent in descriptions of financial doings, one's inclination must be to explain the size of discount rates by looking to dealings in finance markets.

But it would be dangerous to assume that market rates alone should govern all discount calculations. In particular, a firm's internal operations are not always linked closely with finance markets, notably where it cannot borrow as much as it wants, and so must *ration its capital* between various uses; then some private rate may be better for the calculations. This is perhaps the most interesting and revealing situation, so we shall start with it (Chapter II).

The argument gets more complicated where the £'s purchasing power changes (as during inflation). We shall therefore postpone this part of the subject till chapter *VI*.

13

247

Discounting, value, and comparison

How is the right discount rate found? To answer this question, one must remember that discounting is one form of *valuation* – that the NPV budgeter is just as much a valuer (of projects, etc.) as the appraiser who puts a value on (say) your home. So it is worth-while to recall the principles of valuation.

"Every valuation is a comparison" a famous economist tells us. The role of comparison becomes plain if we look at the way in which a market valuation is made by an appraiser such as a house agent. In effect, he compares the given asset (call it X) with some other asset (Y) whose price has been established in market deals. Thus, if he is to value your home (X), he will refer to recent sales of similar houses to find a Y. If he finds a Y that is very like your home, and it sold for £90,000, then he will value your home at about £90,000.

However, not all markets can include a Y that resembles X closely. When the market provides only a Y that varies a good deal from X, the valuer has the delicate task of gauging the variance in money terms. If, say, your home is somewhat bigger than Y, he may convert Y's price into a rate per square metre, and apply this rate to your home's area.

Share valuation gives us a closer example. Suppose you are valuing unquoted shares in Company X. They yield a dividend of 10p. per share. You find a Y of similar size, risk, total dividend, etc. Y has more shares than X, and so its dividend rate is lower — 8p. The price of Y is shares is 160p. You argue "Y's dividend yield is 8/160, i.e. 5%. Using this to discount (capitalize) X's dividends, I get a value of 10/.05, i.e. 200p". Here the discount rate is very clearly a way of valuing X by comparison with Y. But, where all the steps are not spelled out – e.g. if we rely on generalizations such as "current discount rates seem to be about 7%" – there is some danger of our failing to identify Y and allow for variances.

So we should remember that, where a budgeter studies a potential business project with the help of NPV arithmetic, he is valuing an intangible X – expectations of the project's future cash flows, possibly spread over many years. If the firm can borrow and lend readily in financial markets (i.e. is not subject to capital rationing), these give him a helpful Y. He can for instance reason "if the firm puts funds into the market, they would grow at such-and-such a rate. So I can use that rate to test whether the alternative of investing in X is worth-while". Again, where X would be financed by a loan, this acts as a kind of Y; X is not worth-while unless it grows more steeply than Y-cum-interest.

14

II CAPITAL RATIONING

What discount rate should the budgets use if the firm is denied access to finance markets? Such a situation could readily arise where, for instance, lenders deem the firm too poor a risk; this is likely if the firm is small or unknown, or when its trade has struck a bad patch, or when it wants to expand at a pace that strikes outsiders as over-ambitious. Again, the firm may voluntarily restrict its borrowing, e.g. to avoid the perils of indebtedness (high gearing), or the strains of undertaking more work than managers can handle.

In this cramped situation, various projects may compete with one another for the firm's limited funds, and it must decide which of the rivals to invest in and which to reject. External interest rates may here have scant relevance, and decision budgets can hardly be of great service if they use such rates. To ration out its capital, the firm must use some rate of its own (possibly much higher than external rates). It must seek another Y within its own boundaries: project X must be compared with other internal activities.

Usually a firm faces a range of other possible projects – good, bad, and indifferent. It will probably look on one (or a group) of these as its Y. But such a Y could take many shapes, possibly very different from X. The variances between X and Y could then be considerable.

Comparison of activities within a firm: opportunity cost

Suppose a firm is offered jobs A and B, involving much the same outlay and time-span. The firm is too small to do both (i.e. the jobs are "mutually exclusive"). If its budgets show that A would yield a profit of £1500, and B of £1000, presumably it will refuse B in order to do A. Then B can be described as the opportunity (or alternative) forgone.

It is sometimes convenient to describe B's £1000 as the *opportunity cost* of doing A. The profit of £1500 shows the gain from doing A rather than nothing at all; the net surplus of £500 (£1500 less opportunity cost) shows the extra gain from doing A rather than the best alternative.

Comparison via end-values

In deciding between A and B, we have compared end-figures. Project comparison would often be easier if this could be done; the end-values reveal the heart of the matter more clearly than other figures.

15

249

Diagram Comparison of end-values is illustrated in figure 1a. Here OD shows the life-span of two rival projects, X and Y, as predicted in budgets. OA is the starting investment for either. The curve AX traces the growth of project X till it realises DX. AY traces Y's growth till it realises DY. Profit on X is FX; on Y is FY. FY (common to X and Y) is X's opportunity cost; so YX is the measure of X's superiority over Y. Presumably the firm will chose X.

Figure 1

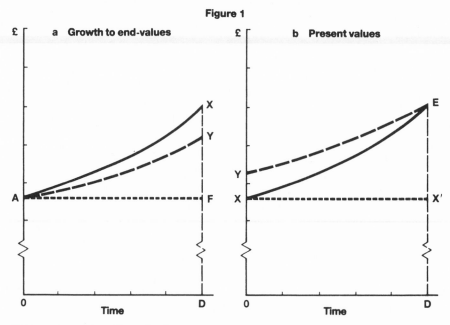

Comparison via *rates of return*

However, the worth of a project (like that of X's unquoted shares considered earlier) may be tested with a growth *rate* per year rather than a sum of money.

For convenience in arithmetic, rates are often expressed not as percentages but as fractions of 1. Thus 5% becomes .05.

Comparison of IRRs.

One possible rate is that of the project itself (the internal rate of return – see page 12). Thus we can find X's internal rate, and compare it with Y's.

Suppose the starting investments in X or in Y to be £100; the life of such projects to be a year; X's end revenue to be £130, and Y's £120. Then X's internal rate is 30%. Similarly, Y's is 20%.

16

Some firms use such rates to compare projects. In our simple example, this IRR method yields the right answer: 30% is higher than 20%, so X ranks above Y; and X does in fact give the bigger return. With less straight-forward conditions, however, the IRR can on occasion prove a false guide (particularly where there is a series of outflows mixed with inflows).

IRR rates look simple, and so may be attractive to a manager who has no time or taste for arithmetical subtleties: he can readily decide that 30% is better than 20%. Thus some managers, faced with the need to test projects as they come along day by day, use a rule-of-thumb: accept if their IRR exceeds a given "cut-off" rate, otherwise reject. Here the Y is probably not one clearly-seen alternative, but a vague level of activities that are better not accepted.

Finding IRRs can be tedious (though you can get computer packages that do the job). Consider this example. A project's flows are expected to be:

			£
End of Year 0	Invest		100
	1		Nil
	2	Withdraw	20
	3	Withdraw	30
	4	Withdraw	85

We must find the rate that will reduce the total of discounted future flows to the starting investment of £100. Our simplest plan is to use trial and error. If we first try a rate of 8%, the answer is too big (£103.4 – see below). If we next try 10%, the answer is too small (£97.1). At 9%, the answer is almost £100; so 9% will be good enough for most purposes.

		Rate		
		8%	9%	10%
	Flow			
Year 2	20	17.1	16.8	16.5
3	30	23.8	23.2	22.5
4	85	62.5	60.2	58.1
		103.4	100.2	97.1

17

Comparison via *net present value (NPV)*

This method gives us another way (more reliable than IRR) of using growth rates as aids to comparison. With it, we work backward from X's end-value to find a present value. We do so (with capital rationing) by using the IRR of alternative work as the discount rate.

Sometimes this alternative (again call it Y) may be obvious (e.g. a specific rival job). Sometimes it is less obvious – for instance where the size, nature and timing of possible alternatives can be seen only vaguely (so that a manager must make do with an estimated rate). Obvious or not, Y is what gives the discount rate its validity.

Take again our example in which £100 in X will yield £130 a year hence, and in Y will yield £120. These end-values make us regard X as a good project; they show also that our reasoning stems from comparison of X with Y. If we prefer instead to make the comparison in terms of starting value, we discount X's future cash flow of £130. To do so, we assume the existence of Y-type work that will also, at its growth rate of only 20%, reach £130. The initial investment in such work must plainly differ from £100 – in fact must be $130 \times \frac{100}{120} = £108.3$.

We use this figure (the potential investment in Y) to test X, by saying that £108.3 is the present value of X's £130. Comparing the initial investments of £100 and £108.3, we again decide that X is better.

Y has in this arithmetic become anonymous as the hidden father of the 20% interest rate (the "opportunity cost of capital"). There is an obvious danger that Y's transmogrification into the interest rate will mask its nature and indeed existence. To acknowledge its importance, we shall here call it the base-project.

Diagram. Figure 1b looks at projects from the NPV stance. OX is the starting investment in X; DE is its end-value. The discounting arithmetic works backward from DE. It assumes that there is, conveniently, alternative work of Y-type that would grow also to DE. To do so, the alternative would – because of its lower growth rate – need a higher starting investment than X. The arithmetic finds this starting investment, OY, by discounting DE with Y's IRR. It thus shows X's superiority (in opening terms) of XY. However, it gives no clear picture of the end merits of either X or Y.

If a given base-project ceases for some reason to be available, the budgeter must turn to whatever alternative project ranks next, and promote it to base. Its lower IRR becomes the new discount rate. Y moves up the vertical axis in
18

Ib; X's present value OY rises. Such a move accords with common sense: the worse the alternative, the more we like the given project, and so the higher its present value.

Thus X's value can change, not because of any change in X's own flows, but because of change in the all-important understudy Y. Values move "in sympathy".

Meaning of a present value

What does our example's £108 signify? A possible reply is that the firm is indifferent as between £108 now and £130 a year hence. But why? Perhaps the best justification must follow the reasoning of "deprival value": if the firm were somehow deprived of (prevented from starting) project X, fair compensation would be £8; for the firm could then put £108 into base-projects earning 20%, and so would still end up with £130. Present value is thus the size of the investment needed to achieve the same end-value by the best alternative route.

If one wants to explain the matter with more stress on valuation theory, one must alter the above words slightly. A valuer, asked to appraise X, would look around for comparable projects. He would then find that investment of £108 in type Y also promises to yield £130; so he pronounces X to be worth £108. Thanks to its ability to do X, the firm can thus "buy" something worth £108 for only £100, and should snap up the bargain.

Interest tables as aids

In the example, we "translated" the £130 with a present value factor *(v)* of $\frac{1}{1\frac{1}{2}}$ or .833. The mechanics of such factor calculations can be eased by using compound interest ("actuarial") tables. Such tables give, in a column probably headed *v*, the present values of 1 for the successive periods. Thus the 20% table gives, for 1 year, .833; for 2 years *(v²)*, .694; and so on.

Weakness of discounting

Use of present value has great practical advantages. But we may perhaps be excused for deeming our example's £130 end-value more real than the £108 present value, since we expect that its £130 will one day actually grace the cash account; whereas the £108 is much more of an abstraction, dependent on various "ifs". The fact that NPV exceeds £100 is a strong argument for doing X; but a theorist must have considerable doubt about whether £8 is the exact measure of X's superior worth.

19

The "ifs" hinge largely on how suitable Y is as base-project. In real life, the "jobs" forgone may not be known with any precision, or may be different from X. In particular, they may vary in degree of risk. And they may come in a "lumpy" range of sizes; thus, if our projects call for investment in a machine, a small Y may be available for £80, a bigger one for £140, and none at £108. Moreover the IRR on different sizes is not likely to be constant at 20%.

Again, there are awkward problems where X and Y end on different dates. Thus if X ends in 1989, and Y in 1987, X's 1989 end-value ought to be compared with:

(1) Y's 1987 end-value; plus

(2) some kind of variance allowance for the growth to 1989 of Y's successors, i.e. of the projects in which Y's proceeds will be re-invested (and which may not end till long after 1989).

Here the blind use of discount arithmetic may appear to offer an easy escape from protracted guesswork. But it must in fact rely on simplified and perhaps wrong assumptions about Y and events after 1987.

In many situations, then, the results of alternative "jobs" may be far from clear-cut. Thus Y and the discounting method are best thought of as useful but somewhat rough-and-ready guides. Arithmetic can never supplant judgement and luck.

Can present values dampen investors' enthusiasm?

Perhaps it is not altogether fanciful to think that the form of the NPV answer may on occasion play down X's charms so much that the investor will become apathetic when he should be eager. This could happen where both X and Y are excellent projects, but X is only a shade better than Y, e.g. where the same end-sum can be got by investing £100 in X or £101 in Y, so that the discounted inducement to go ahead is put at only £1. In terms of diagram 1a, FX is big but Y is near X; so, in 1b, XY is small. A more effective study would also compare X's £100 with the end gain (FX), i.e. compare X with a policy of doing nothing at all. Here, at least, IRR might be a more helpful guide.

Summary

To re-cap. An NPV calculation compares the given project with a hidden rival. To do this, it uses the rival's IRR as discount factor. The resulting present

20

value tells us whether the project is better than the rival, by showing how much more might have to be invested in the latter to reach the same end-value.

Capacity for many jobs

So far, we have for simplicity assumed that the firm can accept only one project. In real life, it often is able (even with capital rationing) to accept several. Thus we must picture a firm that (say) can spend a total of £10000, and must make up the best possible portfolio by selecting projects from candidates A (needing £2000), B (£7000), C(4000), . . . and Z(£5000). How does it pick the winning team?

This is an intractable problem. Theorists have suggested various methods (e.g. mathematical programming) that may in some circumstances be helpful, but do not provide a complete solution. Probably the most reasonable procedure is to find the present values of each project; then to try out various teams of projects (each with total costs not exceeding £10000); and to pick the team whose total of present values is highest.

But, alas, the last paragraph fails to explain how the discount rate is chosen in this situation. Logic here goes round in circles: to find the base-project Y, one needs first to know X (all the projects better than Y); but to find X by discounting, one needs first to know Y.

And there are many complicating factors. It may or may not be possible to postpone a job. It may or may not be possible to vary a job's size. It may or may not be possible to get more capital later in the budget period. And – a very likely snag – jobs may start and finish at different dates; so the firm cannot pick a whole team at a given starting date and for a neat period, but will have to start new jobs one-by-one as some space becomes free. Y can here be no more than a stream of vague possibilities.

The arbitrary cut-off rate

In view of these difficulties, common sense tells the firm to test projects with an arbitrary rate. Past experience and market mood may – or may not – point to a rate that works reasonably well, i.e. approximates to the opportunity cost of the scarce funds. Such a rate may be called the "hurdle" or "cut-off" rate.

Thus the statement "we use a 15% rate in NPV appraisals" may mean nothing more precise than "we hope a 15% rate will point to a serviceable frontier between good and less good projects".

21

255

Market rates and rationing

So far, we have assumed that the firm subject to rationing will ignore market rates. But there may be occasions – particularly in the short-run or at slack times – when even this firm finds that investment in the finance market looks attractive, and so gives a new base-project.

Then, if the best use of spare funds would be (say) to put them on deposit, the interest rate on deposits would point to the discount factor. Sometimes however the best plan might instead be to repay loan, etc. Here the potential saving on loan interest would show the factor. The next chapter sets these possibilities into a broader framework.

22

III UNRATIONED CAPITAL

When a firm can borrow readily (the most usual starting-point in discussions of discounting), the above argument changes. "Discount rate" takes on its everyday meaning of a rate in the financial markets.

Projects financed by loan

As before, a budget could here test projects most simply by using end figures. It could then show whether net revenue (revenue less operating costs) would exceed interest cost and loan repayment.

If instead the budgeter prefers opening figures, he uses the loan's interest rate to discount the revenue (net of costs rather than interest), and finds whether the latter's present value exceeds the loan.

Diagram Figure 2a stresses the end position. The firm starts by borrowing OX. At the end, interest cost (still to be paid) is X'A, so the liability has grown to DA (loan plus interest); net revenue is DE; after payment of DA, a surplus of AE will be left.

Figure 2

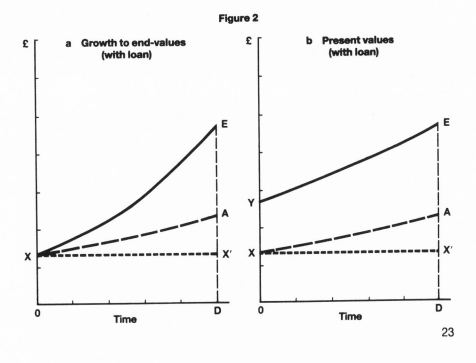

23

257

2b stresses instead the starting position. It discounts DE (using a rate found from XA, i.e. the interest rate to borrowers), and shrinks it to a present value OY. This exceeds OX by XY, and so predicts that the project will at the end yield a surplus.

Interest expense and opportunity cost

When capital is not rationed, one is tempted to say that budgets shed internal opportunity cost and replace it with ordinary expense (interest charges). However, it may be just as true (and more perceptive) to say that the opportunity cost rate has sunk to the level of the interest rate.

The argument often runs thus. If the firm has capacity for many jobs, the budgeter's problem is not comparison of job X with job Y, but how far to raise more loan so as to finance extra jobs. Picture the projects in a list ranked in order of descending merit. Projects will be accepted until one is reached that barely yields a surplus after interest and repayment of loan. The IRR of this marginal project is the opportunity cost rate; and it may well be very close to the interest rate.

The variety of market rates

However, phrases such as "the market rate of interest" are in fact ambiguous. My bank charges me a higher rate on overdrafts than it credits on my deposits, i.e. the market has a borrowing rate and a lending rate. And there are further complexities. The budgeter faces problems of finance as well as investment, and may have to consider:

a. *Fluctuating rates*. A loan contract may stipulate that the interest rate will vary in step with market rates. Here the budgeter should in theory guess all the future rates of the budget period, and use this array in his calculations. But such guesses are likely to be far from accurate. Common sense tells him to be content with a rough average of expected rates, perhaps raised somewhat for caution's sake.

b. *Short-term* versus *long-term*. Often rates vary with different lengths of loan period (e.g. the rate on a 10-year loan may be higher than on a 3-year loan).

c. *Size of loan*. Again, the interest rate may vary with size of loan outstanding.

d. *Type of finance*. The market offers many ways of raising funds. A budgeter must at times consider not only "loan" (or "debt") in the strict sense, but also preference and equity capital, convertible stock, etc. The rate of "interest"
24

258

(including dividends) then varies with type of security, and with the standing of the borrower.

e. *The composite cost of capital.* Moreover, it can in some circumstances be wrong to link a given project with a given loan. Over the years, a firm may raise funds from various types of "loan", and invest the receipts in various projects. One should therefore picture the receipts as flowing into a common pool; this merged source will provide cash for many projects. Here the best interest rate for budgets (a popular argument runs) is a composite. It is a weighted average of the rates on the different types of finance. Suppose the firm will be financed by equity (cost 12%) and loan (cost 9%) in a 2:1 ratio. Then:

$$\text{cost of capital} = .12 \times \tfrac{2}{3} + .09 \times \tfrac{1}{3} = .11$$

Note that "equity" is here not a book value, but the market value of all the ordinary shares.

The case for a composite rate seems valid where a budget previews a length of time, and a scale of investment, so big that finance will in fact be raised in several ways.

Meaning of present value if finance is borrowed

Flexible terms. The argument of this chapter may so far have implied that the firm can borrow and repay on flexible terms, i.e. that the size and duration of loans exactly match the needs of projects X and Y. In these simple circumstances, present values can have a clear meaning. Thus the surplus XY in Figure 2(b) is the extra amount that the firm would have to borrow to reach DE *via* project Y instead of X.

Fixed terms. However, arrangements are not always so flexible. The firm may already have borrowed (or committed itself to borrow) a given sum to cover all its likely needs. And the terms may be rigid, i.e. preclude rapayment at such dates, and in such doses, as the firm pleases. Here the loans, and their interest, have become "fixed" in the sense that they will not be varied by decisions on projects X and Y; and so (like other fixed costs) they should surely be regarded as irrelevant by a manager wise enough to use the incremental ("what difference does it make?") approach for his decisions. Suppose, after finance has been raised for a fixed period, a short-term project will use idle funds that otherwise would be put on deposit at a low interest rate; the latter, and not the borrowing rate, would here seem to be the right basis for calculating present value.

25

Value as "so-many years' purchase"

A valuer somtimes uses phrases that seem neatly to side-step the troubles of discounting for risk. Thus he may say "the value of this prime shop, in its first-class location, is twenty-five years' purchase of its yearly rent", or "this run-down warehouse is worth only six years' purchase of its rent". What he here is really saying is that the shop's value is its rent discounted at 4% (i.e. 100/25) – a low rate suitable for ultra-sound investments; whereas the warehouse's value is rent discounted at $16^2/_3$% (i.e. 100/6) – a high rate suitable for dubious investments. He certainly does not mean that what are for sale are 25-year and 6-year annuities. (Their capital values work out at less than his suggested prices.) Both investments have unknown future lives, but the shop rents look more reliable (in duration and size) than the warehouse rents.

A high rate as executioner

As under capital rationing, the size of the discount rate can have a decisive effect on a project's fate, particularly if the project will last for many years. Low rates encourage investment; high rates discourage it. Professor K. E. Boulding, when sitting on a committee charged with the cost-benefit analysis of a vast state project, put the matter into verse:

> At 4 per cent, the case is clear.
> At 6, some sneaking doubts appear.
> At 8, it draws its latest breath.
> At 10, it meets with certain death.

Incidentally, the government decided that the committee's realistic report would lose votes, and suppressed it.

26

IV   EXAMPLES

To avoid confusion over the mechanics of budgets, it will be as well to classify projects into two types, which we may (rather clumsily) call "satellite" and "integral":

1. *Satellite.* Here the project can be viewed almost as a separate firm, in the sense that its day-to-day cash flows are kept apart from those of the owning firm. Thus it keeps revenues and makes outlays, and it has its own cash float and bank balance. Its cash links with the owning firm are confined to the latter's "financing" flows – namely "in-payments" to the project's cash account, e.g. to cover start-up outlays, and "out-payments" of any surplus cash sent to the owner from time to time (perhaps as dividends) and residue at end of life. A distant branch could be a clear example of a satellite project. A budget to find whether such a project would be worth-while can confine itself to the flows that affect the owning firm directly, i.e. the in-payments and out-payments.

2. *Integral.* Here the project is part-and-parcel of the owning firm's cash system. A factory's purchase of an extra machine is an example. All the project's receipts and outlays affect the owner's cash directly, and so must go into the budget. There are no financing flows (or, if you will, *all* the flows are financing).

Example of budgets

The flows of a new branch are expected to be:

Year 0   £700 is paid in by the owner, and £500 is borrowed at 20%, to finance purchase of assets (£900) and the cash float (£300).

Year 1   Trading receipts £700, payments £400; interest £100; sent to owner £200.

Year 2   Trading receipts £900, payments £500; interest £100; sent to owner £300.

Year 3   Trading receipts £1100, payments £700; interest £100. The assets are sold off for £1300, the £500 loan repaid, and the cash balance (£1400) sent to the owner.

The owner's cut-off rate is 25%. Assume flows to take place at the year-end.

27

Possible types of budget (first for a satellite, then for an integral project) are as follows:

Satellite project. In a budget to show whether the project will be worth-while, only the in- and out-payments are needed:

Year	0	1	2	3	*Net Total*
		£	£	£	£
In-payments	700				
Out-payments	___	200	300	1400	
Present values, at 25%	(700)	160	192	717	369

The project yields a surplus of £369, and so should be accepted.

Integral project. Let us doctor the example, by merging the project's funds with those of the owning firm – so that there are no in-payments and out-payments; however we can suppose (as is not unrealistic) that the firm must keep £300 more cash on hand to deal with the increased volume of trade. The budget test at the start now runs:

Year	0	1	2	3	*Net Total*
	£	£	£	£	£
Loan received	500				
Trade revenues		700	900	1100	
Assets sold				1300	
Cash released				300	
	500	700	900	2700	
Assets paid for	900				
Extra cash-on-hand	300				
Trade outlays		400	500	700	
Interest paid		100	100	100	
Loan repaid				500	
	1200	500	600	1300	
Net receipts	(700)	200	300	1400	
Present values at 25%	(700)	160	192	717	369

Here the budget shows the same surplus of £369. But, where a satellite does not promptly remit all cash in excess of a fixed float, the two budgets will end up with different surpluses.

28

Cash adequacy

Suppose the budget is intended to show, not whether the end result is good, but whether the cash-on-hand for each year (or month) is big enough for fluctuating needs. Here the budget will take a slightly different form, i.e. become a summary of each period's cash account, including opening and closing balances. The latter will signal any current cash shortage or excess. Discounting is not needed.

29

V   SOME FURTHER POINTS

Risk

"Never prophesy — particularly about the future", S. Goldwyn allegedly warned us. Fortunately perhaps, mankind lacks the power to foresee with sureness. However impressive a budget's looks, however powerful the computers that work out its figures, it must remain a prey to risk: the figures are likely in the event to prove slightly or wildly wrong. Indeed, coping with risk is the essence of the businessman's task; there would be small need for him in a world of certainty.

The wise and voluminous suggestions of text-books do not help him much. They tell him, for instance, to put eggs into different baskets. They tell him too that it may be useful to draft not one but a range of budgets for a project. These might show e.g. a poor result, a middle result and a very good result. They might be adjusted with probability factors. Or they might show how sensitive the project is to change in any one of the ingredients (e.g. wage rates). And so on.
Businessmen respond to high risk in various ways. Some reject budgets entirely, and rely on their gambling instinct. Some accept only projects with a short payback time. Some put very cautious figures into their budgets. And some look for a high IRR, or find net present value with a high discount rate.

High discount rates and risk

Use of a high rate is popular and accords with common sense. But, alas, it brings its own problems.

To understand these, it is often illuminating to split up *i*, the high interest rate, into components. Thus we can expand the discount formula

$$\frac{1}{(1 + i)^n} \quad \text{into} \quad \frac{1}{(1+t+r)^n}$$

where *t* is the time rate of interest for riskless projects, *r* the extra rate ("premium") for risk, and *n* the number of years. The split between *t* and *r* points to various difficulties:

1. What is the size of the risk premium *r*? Few of us could pick it with any assurance.

2. Projects are likely to vary greatly in risk. So different projects should be discounted with different rates of *r*.

30

3. The ingredients of a given budget may also vary in risk (e.g. sale prices may be less sure than material costs). Then the different ingredients should be discounted separately, with different sizes of *r*.

4. If you try out various sizes of *n* (length of time) when applying

$$\frac{1}{(1+t+r)^n}$$

you will of course find that the present values fall fast as *n* grows. This is proper so far as *t* is concerned, and where (as is often the case) risk seems to mount steeply in each successive year. But it is not proper if the successive years bear equal risk (cf. premium bonds).

5. Attitudes to risk, and therefore to the size that should be given to *r*, depend on emotion rather than cold calculation, and vary from person to person. To some people, the unexpected is what gives interest to business; they may revel in risk, i.e. would like their firm to use a low *r*. Other people are risk-averse, and would like a high *r*; and mood can change from day to day. But budgets are probably controlled by a team of different people (say, the directors); how do they pick their collective *r*; and do they try somehow to reflect also the views of the shareholders, often a remote group whose emotions vary from person to person, and anyway are unknown to the directors?

Alternative projects and risk

The above arguments could perhaps be re-stated more simply within the framework used in earlier chapters, i.e. with reasoning and diagrams that stress the firm's alternatives X and Y.

Diagrams such as la are still appropriate for risky ventures, but the end values are no longer known precisely. The size of DX now becomes only the dominant guess from a range of other guesses; it may be the most likely outcome, or an average of the likely outcomes (perhaps weighted by probabilities), or just a hunch figure. Similarly DY reflects guesses at the possible outcome of Y; and , if the NPV method is to act as an effective comparison, Y must be a rival venture of much the same risk as X. Presumably the firm would not be willing to undertake the risky Y unless lured on by the chance of a high IRR; this is what justifies the discounting of X with a high rate.

31

But the firm may have no Y with risk exactly comparable to that of X – in which case, the NPV method cannot do a very good job (i.e. does not reflect close alternatives). And anyway the assessment of degree of risk must often be arbitary and unreliable.

The argument can be repeated, perhaps more forcibly, where risky projects are financed by loan. Then figure 2a compares a certain end-liability of DA with X's uncertain end-revenue of DE – hardly reliable guidance. Present value will also give dubious guidance when risky growth is compared with safe growth. In 2b, the present value of OY becomes suspect if it is found by discounting DE at the loan's interest rate. But what would be the "right" rate? A theorist might guess it to be the high rate at which a firm – specializing on jobs of X-class risk – would have to pay to raise equity capital. But such a notion cannot be quantified with any sureness.

Once again we must conclude that a discount rate, despite its air of precision, is only a rough-and-ready guide.

These are problems on which theorists are expending great ingenuity. Until they come up with adequate solutions, we must sadly admit the high-rate method to be a black box which we do not fully understand – but which may be the least-bad ritual available to us in an uncertain world.

Prophetic team work

Because of all the uncertainties, even the best budgeter can hardly fail to go astray in lesser or greater degree. Clearly it would be unreasonable to blame him unduly for all variances between his guesses and the actual figures found later.

In practice, two devices can ease his burden:

(1) The longer the forecast period, the bigger the chance of error. So budgets may be classed as "short-term" and "long-term". Then large errors in the short-term can involve the budgeter in awkward explanations; whereas his long-term errors can be viewed leniently.

(2) In a big firm, the job of prediction can be split. An economics department may act as chief soothsayer, and issue half-yearly forecasts on such macro-economic factors as inflation and exchange rates, GNP, and oil prices; and a technical department may produce an index of likely construction costs. Thus the final budgeter's responsibility is eased. Probably his chief worry is the estimation of physical volumes.

32

However, though such comforting arrangements spread responsibility, they do not extinguish the risks.

And it is worth remembering that, at the various stages in the budgets' preparation, the budgeter may well be a team (e.g. heads of various departments). Then the choice of figures must tend to be a compromise, perhaps unwise, between conflicting views.

Net-of-tax rates

Tax is likely to loom large in the flows that a project causes. Indeed, tax may play a decisive role in some circumstances, for instance where plant attracts capital allowances, and where there are interest charges (like other expenses, allowable for tax purposes). The budgeter should therefore be at pains to allow fully for tax (at dates of payment, not accrual).

It follows that, if project X is to be compared properly with base-project Y, *both* must allow for tax. Y's budget then provides a discount rate that is net-of-tax.

Example Suppose that the figures of our original example (see page 16) are for an investor who pays tax at 60%. Recall that before tax his £100 in X grows to £130 gross, in Y to £120 gross; so X's present value is £130 × $\frac{1}{1.2}$ = £108. After tax, the figures become:

	X	Y
	£	£
Gross proceeds	130	120
less Tax at 60% on gain:		
On 130 − 100 = 30	18	
On 120-100 = 20		12
Net proceeds	$\overline{112}$	$\overline{108}$

So Y's growth rate shrinks to only 8% for the period; and X's present value becomes:

$$£112 \times \tfrac{1}{1.08} = £103.7.$$

X's superiority over Y is no longer so marked, thanks to Y's lesser tax.

Thus, to find the most useful present value, one must apply a post-tax discount rate to post-tax future flows.

33

VI INFLATION

Let us now turn to inflation.

There seem to be three main ways in which the budgeter can approach inflation;

(1) He can act as if he expects the price-level to stay constant, i.e. he can "freeze" his figures.

(2) He can estimate the future's rising prices and flows.

(3) He can mix (1) and (2), by using rising prices for the first few years, and frozen ones for the dimly-seen thereafter.

It will be best to start by considering how these methods apply to budgets of actual (i.e. undiscounted) cash flows, leaving DCF till later.

(1) Frozen Figures

Here the budgeter looks only at the price-level of (say) the starting date of the proposed activity, and seems to ignore probable changes thereafter.

This is perhaps the most usual procedure. And, in view of the whopping uncertainties of forecasting prices and exchage rates, common sense must often give high marks to this seemingly crude method.

A more sophisticated defence lies to hand when all the figures in all years are likely to keep closely in step with inflation. Here the budget in effect assumes that frozen figures are much the same as "stabilized" ones, i.e. as the rising figures of each future year deflated with annual factors based on the general index.

Thus a Brazilian businessman may reason:

"Project A needs a starting investment of 1000; it will – at today's price-level – earn 200 a year. If in fact prices double each year, the earnings should double too; so the real return stays the same."

Or again:

"At today's price-level, project B will each year earn 250, and cost 150 in wages; so it will yield 100 net, and will need no extra cash. If in fact

34

general prices double each year, the 250 and 150 will probably double too; so the project will still need no extra cash.''

However, the reasoning on B may hide a pitfall. As we shall see later, inflation often in fact brings great need for more cash.

(2) Figures allowing for price-change

Here the budgeter estimates the actual (inflated) flows of each future year.

This may be helpful, not only to spotlight cash needs from period to period, but where the budget items are likely to rise at different speeds. For instance, experience may suggest that wage rates will outstrip sale prices; and construction costs of the set-up period may be governed by forces different from those of subsequent trade. In other words, if items are compared with the *general* price index, some may be found to march in close step with it, while others rise much more (or less) steeply; and some items may not rise at all, because they are fixed by contract (e.g. rent).

If the budgeter seeks a clearer view of trends over the years, he can once again get help from ''stabilization'' – i.e. by re-stating the flows with general index factors, in £s of a convenient base date (say, the starting month). In the jargon of inflation accounting, he turns the ''raw'' figures into units of constant purchasing power, and thus shows *real* changes. For instance, slowly rising raw figures for sales may hide a falling real trend. Arithmetical examples are given later. But of course stabilization unfortunately lands the budgeter in fresh uncertainties, since he must guess the future of the general index.

(3) Mixed Methods

Here the forecaster makes detailed estimates of the price-levels and main flows for (say) years 1 to 3. For year 4 onwards, he relies on the frozen figures of 3, modifying them only for big changes such as the end of construction payments.

The freezing date can be arbitrary or set by some obvious break. Thus sale prices may be agreed in a contract for a given number of years; construction may extend over a predictable period (e.g. one year for planning, four for building); and firm arrangements may cover foreign exchanges for a given term.

35

Real change in relevant prices

Perhaps one could best sum up the above paragraphs by stressing the importance of real change. The budgeter must be alert for deviation from general prices. Over the years, the specific indices of various input and sale prices are likely to fan out widely from the general index. Stabilized figures can automatically allow for such deviation: if (say) the general index rises annually by 20%, but wages by 30%, a stabilized budget should increase each year's wages by 10%. Particularly important are items that are glued to the £. Thus some flows may be tied to a fixed number of £s per year (e.g. rent, loan interest, and payments for ship charters). These become less and less significant each year as inflation cuts the £'s value and raises the other flows. Stabilised budgets rightly portray fixed money flows as sinking over time.

Again, deviation becomes important if there is holding gain. Suppose buildings are sold off at the project's end. Thanks to inflation, their proceeds are likely to be much bigger than their historical cost. But the owner will not have gained anything – in terms of his purchasing power – unless this appreciation outweighs the inflation. A stabilised budget gets rid of the spurious gain: by expressing proceeds and cost in £s of the same worth (say, that of date 0), it makes sensible comparison easy. Much the same argument applies where the firm holds "monetary assets" (such as cash and debtors): these inevitably bring real loss as the £'s worth falls. Suppose the firm holds £x of cash throughout the budget period. A stabilised budget shows the loss by re-stating the £x of the end-year as a lower number of beginning-£s. Likewise it allows for holding gain on fixed-money obligations (the lessened strain of repayment after the £'s worth has shrunk).

Examples of budget stabilization

Firm A – items move freely, at different rates.

Suppose that at the end of the first year (general index 100), a project's expenses will be £100 and sales £110. The budgeter expects the same physical activity during 11 more years, and the rates of price-rise to be:

expenses	12% per year, i.e. year 12 specific index is 348
sales	14% per year, i.e. year 12 specific index is 423
things-in-general	10% per year, i.e. year 12 general index is 285

36

His calculations for the first and last years might run:

Year	1		12	
	Actual		*Actual*	*Stabilized* (£ of year 1)
Expenses	100	348	$\times \frac{100}{285}$ =	122
Sales	110	465	$\times \frac{100}{285}$ =	163
Profit	$\overline{10}$	$\overline{117}$	$\times \frac{100}{285}$ =	$\overline{41}$

Here the stabilized figures predict a less brilliant outcome than the "actual" figures. Nevertheless they show a rise from £10 to £41; the project beats inflation handsomely.

Note that quite a small variance in the forecast indices can give long-term budgets a very different hue. Suppose the predicted rates for expenses and sales are each changed by two points in opposite directions, so that they are reversed to 14% and 12%. The table becomes:

Year	1		12	
	Actual		*Actual*	*Stabilized* (£ of year 1)
Expenses	100	423	$\times \frac{100}{285}$ =	148
Sales	110	383	$\times \frac{100}{285}$ =	134
Profit (loss)	$\overline{10}$	$\overline{(40)}$	$\times \frac{100}{285}$ =	$\overline{(14)}$

i.e. the surplus becomes negative.

The moral is again that a forecaster, faced with risk, should draft not one but several budgets, to show the effects of a range of possible price-changes (e.g. "best guess" and "worst case".)

Firm B – some cost items fixed, others changing.

Now consider a fuller series of figures. The budgets show flows over four years. Inflation runs at 25% per year. The budgeter expects that, at the prices of the first year, outflows will be 500 and inflows 600; and that inflation will affect all items alike. His figures will be:

37

Year	1	2	3	4
General index	100	125	156	195
Outflow	500	625	780	975
Inflow	600	750	936	1170
Surplus – nominal	100	125	156	195
– real		100	100	100

Here, because all items keep step with the general index, the real surplus sticks doggedly at 100 per year. There would be little harm in relying on frozen figures (i.e. those in the year 1 column) as a test of worth-whileness.

But now consider what happens if the outflows in fact include a fixed item (say rent) of 200. Nominal figures become:

Year	1	2	3	4
	£	£	£	£
Outflows: Variable	300	375	468	585
Fixed	200	200	200	200
	500	575	668	785
Inflow	600	750	936	1170
Surplus – nominal	100	175	268	385
– real		140	172	197

Thanks to the fixed rent, surplus mounts steeply. Frozen cost estimates would fail to reveal this golden prospect.

Stabilized figures, in £s of the beginning year ($£_B$), make the facts stand out more clearly:

Year	1	2	3	4
General index	100	125	156	195
	$£_B$	$£_B$	$£_B$	$£_B$
Outflows: Variable	300	300	300	300
Fixed	200	160	128	103
	500	460	428	403
Inflow	600	600	600	600
Surplus – real	100	140	172	197

The real burden of the fixed payment sinks till it is almost halved. This is what makes the real surplus rise fast.

38

Tax and the time-lag error on income

As the advocate of inflation accounting rightly points out, historical cost accounts tend to overstate income during inflation. They will do so where – as is very usual – there is a time-lag between input date and revenue date. Then input costs are measured in the relatively sound £s of (say) January, but the resulting sales are measured in the less sound £s of (say) the following December. So cost is too low, relative to revenue, and nominal profit is to some extent spurious: if it is paid out as tax and dividends, the purchasing power of capital is not maintained. And tax is in fact levied on nominal figures.

Again consider our Y-type project where (with stable prices) input costs £100 and revenue is £120. Suppose now that general prices are expected to rise 10% between input and sale dates, hoisting sales to £132, and that the owner's tax rate is 60%. A forecast income statement can show either (a) nominal (historical cost) profit, or (b) real profit – here stated in the beginning-£:

	a Nominal £		*b* Real $£_B$
Input cost	100		100
Sales	132	$\times \frac{100}{110} =$	120
Profit	32		20
Tax: 60% of £32	19	$\times \frac{100}{110} =$	17
Post-tax profit	13		3

Such figures explain why the time-lag error causes nominal profit to outstrip real profit (a likely danger where stocks and depreciating assets are owned). They show too how harsh our tax rules are because of their refusal to accept inflation accounting.

This matter is important in budget making, for at least two reasons. It helps to explain why (after making tax and dividend payments that are based on nominal profit) firms may during inflation run short of cash; and it points to the need for distinguishing between real and nominal growth rates. We must now consider these topics.

Inflation brings cash shortage

To trade safely, usually a firm must keep net liquid assets (e.g. cash and short-term deposits, less creditors) up to some suitable level compared with

39

273

other items in its balance sheet (so that it can pay its creditors, buy stock replacements, etc., etc.).

In practice, the volume of net liquid assets may not automatically rise in step with inflation (i.e. the Brazilian's reasoning on page 34, project B, can go astray). For instance, there may be a time-lag before debtors pay for their dearer purchases, and (as we have just seen) tax payments are very apt to grow faster than inflation. Businessmen therefore tend to regard cash shortage as a major mischief of inflation. So they may feel that they get more help from each year's cash budget than from the calculations that accountants deem more important, e.g. the income statement.

40

VII   DISCOUNTING DURING INFLATION

Real versus *nominal rates*

Look again at the last example, where a £100 investment during inflation yields a nominal profit of £32, and a real profit of only £20. Should we describe its growth rate as:

    (i) 32%, i.e. the nominal rate: or

    (ii) 20%, i.e. the real rate (and perhaps the pre-inflation rate)?

The answer is that with rates, as with income, we must beware of the time-lag error; their presentation too can be improved by stabilisation. We must remember that the beginning-£ ($£_B$) and end-£ ($£_E$) are changed by inflation into unlike units (i.e. units of different purchasing power). Arithmetic errs if it treats (say) francs and dollars as like units, e.g. by adding them; it errs in the same way if it treats the $£_B$ and $£_E$ as like. Confusion is lessened if we express beginning investment and end assets in units of like purchasing power; we could say that, in our example, $£_B$100 grows over the year to $£_B$120 (i.e. by 20%), or alternatively that $£_E$110 grows to $£_E$132 (again 20%). The nominal rate is the offspring of unlike units, $£_B$100 and $£_E$132.

The DCF budgeter must during inflation recognize, and choose between, the nominal and real interest rates. However, fortunately his situation is simpler than it sounds: both rates will lead him to the right present value – provided he is careful to use the nominal rate for nominal (rising) figures, or the real rate for frozen figures. A mix of nominal and real can land him in a sorry mess.

Diagram. Figure 3a adapts la to illustrate growth rates during inflation. In nominal terms, an investment of OA in project X again grows to DX, in Y to DY (broken curves). But we know that such growth is to some degree illusory; the diagram now misleads because the units on OA (January £s) are worth more than those on DX (December's depreciated £s). By stabilizing, we in effect improve the calibration of DX, and change to less steep (unbroken) curves for real growth, AX', and AY'. The rates of growth fall too, but here (as Y' is above A) are still positive.

When the budgeter works backwards from date D to find discounted value (as in 3b), he must choose between two methods. He can use either the broken curves, and discount nominal end-value DE with project Y's nominal rate (suggested by AY) and so derive YE; or he can use the unbroken curves, and

41

275

discount the deflated amount DE' with project Y's real rate (suggested by AY') and so derive YE'. Both methods lead to the same present value OY.

Figure 3 Nominal and real growth

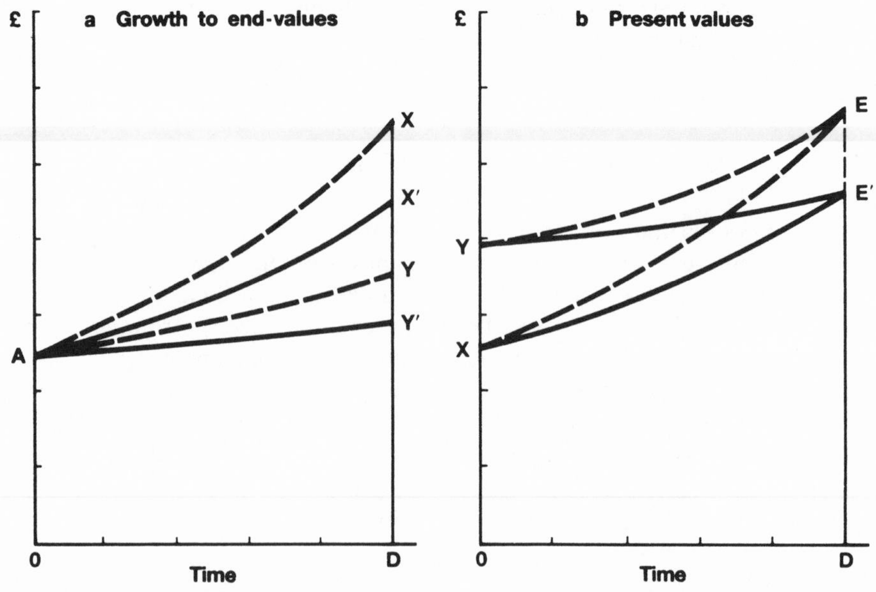

Real and nominal rates in arithmetic

It follows that the budget arithmetic can take two different forms. It can, as a one-step calculation, discount inflated figures with the nominal rate; or it can use two steps – first deflating the actual figures, and then discounting with the real rate.

Suppose again that our £$_B$100 base project grows to £$_E$132 during a year of 10% inflation (i.e. Y's nominal and real growth rates are 32% and 20%), but X now grows to £$_E$138.6. The alternative methods are:

(1) *Single step.* The budget can discount the actual figures with Y's high *nominal* rate.

Receipts of X, end of year .... £$_E$ *138.6*
Discounted equivalent, start of year:
   138.6 ÷ 1.32 .... £$_B$*105*

42

(2) Two steps. The budget can first stabilize the actual figures, and then discount with the low real rate:

Step 1. Receipts, end of year..£E *138.6*
        Stabilized: 138.6 ÷ 1.1 ....£B *126*

Step 2. Discounted equivalent, start of
        year: 126 ÷ 1.2.. £B *105*

Either method works. (1) is here the simpler. The important thing is to separate them clearly in one's thinking.

One should for instance be at pains to distinguish the two rates when using interest formulae. One can lessen the risk of confusion by writing the nominal and real rates as *i* and *i**.

The likelihood of confusing the rates

It is harder than one might suppose to keep the two rates apart in the mind. Confusion is the most likely where we think, like our Brazilian of page 34, that actual future figures will keep in step with inflation, and so the budget can rely on today's frozen figures. Here we are in effect using the second step of method (2); therefore discounting must be done with a real rate. But this rate may well be unfamiliar, i.e. below the current nominal rates which everyone has grown accustomed to use. So there is a great temptation to apply the high nominal rate to the low frozen figures.

Once again the notion of a base-project (Y) can help to clear the mind. Suppose Y is a bank deposit that will grow (thanks to current high rates of interest) to a big end-value. We can sensibly compare X with Y if X's end-value also allows for inflationary growth. If instead X's budget uses frozen figures, the comparison cannot but favour Y and possibly cause the mistaken rejection of X; for a clearer view, we must either inflate X's end-value or deflate Y's growth rate. We may reasonably wonder whether failure over this arithmetic explains the stagnation of some firms.

Unfortunately no-one can feel sure about the right size of real discount rates. The budgeter can only guess how much prices will rise during the project's life, and use this rate to cut his guess at Y's nominal end-value. Inflation thus increases uncertainty.

43

Tax and real rates

As we have seen, tax can have an important effect on real rates. If tax officials assess a project's income on figures swollen by the time-lag error (as is their wont), the real net rate of income can all-too-easily sink to tiny size, or even become negative.

Look again at the figures on page 39. With stable prices, the profit would have been $120 - 100 = 20$; and tax would have been 60% of £20, i.e. £12. With 10% inflation, one might have expected this £12 to become

$$\tfrac{110}{100} \times 12 = £13.2.$$

But, because of the time-lag error, tax jumps to £19; and so the real post-tax growth rate (see foot of column *b*) is mercilessly slashed to 3%.

Budget examples with inflation

Let us again use the raw figures in our budget of page 28, but now suppose the same figures cover a time when inflation runs at 12% per year.

There is no overwhelming need to change those figures if the 25% interest rate is nominal; net present value is still £$_B$369. The budgeter has used the one-step method.

44

But the two-step method tells a clearer tale. Its real discount rate is only $\frac{125}{112} - 1 = .116$ per year.

	Year	0	1	2	3	Net
	Factor	1	1.116	1.25	1.39	Total

Step 1. Stabilize	£B	£B	£B	£B	£B
Loan received	500				
Trade revenues		625	717	783	
Assets sold				925	
Cash released				214	
	500	625	717	1922	
Assets paid for	900				
Extra cash-on-hand	300				
Trade outlays		357	398	498	
Interest paid		89	80	71	
Loan repaid				356	
	1200	446	478	925	
Net receipts	(700)	179	239	997	

Step 2. Discount

Present values, at 11.16%	(700)	160	192	717	369

This stabilized budget shows some important things, e.g. that the £500 loan burden shrinks a lot (real holding gain), but that value of the £300 of cash shrinks too (real holding loss); that the seemingly big holding gain on fixed assets is in fact small; and that the interest burden slides downward each year.

If .25 is instead a pre-inflation (or real) rate of interest, the nominal rate must be raised to allow for the 12% inflation, and becomes $(1.25 \times 1.12 - 1) = .4$. At this rate, the more remote flows shrivel, and the budget gets less cheerful, e.g. in its satellite form is:

					Net
	Year	0	1	2	3	Total
		£	£	£	£	£B
Actual flows		(700)	200	300	1400	
Present values at 40%		(700)	143	153	510	106

45

The gain of $£_B106$ shows that the project is still worth-while, but the higher discount rate has made its lead over the base-project less convincing.

As we have seen, such a budget may in real life have to embrace various complicating factors, such as rising tax and also the need for more liquid capital (embarrassing at the time, and thereafter bringing holding loss on money).

Low and negative real rates

We expect financial interest rates to rise during inflation; unless lenders get some compensation for their money's loss of real value, they will tend to withhold funds (preferring to spend more on consumption, houses, etc.). We likewise expect (but perhaps with less justification) business profit rates to rise. These increases in nominal rates seem however to have often been too small to maintain real rates.

Indeed, it is by no means impossible for a firm to face negative real rates of profit. This is particularly true for net-of-tax flows (tax being levied on profit swollen by the historical cost error). Probably post-tax rates in Britain were negative for most of the early 1980s.

Low and negative borrowing rates have had important social results. Thanks to these rates, capital projects have become relatively more attractive: firms have tended to buy machines rather than hire labour. This may perhaps have contributed to Britain's sorry unemployment record. Again, the buying of homes on mortgage has been made easy, and has led to a major re-distribution of wealth.

Arithmetic and negative rates.

Our understanding of negative rates can be sharpened if we use them in some arithmetic. So let us once more go to our very first example, where 100 invested in Y grows to 120, and in X to 130, so that X's present value is $\frac{130}{1.2} = 108.3$. Now consider these same nominal results (suggested by the broken curves in Figure 4) in two scenarios with brisk inflation.

(1) *X's real rate positive, Y's negative.* If the inflation rate is (say) 25%, X's real end-value sinks to $\frac{130}{1.25} = 104$, and Y's to $\frac{120}{1.25} = 96$. Y's real growth rate is thus -4%. X is just worth-while, Y is not.

In Figure 4a, the unbroken curves show the real results. X' is barely higher than A; Y' has sunk below A.

46

Figure 4 Negative real discount rate

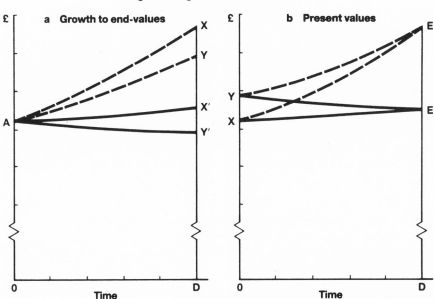

When we instead work backwards from end values, X's nominal end-result of 130, discounted with the .2 nominal rate, still reverts to the present value of 108.3; see the broken curve EY in Figure 4b. The real figures lead to this same present value; by discounting with Y's negative rate, we *increase* end-value from 104 to $\frac{104}{1-.04} = 108.3$; see the broken curve E'Y. We are now in a topsy-turvy world where discounting raises present value instead of lowering it.

(2) *Real rates of X and Y both negative.* Next suppose that inflation runs at 50%. As nominal values remain the same, they again give X a present value of £108.3.

X's real end-value here sinks to $\frac{130}{1.5} = 86.7$, and Y's to $\frac{120}{1.5} = 80$, so both have negative real growth. Y's real rate is -20%. With these real data, discounting raises end value to a present value of $\frac{86.7}{1-.2}$, again £108.3.

We could readily adapt Figure 4 to these new facts – in 4a, by lowering X' and Y' to well below A; in 4b, by lowering E' to below X.

Real figures show the facts more revealingly than nominal figures, but the latter reach the same present value by a one-step route that is easy and familiar. One must choose between the informative and the simple.

47

Weakness of discounting during inflation

In scenario (2) above, the budget's real flows argue strongly that project X (initial £100 sinking to £86.7) is not worth accepting. Yet its present value of 108 gives a contrary impression.

This is not surprising when we recall the role of present values. Discounting shows how much must be invested in X or in Y to reach the same goal, and thus Y's extra cost. It does not show whether the goal is worth-while – merely whether, and how far, X is the better vehicle for attaining it.

The moral is surely that, during severe inflation, a project should be given a double test:

i A DCF budget will as usual show whether the project is superior to the base-project. (The one-step method is adequate for this purpose).

ii A full set of stabilized flows (as in the budget example of page 45) will show the outcome in real terms.

Should real loss projects be abandoned?

When even the best projects bring real decline, as in scenario (2), it is natural to suppose that they should be abandoned – that idleness is preferable.

However, idleness can of course bring many ill results. Customer relations may be upset, and good workers lost. In the short-run at least, it may be less harmful to accept projects at a small real loss than to reject them.

Moreover, the argument for rejection presumes idle funds to maintain their real value. With inflation, any surplus money – even if earning high nominal interest on deposit – may lose real value faster than does investment in projects. The frying pan is preferable to the fire.

48

VIII   CONCLUSION

These pages have tried to explain the nature of discounting, in order to show its strength and weakness. Often it is a valuable aid. But there are circumstances in which failure to understand its nature will do harm. In particular, the base-project Y of our examples can often be no more than a very rough guess about future yields from investment within the firm or in financial markets.

Some businessmen achieve success without using or even understanding DCF. But they might achieve still more if they did use it – not because it can in the end replace judgement, but because it demands careful study of timing and alternatives. Such study must surely prompt searching questions and clarify key facts – and so make judgements sounder.

SUGGESTIONS FOR FURTHER READING

Two important pioneering books, respectively from U.S.A. and Britain, are:

H. Bierman and S. Smidt *The Capital Budgeting Decision,* MacMillan, N.Y., 1960.

A. J. Merrett and A. Sykes, *The Finance and Analysis of Capital Projects,* Longman, London, 1963.

Two highly recommended paper-backs are:

M. Bromwich, *The Economics of Capital Budgeting,* Penguin, London, 1976.

S. Lumby, *Investment Appraisal,* van Nostrand Reinhold, Wokingham, 1981.

These give references to the many articles, on special aspects of the subject, in journals. For value theory, stabilization, etc., see W.T. Baxter, *Inflation Accounting,* Philip Allan, Oxford, *1984.*

49

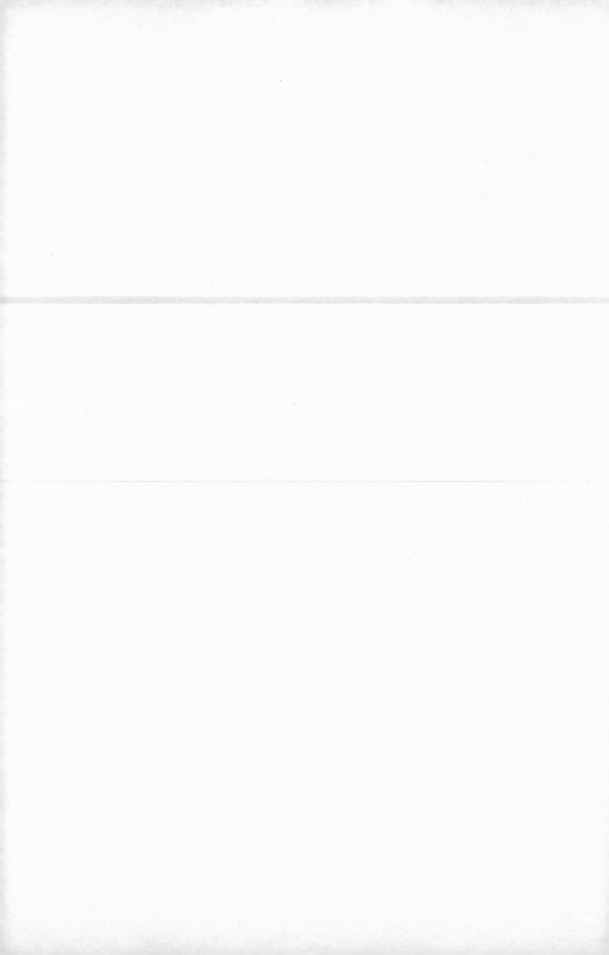

ACCOUNTING RESEARCH

Academic Trends *versus* Practical Needs

INTRODUCTION

In the last twenty years or so, accounting has burgeoned as an academic discipline. Almost every British university has set up an accounting department. Student numbers in these departments have soared; and staff numbers too have become big.

As might be expected, growth in teaching has been paralleled by growth in output of research articles. Until 1970, Britain had no journals for these (if we tactfully ignore the short-lived Accounting Research, published by the Incorporated Accountants, and suppressed after that body's amalgamation). Now we have several; and the many writers - even when fortunate enough to win an editor's imprimatur - have to wait in a long queue till publication. There is a similar flow (rising at an exponential rate) in USA, Australia, etc.

The job of the university departments is to study a "practical" activity - the important and demanding work of accountants in the profession, management, etc - and to train students who will gain their livelihood in that activity. So it would be not unreasonable to suppose that the research would centre on various practical aspects of an accountant's daily work; and that the spate of papers would cast a fresh and helpful light on such work. We might then picture the practical accountant turning eagerly to the latest research journal, and finding just the right ideas for improvement.

But, alas, this picture would seem far from accurate. I fear that a great gap separates much research from practice.

One can make some test of this view by scanning the content lists of research journals. My own snap conclusion, no doubt arbitrary, is that nearly fifty out of a hundred titles must be incomprehensible and repellent to most accountants. And of

287

course an innocent-seeming title may disguise a less-innocent content.

The editorial boards of some research journals have lately furnished proof of the gap's existence and size, by adopting plans for lessening its bad effects. The <u>Accounting Review</u> has launched a sister journal, <u>Accounting Horizons</u>, for articles that may appeal to practical men. The <u>Journal of Accounting, Auditing and Finance</u> (NYU) publishes twin articles simultaneously:

> "high quality, academic refereed articles will be accompanied by non-academic renderings . . . . Upon acceptance of a paper, the author will be asked to provide a concise, non-academic version, describing the research problem, design, methodology, results and implications for practitioners. A professional editor will be available to assist the author in editing and styling the abbreviated version. As a result, the work will be read by both academic peers and a wide audience of practitioners, the latter typically not having been exposed to research written in technical, academic language. Thus, the condensed version will provide the critical bridge between the academic and professional communities."

2

What Has Caused The Gap?

One can readily think of explanations for this gap. I suspect there are faults on both sides.

Practical men give plenty of reasons for ignoring, and sometimes disparaging, academic research. Thus they find its subject matter remote. They shy away from its statistical tables and mathematics. They regard its jargon as pretentious ("hermeneutic", "stochasticity", "systematic heuristics" and "protocol analysis" are perhaps not yet part of the everyday chat in some offices). They feel that the writers are excessively concerned to demonstrate familiarity with "the literature"; the many bracketed references in the text are irritants, as is the end-loading of full references. Research (they tell us) should be written up with brevity and clarity. Where it is specially commissioned, it should be done without the long delays, and for a modest fee. It should possess practicality, ie suggest improvements that are simple, quick and foolproof; yet (despite the requirement of simplicity) it should be detailed enough to reveal a full and well-digested scheme. And so on.

The academic researcher will put the case somewhat differently. He can argue that new ideas demand new terms and new ways of study, and that he can hardly preface each article with a background guide. He can say that mathematics on occasion provides not only a useful shorthand but also a means to clearer thought. He can point out that professional bodies such as the Accounting Standards Committee also are accused of failing to achieve the simple and practical. In a less kindly mood, he might hint that practical men may lack the training and energy that are needed for the understanding of research. He might even suggest that his harsher critics joined the profession in years when a degree was not yet needed - so that their attacks

3

are in fact an admission of weakness. And he might sourly add that, to be welcome, some research would have to pander to selfish policies; thus the logic of inflation accounting is unacceptable because it cuts profit.

It would of course be wrong to say that research has had no impact at all on practice. Some contrary instances come at once to mind. Discounting, long looked on as highly academic, has percolated from university to practice: many accountants now accept that DCF calculations are superior to the payback method of testing projects. Sampling techniques have spread from the university statistician to the auditor. Bonbright's reasoning on deprival value has affected revaluation. Academic studies have helped to improve financial controls in the National Health Service and to check the creativity now said to be spreading in local government accounts.

4

THE NATURE OF "RESEARCH"

The Nature of "Research"

When practical men complain that academic research is remote from their needs, to some extent the reason lies in different interpretations of "research" in university and office.

1. <u>University</u>

   Here "research" implies a quest for knowledge, of a non-trivial nature, and often in the form of principles rather than facts. The knowledge may or may not bring material dividends; the researcher will in many cases make best progress if he is left free to follow his own interests and hunches, regardless of dividend prospects. Indeed, a somewhat extreme view holds that "applied" research (eg on how to cure the common cold) is less likely than "pure" research to yield benefits; we never can tell what blessings may not come as unforeseen by-products of "pure" research. So, if practical men protest that accounting research is off-beam, a possible - though not always convincing - retort is that the best research ought to be pure and offer no prospect of instant benefits.

   In some other fields of learning, academic research can indeed cater directly to practical needs (notably where there are contracts with government or industry); in science, surgery, etc university staff do applied work that yields obvious benefits and acclaim. So why not in accounting? The most likely answer hinges on the availability of raw materials. Chemicals, rats, the sick, etc can be taken into a university's laboratories or hospitals; whereas financial transactions and personnel cannot. Accounting research must usually be rather abstract.

5

2.   Office

In the big auditing firms, "research" is likely to have a somewhat narrow meaning. A main task of the research department - significantly, often called the technical department - is to offer fast solutions to problems that crop up from day to day. Thus if auditors come across a worrying feature in a client's accounts, they can phone to the technical department for guidance. A member of that department must then give a prompt answer; if in doubt, he may find out how the firm has in the past dealt with similar cases (perhaps by consulting colleagues, or records that have been kept for this very purpose), or he may look up external rules (company law, standards, etc). When faced with a situation in which there are no clearly-defined rules, he may apply his analytical skills to more fundamental ideas, stemming, for example, from "true and fair".

In some firms, the research department has the extra task of monitoring developments in computing, tax, etc.

A big company, especially a multi-national, also may have a department for accounting research. Here again a chief concern is likely to be with external rules.

These departments obviously do "research" in the sense of noting and digesting each rule as it appears, both in Britain and abroad. And they often will try to influence proposed new rules - by studying their likely impact, getting evidence and arguing a case before the issuing body.

All these activities can demand an enviable degree of expertise. But they can seldom grow into a sustained

6

search for principle. So, despite its name, the work of a research office is apt to differ greatly from university research - in both aims and subject matter. True, its members will at times scan academic journals, in the hope of detecting something of use to the firm. And fortunately they do occasionally contribute to the journals and publish books. They may do so for disinterested reasons, or because publication can enhance the firm's standing, eg with those who advise students on career choice. However, if audit firms are as profit-driven as is often suggested, there is not likely to be much encouragement for such non-chargeable work.

Practical men do of course meet problems with overtones of theory, and may seek to explore them in some depth. To meet this demand, entrepreneurs lay on expensive conferences. The contents lists of such conferences thus identify the problems of the day. Popular topics of recent times (in some cases selected by the audience) are listed in the note below.[1]

These certainly do not lack intellectual interest. A researcher with marketing flair might regard such lists as guides to subjects that are worthwhile and would tempt editors of professional journals.

---

[1]   Merger and acquisition accounting. The seventh EEC directive and group accounts. Pension fund reporting. Off-balance sheet finance. Property company accounts. Deep discount bonds. Accounting for overseas operations. Depreciation. Lease classification. Valuation of current assets.

UNIVERSITY DEPARTMENTS OF ACCOUNTING

University Departments of Accounting

To understand the academic accountant's drift from practice, we must consider trends in staffing and syllabus at the universities.

1. <u>Staff</u>
    In our lifetime, there has been a marked shift of personnel from office to campus. The opinion used to be that a sound teacher must not only hold a professional qualification but be part-time: full-time work at a university would inevitably mean loss of touch with what matters. This view was presumably held by the chartered bodies of Edinburgh and Glasgow in the early 'twenties when they pioneered in education by persuading the two universities to teach accounting: apprentices attended classes part-time, and professors like William Annan managed somehow to put in long hours at both the North Bridge and Charlotte Square.

    Subsequent change has been big. Many of today's teachers hold qualifications other than those of a professional accountant and are full-time. The change is well-illustrated by a recent advertisement for a lecturer:

    > "Candidates should have a good degree in accounting or a related subject and teaching experience in accounting. An accounting qualification and/or professional experience will be an advantage. Applicants are invited from any specialist area of accounting or finance."

8

Several reasons for this change suggest themselves, including:

(a)   Part-timers cannot do all the administrative work that a university exacts, particularly when student numbers grow large.

(b)   Part-timers are too rushed to teach with conscientious care, or to do the reading and research expected of a scholar.

(c)   University training has become more thorough. A degree may (at least in some areas) compare not unfavourably with a professional qualification.

(d)   Accounting (both in the outside world and university) has increasingly been forced to absorb fellow disciplines, such as mathematics and computing. A teacher whose primary training is in these disciplines (let us call him, with no disrespect, a fellow traveller) is likely to be better at them than is a "pure" accountant.

(e)   (A rather improper thought.) Accountants can command high pay. Fellow travellers are content with the other kinds of rewards found in university life.

The ideal is of course a mix of full- and part-timers, and of professional accountants and fellow travellers. But getting the best mix may not be easy.

9

2.   Syllabus

For several good reasons (eg the use of computers in business, and the economist's shift to mathematics), an accounting course now includes many novel topics. Students must use an impressive array of skills (largely mathematical) when tackling economics, finance, DCF, portfolio theory, etc.

In many ways, this change is good. The new subjects can be a rigorous intellectual diet. Young accountants no longer shy away from mathematical equations, compound interest or probability. But there are dangers. Stress on the intriguing new topics may lead to neglect of what is old but essential. To quote a paper from the American Accounting Association (a teachers' society),

> "a growing gap exists between what accountants do and what accounting educators teach . . . a complete reorientation of accounting education may be needed".

An economist can very reasonably define his subject by saying "economics is what economists do"; but we can hardly argue that "accounting is what academic accountants do".

A glance at the syllabus of any lively department will show how big has been the shift from traditional ground. Subjects can now include behavioural budgeting, computer-based information systems, artificial intelligence, information economics, stock market efficiency, mathematical financial modelling, etc. (In passing, we may wonder how all these novelties, plus the flow of extra

10

rules on traditional topics such as tax and company law, can be pumped into students in three years. But that is a different problem.)

In these conditions, it is not surprising that a teacher's ideas on research should often be remote from practice. He is under pressure to write about something; university rules sternly link his advancement with publication. Yet, when he looks for a topic, he increasingly feels estranged from the problems of the office. Other subjects dominate his colleagues' discussion and articles. Inevitably he too is drawn to these subjects. And he is likely to find that his prowess with statistics and computing points to his path of least resistance: there are plenty of problems, not too remote from accounting and finance, that give scope for measurement - unfortunately, often only of the "handle-turning" kind. No-one can deny that the resulting tables are fresh knowledge; and they demand only slight ability to write the simple and grammatical. But they may interest and enlighten few readers save specialists.

An outsider cannot perhaps appreciate the power of fashion in research. Suddenly a writer of originality propounds a new idea, and so starts off an intellectual hare. Soon his idea dominates discussions, seminars and journals. Old topics may be abandoned - perhaps before they have been explored thoroughly. Anyone who stays faithful to the old feels shut out; he may be regarded as a dull plodder and is unlikely to find favour with selection committees. This bandwagon trend is common to many subjects besides accounting; for instance, language departments may concentrate for a time on place names, then on dialects, then on psycho-linguistics and so on. Editors can further bias the direction of research (and in US - the complaint

11

is - may even announce what are acceptable topics and methods, before receiving manuscripts). If editors and their referees feel enthusiasm for some new approach, then writers who adopt it are likely to dominate the journals.

12

The Methods and Matter of Academic Research

Any short description of academic research must be naive. No summary can do justice to the wide variety of theories, topics and methods.

It may perhaps be helpful to regard the researchers as belonging to one or other of two different schools, even though these are not in fact divided by hard walls. We may call the schools the classical and the radical. Most early researchers belonged to the former. The latter became conspicuous about 1970.

The classical school tends to believe that principles and methods should be established by careful reasoning; the goal is the logical what-ought-to-be. The new school tends to reject this normative approach, and to substitute empiricism; the information value of rival accounting methods must be determined not by logic but observation, backed up by statistical testing.

1.   The classical school

        This school began, like the writers of textbooks, with descriptions of book-keeping technique. Then however it went on to look for principles behind the traditional records. But "principles" turns out to have two rather different meanings:

        (a)   Codification of practice. The researcher describes "what is" and reduces it to settled rules of procedure.

        (b)   Discovery of fundamental truth. The researcher seeks for "a comprehensive law or doctrine, from which others are derived" (the definition in Webster's

13

Dictionary).

Thus pioneers like Paton, Hatfield and May studied practice and then reduced it to rules of type (a); for instance, Paton described and justified accruals in terms of the (to my mind, unfortunate) "matching" notion; and "conservatism" and "the realisation test" were rationalised. But May was also leaning towards type (b) when, examining the rules of book-keeping, he detected GAAP (Generally Accepted Accounting Principles). This premonition of a conceptual framework enabled him to nudge accounting forward in a consistent way.

The early members of the classical school did not advocate much change in the traditional subject matter of accounting, ie historical figures of actual arms-length transactions (plus accruals and allocations based on the historical figures). By the mid-1930s, however, critics began to question the historical cost doctrine. Young teachers at the London School of Economics (R S Edwards and Ronald Coase) led the way in a memorable series in The Accountant; inspired by the marginalist doctrines of LSE economists, they argued that accounting should demote fixed costs, abandon allocation, recognise unrealised appreciation and pay some regard to ex ante concepts of income. Their what-difference-does-it-make approach also let them readily absorb J C Bonbright's teaching on the valuation of assets: "value to the owner" is the difference in the owner's wealth if he is (1) left free to use the asset to best advantage, or (2) deprived of it.

At much the same time, some American writers were questioning orthodox accounting because of its failure to recognise price change. H W Sweeney published his Inflation Accounting, based on Germany's disaster of

14

1923 - 24. Kenneth MacNeal joined in the attack, though he was concerned with the <u>falling</u> prices of the depression years.

The post-war inflation has inspired many sequels. Almost all of them argue that historical figures should give way to up-to-date values that can better reflect "economic reality".

Though such proposed tamperings with historical cost have seemed outrageous to an older generation, we are perhaps justified in still looking on them as part of a classical (or "neo-classical") tradition. The innovators in this school seek to modernise the figures, but nevertheless accept such traditional accounts as the balance sheet and income statement; they are still concerned with concepts of asset value, and therefore of depreciation and income. Thus they continue the study of subjects familar to practical men (and, for the most part, in language that is acceptable to such men). Indeed, Sweeney and MacNeal were themselves in practice, while Edwards was an accountant before becoming a professor, and he went on to be chairman of the nationalised electricity industry and then Beecham.

2.   <u>The radical school</u>

The classical school has often taken "usefulness" as a test of good accounting. The radical school also accepted this view. But it put far more stress on usefulness to a particular group - namely decision-makers, and especially actual and potential investors.

It therefore reasoned that such persons must regard past and even current values as low-grade information. What decision-makers want is <u>ex ante</u> information. In other

15

301

words, assets and income should be deposed, and accountants should provide estimates of future cash flows and risk.

Some radicals soon took a further step; they changed the methodology too. They argue that usefulness must be established by tests - for instance, of whether security markets do in fact respond to fresh accounting figures. Observation replaces the logical quest for a "desired state".

The better to explore these ideas, the researchers sought help outside of accounting proper. They turned to sister subjects such as information economics and decision theory. They thereby were led to further change in both content and methods.

It is largely these sister subjects, with their recourse to mathematics, that have made accounting research so baffling to the uninitiated. So let us look at them a little more closely. Some of the more important are:

Information economics. This has perhaps had most influence on research. It seeks to answer questions about the quantity and nature of the information that providers (such as accountants) should supply. It regards information as a commodity, ie something subject to market rules of supply and demand; as with other commodities, its producers should weigh the costs and benefits of marginal quantity change. But information is peculiar in several ways; for instance, the producer may be unable to exact a price from the consumer (eg the shareholder and analyst); some researchers therefore ask whether a free market underproduces accounting information.

Moreover, there can be conflict between different groups

16

of producers and consumers. Thus the individual firm may fear that franker accounts will help competitors; yet more information may be good for consumers and indeed - if provided by all firms - may help them all to improve their methods. The investor, company, industry and government can all have different views on the optimum supply of accounting information. Bodies such as the Accounting Standards Committee must make political decisions when trying to resolve such conflicts. Some researchers (staunch upholders of the free market) go on to ask whether any regulation of accounting can be justified, ie whether laissez-faire would not work better than standards and laws.

Agency theory. Where ownership and management are separated, there may well be a divergence of interest between a principal (owner) and his agent (manager). Thus interests may clash where, for instance, shareholders would gain by selling their company, and the managers by not selling. Agency may also entail extra costs, including those of monitoring (eg fuller accounts) and "bonding" (eg auditing). Researchers ask how far these relationships and clashes can explain the accountant's behaviour and choice of methods. Ex post accounting is to some extent vindicated, since its picture of recent history helps owners to assess their agents' skill and probity; agency theory can thus be looked on as a welcome return to notions of stewardship accounting.

Efficient market hypothesis. Researchers interested in this hypothesis ask how far financial markets show "information efficiency", ie react intelligently to information. For instance, can markets distinguish between form and substance in a report? Are they misled by superficial change in accounting methods (change that does not herald

17

change in cash flows)? Are figures as effective in notes as in accounts proper? Can a shrewd analyst spot "mis-priced" securities, and thus outstrip the market? Should standards be looked on as evidence that markets have hitherto not been efficient? Plainly there is great scope for statistical testing of possible links between new information and movement in share prices; the efficient market hypothesis has thus done much to promote the empiricism now found in research.

Behavioural accounting. Researchers in this field ask inter alia how individuals and groups use information. What kind of accounting is "useful"? How do owners monitor managers? Some researchers claim they can find the answers to such questions in the responses to mailed questionnaires or to classroom tests on students. Often the researchers invoke the teachings of other behaviourable sciences, eg psychology, organisational theory and sociology. And they have now won an accolade from the other sciences as these have begun to quote the findings of behavioural accounting.

18

Conclusion

If the argument of foregoing pages is sound, it can hardly lead to any neat and comfortable ending. It suggests that academic accountants have taken the bit between their teeth and are moving far and fast from familiar ground. They seek to emulate the standards and ways of sister departments rather than the office. They find more stimulus in study of the abstract than of practice. They prefer pure to applied because pure comes more easily, is more fashionable and offers better career prospects.

No doubt there are plenty of exceptions to my generalisation. Some academics will continue to study practice and to publish work that is germane and understandable. Tax, computing and other technical fields will still provide a flow of "practical" topics. New standards will give plenty of scope for study and criticism. The conceptual framework may be a chimera, but the fundamentals of financial accounting (value, income, etc) offer ample scope for individual research. Management accounting too has its unsolved problems, eg on the overhead : pricing issue.

If accountants feel that the gap between research and practice is regrettable, there is not much that they can do about it. Schemes of secondment between university and office would be an ideal, but at present sound like pie-in-the-sky. Research committees of professional bodies could usefully commission more work on practical problems, and perhaps suggest lists of topics; more fruitfully - since publication is so important to ambitious academics - they could arrange for approved work to be put into print. Direct pressure on the universities would - very rightly - be resisted.

Are there any grounds for thinking that present trends will in time peter out of their own accord? Perhaps there will be a change of fashion; perhaps a new generation of accountants will

19

be more able to digest research; perhaps researchers will learn to furnish articles with a lucid preface and conclusion; perhaps editors will serve up more digestible fare; perhaps pure research will one day yield unforeseen benefits to practice. But these hopeful notions hardly convince.

So our wise course is to accept philosophically that accounting research has for the most part taken off in an unexpected and probably irreversible direction. We must recognise that the gap is likely to get bigger rather than smaller and that universities and practice will drift still further apart, with disadvantages to both.

20

ACCOUNTING STANDARDS

Boon or Curse?

Accounting Standards—Boon or Curse?*

William T. Baxter

Nearly thirty years ago. when 'accounting standards' were still novel, I was rash enough to write an article that expressed doubts about them. Unlike anything else that I have written, it must have been read by some eminent members of the profession: for it evoked bantering retorts, and no doubt helped to strengthen the distaste then felt for academic accounting. Now that time has given experience and perspective, perhaps a second article will not come amiss—particularly as the Accounting Standards Committee has itself started a discussion in its consultative paper on *Setting Accounting Standards.*

Standards were almost unknown before World War II. Now they dominate the accountant's work. They already fill volumes; and fresh ones keep pouring forth. with no sign of the stream drying up. They are to be found in many lands, and national standards are being topped up with international standards. Any accounting group that is not yet emitting them must feel sadly behind the times, and will no doubt soon be adding its contribution. They have for the most part been accepted willingly enough, and even with enthusiasm. The general expectation is that, in a world made safe by enough standards, accounting will no longer be plagued by scandals, and our noisy defamers will have to hunt elsewhere for a quarry.

Origins of standards

It is perhaps worth our while to look back at the origin of standards. They grew from small and inconspicuous beginnings: I doubt if anyone said at the start: what we accountants need is a set of official rules telling us how to handle every important aspect of our work.

The first milestone of note was the *Statement of Accounting Principles*, published by the American Institute in 1938. Though the Institute commended this book to members in a foreword, it was the work of three authors (Hatfield, Sanders,

and Moore) who were not members but had been prompted by the Institute to carry out this task. Such an arrangement seemed excellent: the Institute encouraged research, but did not lend its authority to any of the findings.

Since then, the pronouncements have become more closely linked with the sponsoring bodies, and the latter have tended more and more to back the findings. Thus the American Institute in 1939 charged its committee on accounting procedure with the task of issuing research bulletins. The committee stated its aim as:

> to consider specific topics, first of all in relation to the existing state of practice, and to recommend, whenever possible. one or more alternative procedures as being definitely superior to other procedures.

Bulletin no. 1 stressed the need for good accounts (particularly because of the growth of companies), and the consequent 'demand for a larger degree of uniformity in accounting'. It said that its rules would be subject to exception, but that 'the burden of proof is upon the accountant clearly to bring out the exceptional procedure and the circumstances which render it necessary'.

Just after World War II, the Institute of Chartered Accountants in England and Wales took a comparable step. It announced its venture in mild words that do not herald momentous change:

> The Council has requested the Taxation and Financial Relations Committee to consider and make recommendations to it on certain aspects of the accounts of companies and it is proposed from time to time to publish approved recommendations for the information of members.

The announcement continues with a clear denial of intent to make the new rules mandatory:

> It is, of course, a matter for each individual member to consider his responsibility in regard to accounts presented by directors, but it is

*Based on an Emanuel Saxe Distinguished Lecture at the Bernard M. Baruch College of The City University of New York.

hoped that the recommendations to be made will be helpful to members in advising directors as to what is regarded as the best practice.[1]

Thus accounting bodies on both sides of the Atlantic drifted into the new system without clear ideas of where it would take them, and with few, if any, formal motions of consent by the members. A revolution took place with far less fuss than would be needed for a minor change in the bodies' constitutions.

Development of standards

There have been several stages in the evolution of the committees that issue standards.

American Developments

In America, the stages have been as follows:

(1) Committee on Accounting Procedure.
Accounting research bulletins (ARBs) were issued by the committee on accounting procedure of the AICPA. The process started in 1939. By 1953, 42 ARBs had come out; in that year, they were consolidated into ARB 43. Only 8 more ARBs were issued during the remaining six years of the committee's life.[2]
The ARBs had a big impact. But the committee was subject to many pressures and distractions. Its members were part-time. Its staff were inadequate in numbers and kept changing. Its critics claimed that it did not rely enough on research, that it was the catspaw of the SEC, that it had no teeth, and that its bulletins were equivocal (e.g. the one on inventories authorised the use of three different methods).

(2) Accounting Principles Board.
Because of this dissatisfaction, the committee was scrapped in 1959 and replaced by the Accounting Principles Board (APB). This had more money, and it engaged distinguished men to run a full-time research division. But otherwise it was much the same as its predecessor. It issued 31 'opinions' on a wide range of fundamental topics. Among other things, these tried to narrow areas of difference, and to settle such debatable issues as accounting for the oil

and gas industry, research and development, and—most controversial of all—investment credits.

The APB too failed to placate the critics. They said that it was cumbersome in size, that it was dominated by the profession to the detriment of business, that its 20-odd part-time members met too seldom and did nothing till the research division sent up material. Its opinions aroused violent debate (that on investment credits inspired over a thousand letters of protest). Perhaps the hostility was a sign that the opinions threatened to be effective: company managers preferred 'flexibility' to binding rules. In his survey of this period, Professor Moonitz sadly concludes that 'a professional body, acting by itself, is incapable of obtaining agreement on a set of accounting standards... the layman simply will not let it do the job.'[3]

Dissatisfaction with the APB led to the setting up of yet another group:

(3) The Financial Accounting Standards Board (1973).
This is composed of seven full-time members, from widely-separated backgrounds. It is generously financed, superbly housed, has a large and able staff, and is independent of the AICPA. It is punctilious about public hearings and first publishing its views as exposure drafts; its final statements are no longer 'bulletins' or 'opinions', but 'standards.' We must wait to see how much better this body functions than its predecessors; at least, its organisation avoids many of their defects.

British Developments

In Britain, the story has been rather different, in part because of the profession's split into six major bodies. As I said above, the English Institute started the issue of 'recommendations'; it continued the process till 1969. Then the other bodies decided to sail in the same boat; their joint committee (the Consultative Committee of Accounting Bodies) therefore set up the Accounting Standards Committee. This has, as I write, issued some sixteen standards.

A noteworthy feature of the story is that on one occasion—when the date approached for imple-

[1] *The Accountant*, December 12, 1942, p. 354.
[2] For full details, see John L. Carey, *The Rise of the Accounting Profession*, New York: American Institute of CPAs, 1970.
[3] M. Moonitz, *Obtaining Agreement on Standards in the Accounting Profession*, AAA Studies in Accounting Research, No. 8, 1974, pp. 67, 79.

menting the standard on inflation accounting—dissenting members of the English Institute put up a motion designed in effect to reject the standard. Despite the admonitions of the leadership, the motion was carried at a substantial poll. We could long debate whether this revolt shows the members as deplorable stick-in-the-muds or as men too wise to swallow half-baked proposals.

Growth of Mandatory Powers

The disciplinary powers of accounting institutes vary from country to country, but usually are mild. Unaided, institutes could hardly force even their own members into complete compliance with a standard. Non-members, including powerful groups such as company directors, are not under the slightest obligation to accounting bodies, and might be expected to brush standards aside whenever it suits them. (And, to complicate matters, the non-members may fall into conflicting camps. Thus the owners of small companies may favour profit rules that minimise early tax. The managers of big companies may favour instead flexible rules that smooth profits from year to year. Ideally, such partisan interests should not influence our reasoning on abstract principle; in the real world, they are likely to carry much weight.)

But the degree of compliance has in fact been substantial. The institutes have high prestige, and can count on the loyalty of members. And the standards boards are reinforced in several ways. First, the auditor of a non-complying company should disclose departures from standards. This threat has been a considerable deterrent. (In Britain, however, there have now been so many qualified reports—with no serious harm to the delinquent companies—that this weapon is losing its edge.) Again, other kinds of (non-governmental) bodies may serve as allies to the accountants. Thus stock exchanges in both America and Britain have threatened to withhold quotations from offending companies. Such threats serve to deter at least companies that are big and want to expand further.

But the above constraints are small beer compared with sanctions imposed by government. These may take oblique forms (e.g. tax requirements) or be more direct. In America, the SEC has made the FASB's standards mandatory for companies under its surveillance. In Britain, the Argyll Foods case has shown that a court may view non-conformity as a crime.

So we have gone far since standards first appeared. They started as gentle guides; they now are becoming firm rules, backed by sanctions.

But they have not yet been tamely accepted everywhere. Perhaps it is correct to say that the most successful rebels are not stray mavericks but powerful companies grouped as an industry and seconded by big auditing firms, e.g. oil companies in the US and property companies in Britain; as I write, notable business leaders threaten to snap their fingers at the new inflation standard (SSAP 16). Strident protest can win dispensation or alter principle. Sometimes protest has become political action; disaffected oil companies in the US are said to have spent $3 million in preventing the rule on dry holes from becoming tax law. A well enough financed lobby could probably amend the law of gravity.

The anatomy of standards

Let us next look at the structure of standards. Usually they consist of three parts:

(a) A description of the problem to be tackled:
(b) A reasoned discussion (possibly exploring fundamental theory) of ways of solving the problem. Then, in the light of decision on theory:
(c) The prescribed solution.

So here we have an instance of authority telling us how both to think and act.

Rules of Action versus *Truth*

It is important for our argument to distinguish between the two forms of pronouncement by authority.

The first is a bald rule on how we are to act—a command to behave in this or that way. If such commands make life run more smoothly, they may well be good. Thus a law compelling drivers to keep to the left (or right) of the road helps us all; again, the rules of a sports association make games more enjoyable.

The essence of these good 'standards' is that they consist only of part (c) of the above list. They stress *what* we are to do, but say little about *how* and less about *why*. They steer clear of (b), principles. Sporting rules work well though they say nothing about the dynamics of tennis balls or the psychology of footballers. Note that auditing standards can confine themselves to (c), rules of action. This may help to explain why they arouse less criticism than accounting standards.

Admittedly, the men who draft rules of action must sometimes be swayed by theory. A legislature may have to choose between rival theories, e.g. public health law may assume that Pasteur was right. Yet this kind of rule does not set a seal of approval on a theory. It merely enables us to follow a hopeful line of action; if the rule does not work, it can be scrapped without loss of face. A legislature that explicitly endorses a theory—as when Tennessee backed fundamentalism—is straying beyond its proper function, and must antagonise all who value freedom of thought.

Sometimes *definitions* are tacked on to rules. They can be helpful if they make the given rules work better—but not if they are regarded as applicable elsewhere, still less if they are viewed as revelations of truth.

With accounting standards, the frontier between (b) and (c) must often be hazy. You may indeed feel that I am pedantic to stress it. But it lies near the heart of our problem. If a standard confines itself to (a) and (c), it may or may not be a useful rule of action; at least, it can be judged by how it works. When it includes (b), it incurs two extra risks: its reasoning may be false, and it will impede other attempts to reach truth.

Subject Matter of Standards

Such ideas are reinforced when one considers the subject matter of standards. These deal with different subjects, and vary in quality accordingly. Four types can be distinguished.[4]

Type 1 states that accountants must tell what they are doing, i.e. their published reports must explain what 'accounting policies' have been followed.

Type 2 aims at uniformity of layout and presentation. The US and Britain have so far tended to by-pass this type. Germany and France, on the other hand, favour standardisation of layout, with numbered classifications in balance sheet and income statement. The international standards of the future may well impose similar requirements.

Type 3 calls for disclosure of specific matters, notably where the reader ought to exercise his own judgement. Examples of such matters are research and development cost, depreciation, and

extraordinary items. *Type 3* can perhaps be stretched to cover also the demand for a flow of funds statement.

Type 4 tells us how we should measure economic phenomena—i.e. what are the approved concepts for asset valuation and income assessment. It deals for instance with depreciation methods, stock values, deferred tax, and foreign exchange.

Critique of the Four Types

It is hard to quarrel with the aim of *Type 1*—to make accountants explain the assumptions and policies of their published reports: 'It is an elementary but fundamental rule of statistical presentation—and indeed of simple good sense, manners and respect for your audience—to make it clear how your figures have been compiled'.[5]

Standards of *Type 2* are not quite so attractive. Uniform layout has its advantages: thanks to it, we do not need to waste time hunting for given items. But it carries the obvious risk that the layout will become a straitjacket—that it will not suit all kinds of firms, and will stop experiment. The style of published accounts has improved enormously in recent years, and there is no reason to think that the process cannot go further if left unfettered.

So far as *Type 3* merely calls for more disclosure, it is free from objection (unless indeed the flood of standards leads to an indigestible quantity of details and notes). But of course it will not prevent differences of judgment, on e.g. what constitutes 'extraordinary'.

It is *Type 4* that should arouse most doubt. For here a standards committee debates principles (or sometimes tries to think up new ones); it weighs the *pros* and *cons* of different theories, and decides for us that such a one is the best. In short, authority here informs us where the truth lies.

There are now demands that standard-makers should—to avoid error and inconsistency—produce a conceptual framework. The FASB has made some progress to this end. Such a super-standard of ultimate principles would be a fearsome extension of type 4.

The good side of standards

If we are to judge fairly, we must spell out the benefits that standards confer.

They give us handy rules for our daily work; in this respect they somewhat resemble the account-

---

[4] I here follow the classification of H. C. Edey, 'Accounting Standards in the British Isles', in Baxter and Davidson, *Studies in Accounting*, 3rd edition, London: Institute of Chartered Accountants of England and Wales, 1977, p. 294. This, and its companion article by A. M. C. Morison, argue the pros and cons of standards. Rather unexpectedly, the academic author is on balance favourable, whereas the partner in a large firm of chartered accountants is mercilessly hostile.

[5] Edey, op. cit., p. 296.

ing manuals of big firms. Standards of types 1 to 3 have greatly reinforced the process of improvement in published reports. They provide shareholders with figures that are fuller, clearer, and more consistent. In this way, they act rather like additions to company law—supplementing it where it is weak. Often indeed standards have paved the way for new law (e.g. Britain's Companies Acts) and for new regulations with semi-legal force such as those of the SEC. Standards may thus play a useful role as a way of testing out new methods.

Because they foster comparability between firms, standards help analysts and potential investors; there is even something to be said for the view that it is better if all firms issue second-rate figures on the same basis than first-rate figures on conflicting bases. Standards are useful also to government, for tasks such as price control. If Congress is to understand the US oil industry, the producers' figures for cost and profit must be presented on the same basis.

The advocate of standards can easily add to this list of good points (and no doubt could phrase the additions more delicately than I). Thus standards force our weaker brethren to improve their work. An accountant feels sheltered against allegations of misconduct if he acts in step with all other accountants. And, if a tycoon tries to bully his accountants into producing tilted figures, standards may strengthen resistance.

But by far the most interesting claim for standards (type 4) is that they lead us to—at any rate nearer to—the 'right' measures of value. Here the assumption (tacit or otherwise) must be that standard-makers can, thanks to prolonged debate and intellectual gifts, perceive economic truth more clearly than other folk. This idea will be discussed later on.

The grounds for doubt

Let us next look at the counter-arguments, starting with the more practical problems:

(1) The making of standards is becoming costly and bureaucratic. Effective policing will demand still more resources, and will excite much resentment. Standards may also burden companies with high start-up and running costs.

(2) Standard procedures may become petrified procedures. What starts as progress may later become a check on progress.

(3) Accounting figures are not docile, and do not lend themselves to standardisation. Industries differ from one another. So do firms within an industry (or, very likely, straddling several industries). The same firm may change from year to year. And the needs of users vary. So, if standards are aimed to suit the 'average', they may be quite unsuitable for the fringes. The marginal firms will then turn restive.

(4) The wording of standards will inevitably bring difficulties of interpretation:

> If they are broad enough to cover the variety of circumstance, they become platitudinous and admit the very disparity of treatments they were designed to avoid; if they are narrow enough to exclude this, then all sorts of hard cases will come up with a silly result.[6]

Thus the successful accountant and auditor may be he who is best at hair-splitting and casuistry, not he who best pictures the economic facts. And men soaked in rules soon begin to mistake rules for reality. To quote from Bacon: 'The first distemper of learning is when men confuse words with matter.'

(5) Standard-makers may have to bow to political pressures.[7] Already one hears the argument that standards ought to further desirable political and social ends. Most of us would answer that figures can best further desirable ends by being unbiased and accurate. The danger of 'politicisation' is real enough. An obvious and regrettable instance is ASC's switch of inflation standard, under government pressure, from constant purchasing power to current cost accounting. Note too that a group bound by a rigid code can be manipulated by government far more readily than one where individuals act in freedom.

(6) The essence of a profession surely is that each member is willing to think and judge for himself about matters of principle. If members abdicate from such responsibility in favour of a ready-made code, they cease to command respect: in time, moreover, they will become less able to think and judge.

(7) Even if a standard lays down a principle well, it may leave scope for personal estimate:

---

[6]Morison, *op. cit.*, p. 279.

[7]Professor David Solomons argues this point with his usual skill in 'The Politicization of Accounting', *Journal of Accountancy*, November 1978, p. 85.

we must still choose the figures to be slotted into the formulae. And many of the figures must be a subjective compromise, with plenty of room for disagreement. In most fields of physical measurement, disagreement over size will rightly suggest that the measurers (or their instruments) are at fault. In contrast, we expect some disagreement between judges of (say) ice-skating, or diving, or beauty; such disagreement is far from suggesting incompetence. The estimation of wealth is probably closer to judging in a beauty competition than to physical measurement. Sooner or later, our profession will have to recognise that standards cannot guarantee identical estimates by different accountants, and that we must educate the public on the point. Until we do so, we shall continue to be fair game for our critics.

If you are disposed to agree about any of these dangers, then you must agree too that optimism would be misplaced. Standards will bring many setbacks and much disillusion.

The Nature of Principles

The theorist can, however, see a further, and more weighty, reason for mistrusting type 4 standards. His objection springs from respect for scientific method. A good scientist accepts that 'principles' must be regarded as tentative. His knowledge of history strengthens this view: sooner or later, principles are likely to be improved on, if not refuted. Only god-like creatures know where the truth lies. It follows that *ex cathedra* pronouncements by human authority are pretentious, and inevitably must sometimes be wrong. The most eminent authorities erred persistently on, for instance, the shape of the earth, the origins of life, and the circulation of the blood; more recently, the council of the English Institute and the ASC have gone badly off the rails with their pronouncements, from 1949 onwards, on inflation accounting. We cannot with complete confidence expect infallibility in the future. Another saying by Bacon still applies: 'Truth is the daughter, not of Authority, but of Time.'

A corollary is that knowledge flourishes best where there is complete freedom of thought. And this means the absence, not only of crude tyranny, but also of any benevolent authority that makes us respect some ideas and discount others. Ideas should compete on equal terms. The engineer Brunel wrote (to a commission considering compulsory standards for bridges):

No man, however bold or however high he may stand in his profession, can resist the benumbing effect of rules laid down by authority. Occupied as leading men are, they could not afford the time, or trouble, or responsibility of constantly fighting against them—they would be compelled to abandon all ideas of improving upon them; while incompetent men might commit the greatest blunder provided they followed the rules ... Devoted as I am to my profession, I see with fear and regret that this tendency to legislate and to rule, which is the fashion of the day, is flowing in our direction.[8]

The structure of the authority must also be considered. A committee is less fitted than a single person to think boldly and coherently. 'A camel is a horse designed by a committee.' Though committees can be useful for collecting facts, or reaching consensus on what kind of ideas will prove acceptable, they are not likely to produce brilliant new ideas. Their members may think best in solitude; and, sitting together, may be hampered by the need for tact and compromise, or by pressures from outside.

Experience of Other Professions

If standards confer patent benefits, it is perhaps worth our while to ask why other professions have little use for them.

True, other professions are subject to 'standards' in the sense of legal or moral constraints. But they seem unattracted to compulsory type 4 standards. One reason is that standard rules would soon be obsolete rules in a dynamic profession; even the non-controversial best of the present will be the future's second or third-best. Brunel put it more strongly:

rules will 'embarrass and shackle the progress of improvement tomorrow by recording and registering as law the prejudices and errors of today. Nothing has conduced more to the great advancement of the profession and to our preeminence in the real practical application of the science, than the absence of all *règles de l'art.*[9]

A pure scientist would have even less use for type 4 standards. He presumably accepts that his job is

---

[8] *The Life of Isambard Kingdom Brunel, Civil Engineer.* London, Longmans Green, 1870, p. 488.
[9] *Op. cit.* p. 488.

to attack and test hypotheses—that he functions best as a Doubting Thomas, not a believer. We cannot imagine a society of physicists or astronomers setting up a committee to issue solutions to problems of the unknown: any such attempt would be laughed out of court.

History

Accounting standards have much in common with the rules of gilds in medieval and Stuart times. Those rules, like ours, were made partly because of scandals, and were meant 'to guarantee the consumer a supply of sound and serviceable commodities at reasonable rates'.[10] Enforcement was 'committed to men of gravity' so that 'the particular grievances and deceits of every trade might be examined, reformed, and ordered'; these men had even the right of search. The state backed the gilds with legislation. By 1792, there were 311 laws on the wool trade alone. 'The minutest rules were framed respecting the nature of the materials, the use of mechanical devices, and the form of the finished product'.[11]

The long-run results of these controls were disappointing. Authority did not 'succeed in destroying the evil which it lamented'. The multitude of rules tended to confuse business and thus defeat their own purpose. Enforcement proved hard; and, where it was effective, it hindered progress and mobility. In the end, the rules degenerated into 'the obsolete restraints of a static society', and by the time of the Reform Act were abolished or forgotten.[12] Thus history does not afford us much comfort.

Collective Controls in the Political Sphere

At this point, we should perhaps dwell for a moment on a rather odd thing. It is a safe bet that some 90% of accountants are not excessively fond of government. Their political philosophy holds that the state should interfere little in the affairs of good citizens, and that state controls soon reach a point at which they do more harm than good. Such men would scoff at the notion that, by entrusting difficult problems to political authority, we bring the millenium closer.

Yet these very men have now erected, and are submitting to, an extra form of authority within their own profession. Some of them hungrily demand still more controls over their daily work,

and do not doubt that the outcome will be good. Is this not a puzzling paradox?

My critics can reply that the rules of the state are very different from those of a profession; indeed, this view has led some liberal US accountants to condemn SEC regulations yet welcome FASB standards. I think the difference is one of degree only. The essence of the matter is that external authority compels the individual to respect a given code of thought: the nature of the authority is unimportant.

Conclusions

So where has our discussion got us? Standards have probably led to many improvements. So long as they are bland and avoid sensitive areas, they are popular. If however they threaten to plunge the accountant into ill-understood complexities, or to slash the profit figures of business, they are attacked and sometimes defeated. And a theorist must suspect that, by the tests of both logic and history, type 4 standards are inherently defective; other men are more likely to view the defects not as fundamental but as remediable faults of draughting or detail.

The process of issuing standards has now acquired such momentum, and aroused such high expectations, that we must accept it as irreversible—at least for the time being. Presumably it will someday reach a point of equilibrium—where those who call for still more standards are checked by those who are sated. That point is not yet in sight.

But if we must willy-nilly live with standards, we should at least be wide awake to their nature and limitations. And we should be careful to adopt as many safeguards as possible.

The possible dangers in accounting standards could be lessened in various ways:

(1) As page 5 pointed out, standards normally lead up to their conclusion with a section that explores various principles, and then backs one of them. The briefer this section, the better: authoritative pronouncements on principle are unwise. There would be a strong case for limiting a standard to a bare statement such as that the recommended procedure is already the most usual one.

(2) The same reasoning tells us to be wary of the *type 4* standards of page 6. They are more prone than *types 1, 2,* and *3* to stray on to thin ice.

---

[10]G. Unwin, *The Gilds and Companies of London*, London, 1924, p. 103.

[11]E. Lipson, *The Economic History of England*, London: Adam & Charles Black, 1956, III, pp. 319–335.

[12]*Ibid*, pp. 344–351.

(3) Pronouncements on theory are less likely to overawe us if they are described as the work of named persons. We all know that individuals can err; we tend to credit institutions with more wisdom. Therefore it would be helpful if standards were signed. Moreover a dissenting opinion adds a valuable dimension. So does an admission that an earlier standard was wrong.

(4) A standard should not pander to political ends.

(5) Standards should be explained in terms of *normal behaviour* (as was stressed in Britain at their introduction). A standard is a rule to be followed so long as it fits the facts. The accountant should be free—and is indeed obliged by the 'true and fair view'—to depart from it when he judges that it will distort the picture. Deviation from standards should of course be described and justified, where possible with a numerical estimate of its effect.

Standards and intellectual training

My paper has (I fear) done more to list doubts than to solve problems. But on one point I am clear. Let us agree for argument's sake that standards—particularly if issued with safeguards—may for a time do more good than harm in the world of practice. I still find it hard to feel anything but gloom about their effect on education.

The study of standards now plays a big part in any accounting curriculum. They must have a profound influence on students just when these are at their most impressionable and uncritical. You have only to look at an up-to-date textbook to see how much weight is given to official pronouncements, how little to the economic reality that accounts are supposed to show. Standards are a godsend to the feebler type of writer and teacher who finds it easier to recite a creed than to analyse facts and to engage in argument. If an official answer is available to a problem, why should a teacher confuse examination candidates with rival views? Thus learning by rote replaces reason; the good student of today is he who can parrot most rules. On this spare diet, accounting students are not likely to develop the habits of reasoning and scepticism that education should instil.

And the student will have little cause to abandon his passive attitude when he leaves the university and enters practice. Here too he must be the respectful servant of standards. We may indeed envisage a brave new world in which an accountant spends his whole life applying rules propounded by others—unless at last, full of years and honours, he himself ascends to the standard setting authority and then for the first time must face reality.

I am sorry to end so glumly. But the trend in accounting education must make one pessimistic. For many years, academic critics viewed accounting—wrongly, to my mind—as unworthy of a place in higher studies. It got in at last. Now that we are substituting rule-of-thumb for reason, one must sadly admit that our critics were right.

EARLY ACCOUNTING
The Tally and The Checker-Board

TYPES OF TALLY

History shows us (or so historians claim) how mankind once coped with conditions that now seem impossibly adverse. Certainly this is true of accounting history. It shows how accounts could be kept when paper was still unknown or costly, coins were scarce and bad, and most men were illiterate.

In these straits, our ancestors made good use of two devices. To record numbers, they cut notches on tallies. To calculate, they used the abacus, notably in its form of the checkerboard.

Meanings of 'tally'

The word 'tally' suggests various things:

(1) A simple record of numbers, such as notches on a stick or chalk marks on a slate.

(2) An object divided into two interlocking bits, thus giving proof of identity, e.g. a split seal or die.

(3) A combination of (1) and (2), such as a stick that is first notched to show e.g. the number of £s lent by A to B, and then is split to give both A and B a record.

All three types have in the past helped business, but (3)—the split tally—probably has been by far the most useful.

First published in *Accounting Historians Journal* (Dec. 1989). I have received much help from M. T. Clanchy and A. Grandell. I am grateful also to: G. de Ste. Croix and D. Wormell (classical references); G. Tegner (Scandinavia); D. Forrester and M. Stevelinck (France); F. E. L. Carter and C. Coleman (England).

Wood's importance for records

Most of the tallies described below were bits of wood. ('Tally' comes from the Latin *talia*, a cutting, rod, or slip for planting.)

To us, wood must seem a clumsy material for records. But our ancestors were short of alternatives. The most obvious was parchment (sheep or calf skin); but this was costly. Such paper as was used in Europe came from the outside till the twelfth century, when its manufacture started in Italy or Spain; Britain had to rely on imports till the late sixteenth century.[1] And wood was in fact a surprisingly suitable means of recording. It could take ink and seals, and was for long regarded as the most important writing material after parchment. Even lengthy documents such as charters could be written on birch bark.[2]

A wooden tally had many virtues. It cost practically nothing. It was easy to score. It was intelligible at a glance to both the literate and illiterate. Its harder varieties withstood rats and decay better than paper and parchment; on many survivors, every notch is still as clean and true as it was six hundred years ago. And, as we shall see, it could serve as a flexible aid to sophisticated systems.

The many roles of the 'carved stick'

Marked sticks have been able to fill many roles in many lands—e.g. management records in Sweden,[3] and 'message sticks' (mnemonic aids for messengers) in ancient Greece and among Australian aborigines, etc.[4] The counting tally must be seen as only one part of a wide range of 'carved sticks'.

Scandinavia in particular has kept many specimens of the *karvstock*, chiefly for their value as a 'rich and subtle' form of folk art. A few date back to the Vikings, but some examples in museums at Stockholm and Helsinki were still in use in the mid-nineteenth century. They have been aptly described as 'neglected bearers of a cultural tradition' because of their importance for administration as well as counting.[5] For instance, some aided village headmen: the 'alderman' had a rod on which was recorded the mark—such as a

---

[1] D. C. Coleman, *British Paper Industry* (Oxford, 1958), 4. Alex Murray, *Reason and Society* (Oxford, 1978), 301 and 475.

[2] M. T. Clanchy, *From Memory to Written Record* (London, 1979), 95.

[3] Scandinavian examples (mentioned on this and later pages) are in museums in Stockholm and Helsinki; many are described in Axel Grandell, *Karvstocken* (Ekenas, 1982). *Tidskrift for Svensk Antikvarisk Forskning*, No. 2 (1986), *Daedalus*, Swedish Technical Museum, 1987, and *Historiska studier i folkliv*, Academic Press, Åbo 1989. (Swedish with English summaries.)

[4] Horniman Museum, London.

[5] Grandell, *Karvstocken*.

variant of the swastika—of each household; he had also a ceremonial staff of office (cf. the university's mace and the magic wand?). Some were used by tax-gatherers to note receipts in cash or kind. Some long and slender survivors were measuring rods (e.g. for checking labour on fencing). Some are carved roughly, others with loving care; thus one ell-stick has been pared into a basket-like frame enclosing loose balls of the wood.

The reckoning tally

Such measuring rods, etc., had more or less permanent markings and functions. But a stick used for recording numbers might from time to time get extra notches, e.g. to note additional payments; and it might have only a brief life.

The unsplit tally (function I of the list above) was a handy means for recording both physical quantities and money. Thus an English monastery used a tally to note milk yields.[6] Surviving specimens show e.g. numbers of seals caught (Sweden), reindeer herded (Siberia), and loaves baked (Albania).[7] The tally's role in cargo checking is recalled by our use of 'tally-man'.

Crude examples of the unsplit counting tally might be no more than a rough stick on which (an English survivor) a wood-cutter scratched a line for each bundle of faggots made, presumably because he was paid by piece-rate.[8] A slight improvement gave a short notch to each unit (e.g. bundles of hides handled at Bergen docks) and an extended notch to every nth unit. And some tallies took elaborate forms. A Finnish survivor, recording day labour (rent by tenant farmers) is a long stick ruled into two columns; the left column shows each man's mark; a small indentation was made on the right column, opposite his mark, after each day's work. Other examples of management records were multi-sided. Thus, where a Swedish flour mill was owned co-operatively, somewhat complex records were needed to keep track of each owner's days of use and his contributions of upkeep work; an octagonal tally met the need. And a sixteen-sided tally of 1863 served a Swedish mine foreman as output record (one side per worker).[9]

The transition from physical measure to money must have been easy. Notches proved a convenient way of showing wage and tax payments, also credit sales at inns and shops. The word 'tally' sometimes meant a credit

[6] Clanchy, *From Memory to Written Record*, 32.
[7] Horniman Museum, London.
[8] British Museum.
[9] Grandell, *Historiska studier i folkliv*, 49.

transaction: 'ye shall not have redy mony neyther, but a taly' (1545);[10] and it was further stretched to cover records on materials other than wood, e.g. a slate.

Antiquity of the tally

In the nature of things, tallies of prehistoric times were unlikely to survive till now. But (a historian of numbers tells us) 'we can deduce that the recording of numbers by notches carved on suitable objects is of great antiquity and was virtually a universal practice' (i.e. function 1 of the list above). A few such objects have been found, including a wolf bone from Moravia, some 30,000 years old; it has fifty-five notches, arranged in groups of five.[11]

Tallies of classical times were also unlikely to survive (though Roman remains dug up in Kent include a bone with scratched notches). But we get help from literary references. The Greeks used the word *symbolon* for 'tally' in the sense of two matching parts, usually of a coin or other hard object. Unfortunately the references do not always make clear whether such a tally filled function 2 (identification) only, or 3 (identification and number); but some early writers were clearly familiar with the use of split sticks in financial transactions.[12]

A moral tale of 500 BC is germane to business. It tells of Glaucus, a Spartan who has a reputation for justice above all other men. A traveller from Miletus therefore entrusts him with gold and silver, and adds 'take these tallies and be careful of them . . . give back the money to the person who brings you their fellows'. But later, when the Milesian's sons come to claim the money, Glaucus is tempted to deny remembrance of the matter. He asks the Delphic oracle whether he can safely swear that he never received it; rebuked, he hands it over, but—for even contemplating the perjury—he and his are 'utterly uprooted out of Sparta . . . there is at this day no descendant of Glaucus, nor any household that bears Glaucus' name'. It is tempting to argue that such *symbola* would not be much use unless they were marked with the *amount* of money—function 3.[13]

Plato gives the tally a role that far transcends accounting. He makes one of his characters suggest the *symbolon* as an explanation of sexual desires, as follows. Originally, humans were united in pairs as spheres. Each sphere had

---

[10] *Oxford English Dictionary.*
[11] Graham Flegg, *Numbers in History* (New York, 1983), 41.
[12] Society of Antiquaries, *Proceedings* (1899–1901), 78. S. West, 'Archilochus' Message-stick', *Classical Quarterly*, 38/1 (1988), 42.
[13] Herodotus, *VI*, 86, a5, b1. S. West, 'Archilochus' Message-stick'.

two faces, four arms, four legs, etc. Some spheres were man–man, some woman–woman, some man–woman. They had surprising strength and vigour, and planned to assault the gods. So Zeus sliced every sphere into two. Each of us therefore is only 'the tally of a man', ever yearning to be grafted again to the tally that will fit him. All men who are sections of man–man delight to be clasped in men's embraces; all women who are sections of woman–woman 'have no great fancy for men'; men who are descended from the hermaphrodite spheres are women-courters and adulterers, and the women are man-courters and adulteresses.[14]

A Latin equivalent to the *symbolon* was the *tessera hospitalis*. This too consisted of two matching halves, normally of something durable such as a die. And it too confirmed identity, e.g. of a stranger bringing a letter of introduction.

THE MEDIEVAL SPLIT TALLY

Thanks in part to its central role at the English exchequer, we have abundant evidence of the medieval tally's use in England. And some references come from further afield. Describing his Chinese trip (1271), Marco Polo tells us that he saw illiterate persons recording their business dealings by notching and splitting sticks 'exactly as it is done with our tallies', i.e. in Venice. The 1407 statutes for university students at Paris include:

Whoever wishes to have wine beyond this portion, whether at table or away, should record it on his tally, and reckon it according to his conscience. Of which tally the one part remains with the servitor and the other with his master, and the receipt is to be tallied as soon as he gets his wine.[15]

Again, monasteries in medieval Italy accepted deposits of goods and money for safe-keeping, giving the depositor part of a split tally (of wood or parchment). This he presented at withdrawal.[16]

According to the late Sir H. Jenkinson (deputy-keeper at the Public Record Office), in medieval England the split tally was the ordinary accompaniment of government and private business. After studying hundreds of exchequer and private tallies, he concluded: 'the more we examine financial conditions . . . the more do we find that all development is conditioned at

---

[14] *Symposium.* 191*d.*
[15] W. Marsden, trans., *Travels of Marco Polo* (London, 1908), 251. Asterie L. Gabriel and Gray C. Boyce (eds.), *Acutorium Chartularii Universitatis Parisiensis* (Paris, 1964).
[16] Florence Edler, *Glossary of Medieval Terms of Business* (Cambridge, Mass., 1938). 21.

every turn . . . by that system of tally cutting that was already well established in the twelfth century'.[17]

Physical form

Tallies intended for splitting were usually made of well-seasoned hazel or willow (woods that split easily), and were square in cross-section. Originally they were slender, and their length often was the space between the tip of the index finger and the outstretched thumb, i.e. was less than six inches if we allow for our growth in physique over the centuries; but, as we shall see, they were later to become much bigger.

Even the exchequer tallies for large sums could be crude: some of the survivors have knots, follow the slight curve of the original branch, and still have bark along one side. A hole might be bored at one end, so that as many as fifty tallies could be strung on a thong or rod.

Stock and Foil

Typically the medieval tally was split into two bits of unequal length. The longer (the 'stock', with a stump or handle) was kept as a receipt by the person who handed over goods or money. The shorter (the 'foil' or 'leaf') was kept by the receiver. Figure 7.1 shows the two parts of a modern Kent tally with notches for physical units (hops gathered).

ILLUSTRATION 1

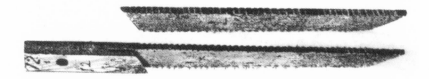

Modern Kent hop-picker's tally. Horniman Museum, London.

The literate often wrote ink 'superscriptions' on both stock and foil, to show the nature of the payment. The writing of the exchequer officials was normally in Latin, but in Hebrew at the 'exchequer of the Jews'. The writing tended to be neat and compact on the short early tallies, but to sprawl across

[17] H. Jenkinson, 'Medieval Tallies, Public and Private,' *Archaeologia* (1923–4), 290.

the later ones. Some private tallies also bore words—occasionally scratched on, and then perhaps rewritten later in ink.[18]

Cutting the tally

An anonymous description (perhaps eighteenth century) of the exchequer's cutting method runs:

A thick stick was put into a vice and roughly squared. On one side was written in Latin the name of the accountant [e.g. a sheriff bringing cash to the exchequer] and for what service the money was paid; on the opposite side the same particulars were written. On the other two sides were written, in front, the test or day of the payment and the year of the reign of the king . . . and on these two sides the sum paid in was represented by notches of various sizes cut in the wood, each size denoting a certain amount. . . . Thus written upon and notched the stick was put into a strong block, and on one of the written sides, about three inches up, a short thick knife was placed diagonally and struck with a heavy mallet, cutting the wood halfway through; the stick was then turned and the knife inserted on one of the notched sides, at the diagonal cut, when two or three sharp blows split it down to the end into two parts, one part having exactly the same writing and notches as the other.[19]

Complex splitting

In Scandinavia, the splitting process was sometimes complex. Where three parties were concerned in a transaction (e.g. the consignor of goods, the carrier, and the consignee), a 'triple tally', split into three parallel pieces, could be used. But the high point in tally technology was the 'fork tally'. The two ends of a four-sided stick were cut apart in such a way that each consisted of a butt with two prongs; the four prongs interlocked neatly when joined. This device was used in eighteenth-century Sweden, and enabled illiterate smiths to record transactions in two currencies—the *daler* (silver) and *ore* (copper), coins whose relative values varied over time.[20] Members of the staff at the Stockholm Museum have recently made copies of the pronged tally, and have found this task easy once the trick is learned.

The tally as a receipt

Thanks to the diagonal cut (the projection seen in the illustrations), stock and foil could at any time be squeezed together again, so that extra cuts for

[18] Hubert Hall, *Antiquities and Curiosities of the Exchequer* (London, 1891), 119.
[19] *Notes and Queries* (1881). 493.
[20] See n. 3 above.

new transactions could be made across the split, or the genuineness of the record could be tested: 'when these two parts came afterwards to be joined, if they were genuine they fitted so exactly that they appeared evidently to be parts the one of the other.'[21]

The split tally thus gave a form of receipt that was simple yet almost fraud-proof—'an intricate but robust form of record, not replaceable readily till carbon copying'.[22]

At settlement, the creditor would often hand over his stock to the payer. The latter could then break both stock and foil, or keep them spliced together as a permanent record. Any balance could be put on a new tally.

The Dialogus

Our knowledge of medieval tallies comes in part from two remarkable books by exchequer officials. About AD 1179, Richard Fitznigel, head of the permanent staff at the exchequer and later bishop of London, wrote his *Dialogus de Scaccario*. It is cast as a textbook for fledgling civil servants, and takes the lively form of question and answer. In 1711, another official (Thomas Madox) again described the exchequer's procedure ('if I do not err in my observation'), confirming that it had hardly changed during the intervening five centuries. An accounting textbook of 1793 still defined a tally, in its dictionary of 'the abstruse words and terms that occur in merchandise', as

a cleft piece of wood, to score up an account upon by notches. They are used by the officers of the exchequer, who keep one of the clefts in the office, and give the other to persons who pay in the money.[23]

Notch language

A simple form of tally had parallel notches of much the same width, each representing a single unit, as in Figure 7.1. But this form was clumsy where numbers were big. Then some of the numbers might be shown by other types of cut. In Scandinavia, the angle was varied; / stood for 5, X for 10, and ⅄ for 20.[24] In England, notches of different breadth and depth have been used for different numerical units. Thus I was denoted by a mere scratch, but 12

---

[21] Thomas Madox, *History and Antiquities of the Exchequer* (1711), 709.

[22] M. T. Clanchy, *From Memory to Written Record*, 27.

[23] Charles Johnson (trans.), *Dialogus de Scaccario* (London, 1950). T. Madox. *History and Antiquities of the Exchequer*. John Mair, *Book-keeping Modernized* (1793).

[24] See n. 3. above.

by a slightly bigger cut, and 240 by a still bigger cut. A tally marked with a 1-notch and 12-notch could be a receipt for one plus a dozen units of goods, or for a penny and a shilling. We must remember that the pound and shilling were for long merely convenient units of account, i.e. coins worth a pound or shilling did not yet exist; the only English coin was the silver penny (240 of which were in theory equal to one pound weight of silver).[25]

At the exchequer, a strict ritual governed the breadth of the notches (and private persons may well have used the same dimensions). The *Dialogus* states that the cut for £1,000 had the thickness of the palm of the hand; £100, of the thumb; £20, the little finger; £1, of a swollen barley corn; a penny, a mere scratch. Later, inches were used as measures. The exchequer then allotted 1½ inches to £1,000, and 1 inch to £100; such big notches tended to be U-shaped. Half-an-inch as a V-shaped notch denoted £20, and ⅜ inch denoted £10; as a v-shaped notch, it meant £1 in late years. ³⁄₁₆ inch meant a shilling; a hair's breadth, 1*d.*; and a small hole 'prickt only by a bodkin', a halfpenny.[26]

If there were many notches of different sizes, they might be grouped on both the upper and lower sides of the tally:

If you hold a tally in your hand with the thick part and hole to the left, and with the note recording the name of the person to whom the business relates and the cause of the payment towards you, then you will find the cuts for the largest denomination—whether thousands, hundreds, scores of pounds or smaller amounts—on the lower edge near the right-hand extremity, and no other denominations will be cut on that edge. The lower denominations are all cut on the upper edge with pennies nearest the right-hand end.[27]

Figure 7.2 shows a stock of 1293, issued as a receipt by the exchequer to the sheriff of Surrey.[28] It has two deep triangular notches, and is thus for 2 × £20 = £40. Figure 7.3 is a diagrammatic view of one end of an exchequer tally acknowledging the receipt of £236 4*s.* 3½*d.* on 25 October 1739, as a loan to the king on 3 per cent annuities repayable out of the Sinking Fund.[29]

Thanks to notches of different sizes, it was easy for even an illiterate stall-holder to cut and to recognize elaborate money numbers. But perhaps we are wrong to dismiss him as completely illiterate, since his notches surely can be looked on as a form of writing. (It has indeed been suggested that the tally's

[25] John Lubbock (Lord Avebury), *A Short History of Coins and Currency* (London, 1902).

[26] H. Jenkinson, *Proceedings of Society of Antiquaries* (1913). 33. J. E. D. Binney, *British Public Finance and Administration, 1774–92* (Oxford, 1958), 222.

[27] R. L. Poole, *The Exchequer in the Twelfth Century* (Oxford, 1912), 88.

[28] PRO. E 402.

[29] *Parliamentary Papers*, 1868–9, XXXV, ii. 339.

Fig. 7.2 Exchequer stock of 1293. Public Record Office, E402.

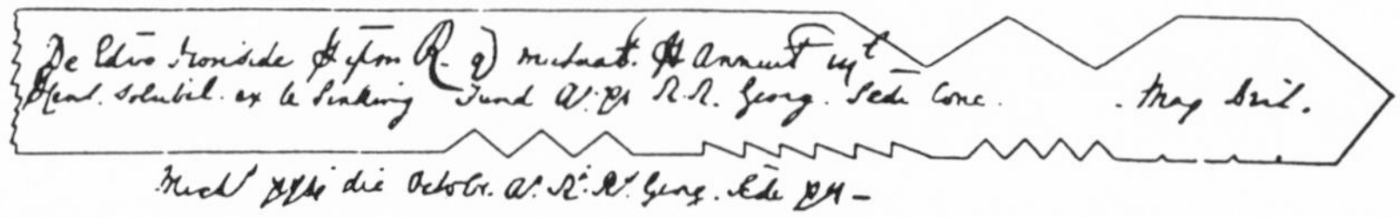

Fig. 7.3 Exchequer tally, 1739, for £236 4s. 3½d.
Source: Parliamentary Papers (1868–9), XXXV, ii. 339.

vertical and diagonal notches may be the ancestors of some ancient alphabets—runic in Scandinavia, and ogham among the Celts—and conceivably of Roman numerals.)[30]

The tally grows bigger

The tally's dimensions could readily be varied to suit the breadth and number of the notches.

Accordingly, as prices rose over the centuries, the tally's length tended to grow. (Maybe its growth could yield a rough index of general prices.) The collection at the Public Record Office (PRO) includes specimens dating from medieval times to the early nineteenth century. Its fourteenth-century stocks are slim and short (say, 5 inches), and thus in outline look rather like a toothbrush. By the eighteenth century, prices had risen perhaps fifteen-fold, and the length of some PRO tallies had stretched to between two and five feet. The famous specimen at the Bank of England is eight feet long. The

[30] Grandell, *Historiska studier i Folkliv*, 9, tells of a Viking tally with cuts for both numerals and Ogham words.

sides grew to about an inch, and the weight to a quarter of a pound or more.

THE MEDIEVAL EXCHEQUER TALLY

From earlier pages, one might well suppose the tallies at the exchequer to have mainly been its own receipts—issued for instance to a lender of cash, and brought back by him for cancellation at repayment date. But in fact some tallies came to concern more than those parties, and took on roles far more ambitious than those of straightforward receipts.

The tally as an order on the exchequer

In one of its extra roles, tallies became rather like a modern bill of exchange or bearer cheque drawn on the exchequer. Various officials other than those of the exchequer (e.g. of the 'King's wardrobe') issued their own tallies in return for goods that the king needed urgently but could not pay: for 'supplies could not wait upon arithmetic'. For instance, when the king and his vast household travelled, he had the right of purveyance, for which large numbers of tallies were issued to suppliers. Other officials might live far afield. A surviving account of the bishop of Carlisle tells how he bought nails on credit for work on the king's behalf at Carlisle castle; he gave stocks to the suppliers, and rendered his account (rolls) to the exchequer with the foils attached by thread as vouchers. Again, kings increasingly decentralized supply work by off-loading it onto sheriffs (e.g. these might be told to send 500 lambs to Westminster); the sheriffs issued their own tallies to sellers, as claims to be paid presently.[31]

The holder of these stocks was presumably paid later by the sheriff, etc. Or he might approach the exchequer for allowance; whether he then got satisfaction was, as we shall see, quite another question.

Orders on distant debtors

In financial matters, the medieval king faced two difficulties. First, he at times needed more ready cash (e.g. for a campaign) than lay in his London

---

[31] H. Jenkinson, *Proceedings of the Society of Antiquaries* (1913), 33; *Archaeologia* (1923–4), 306. Anthony Steel, *Receipt of the Exchequer, 1377–1485* (Cambridge, 1954), p. xxxv. W. A. Morris, *Medieval English Sheriff* (Manchester, 1925), 267.

exchequer. Second, much of his revenue was gathered and held by officials who were scattered across the realm; this cash could not readily be sent to London. He contrived to lessen both these difficulties by promoting the tally to yet another role.

The king's far-off debtors included the sheriffs and various other tax collectors, such as the port officials who levied customs dues on e.g. wool exports (the 'customers', of whom Chaucer was for some years the head). In an age without banks and safe roads, these men had great trouble in remitting money to London. For instance, on one occasion when the Boston customers brought coins, the exchequer had to command sheriffs *en route* to provide armed guards and accommodation, to be paid for out of the customers' treasure.[32]

To circumvent this difficulty, the exchequer had by about 1320 invented an ingenious use of the tally that enabled the king to settle accounts with his remote agents, and moreover to do much of his business without cash. The tally turned into an instrument for many-sided transfers.

To paraphrase Jenkinson: 'If X owes B, but is owed by A, let him—X—make out a receipt to A and give it to B, and let B not part with it till he receives the money'. In other words, if the exchequer—X—was short of funds, it would cajole creditor B into taking not cash but a tally addressed to some tax collector A. The tally purported to be a receipt by the exchequer for such-and-such a sum, paid in by the collector A out of such-and-such type of revenue: in fact, it recorded not A's payment but what he was someday likely to owe. Armed with this tally of assignment, creditor B presented himself to the collector, and—if all went smoothly—exchanged it for cash. The tally would afterwards serve the collector as his acquittance at the exchequer.[33]

On occasion, the tally followed a more roundabout path. The first holder B used it to pay C (at a discount?); C in turn might pass it to D; and so on. It thus circulated like a negotiable bill of exchange before reaching A. It became a kind of wooden money, useful to eke out the poor coinage.[34] Here then was a great innovation, but with the old primitive form preserved.

Assignment and anticipation

These assignment tallies came to play a big part in royal finance. They enabled the king to anticipate revenue: 'a pernicious process by which the

[32] Hubert Hall, *History of the Customs Revenue* (London, 1892), i. 10, 193; ii. 27.
[33] H. Jenkinson, *Archaeologia* (1911), 369; *Proceedings* (1913), 34. T. F. Tout, *Chapters in the Administrative History of Medieval England 11* (London, 1920).
[34] Philip Norman, *Archaeological Proceedings* (1902), 288.

crown sought to stave off present disaster by imposing severe penalties on the future'.[35] Such tallies also let exchequer officials shift the trouble of debt collection onto other shoulders. This was a mixed evil. If creditor B and collector A both worked in London, the system might do them little harm. If they worked in the same remote area, the system was positively beneficial to both, in that it cut out the costs, fatigues, and dangers of taking money to London and back; thus a royal employee B could conveniently get his salary from nearby collector A. But if B worked in London, and a high-handed exchequer gave him a tally on a remote A, the system was grossly unfair. B might be forced to go on a long journey, with no assurance of a favourable reception at the end.[36]

Delays and default at the exchequer

If a creditor's tally was drawn on the exchequer, he could face many troubles. His tally might take the form of an order on the Treasurer, payable at sight out of either revenue at large ('so much of the treasure remaining in your hands'), or some specified source of revenue.[37] But, if the exchequer's funds were running low, such orders could not guarantee payment.

Kings were not systematic in their spending, and the exchequer sometimes faced claims for two whole years of arrears. It therefore had to rank claims in some order of preference. Its chosen system affronts today's ideas of fairness. A creditor was most likely to get paid if he was (1) a member of the king's family or household; (2) a current supplier who threatened to withdraw; and (3) someone who could trade services, e.g. make a fresh loan, or (members of parliament) grant a tax.[38]

If he was not on this privileged list, the tally-holder could follow various courses. He could employ an attorney with inside knowledge to solicit on his behalf. He might pay a fee (perhaps a bribe) to officials who could 'spy out an assignment'. He might try to 'catch the king's ear'—especially by offering to cut down the size of the debt, sometimes by half. The king was apt to drive a hard bargain. If he finally favoured the claim, he gave the creditor a warrant on the exchequer. But even this might not be enough to secure attention there. Some creditors would in the end despair of being paid, and look on their claim as gifts to the king.

[35] T. F. Tout, *English Historical Review*, 39 (1924), 411.
[36] Steel *Receipt of the Exchequer*, p. xxxi.
[37] Hall, *History of the Customs Revenue*, 188.
[38] G. L. Harriss, 'Preference at the Medieval Exchequer', *Bulletin of the Institute of Historical Research* (1957), 17, *et seq.*

Even where the creditor was lucky, he would probably receive not cash but ('with somewhat tempered satisfaction') a tally of assignment. In most years, the exchequer paid more by tally than by cash; in 1381, the assignments rose to £47,000 while cash payments were only £7,000.[39]

Troubles with assignment tallies

The winning of an assignment tally could herald fresh tribulations. If it were drawn on (say) a customer in Cornwall, the holder faced an arduous journey (a prospect that might prompt him to discount the tally in London, with a merchant or perhaps an enterprising official at the exchequer itself). Arrived in Cornwall, he might be met by a harassed customer who was already over-drawn, or who faced a proliferation of preferences. Delay and insolence were common. The customer's difficulties might be genuine, e.g. where he had been ordered (assignments notwithstanding) to send all his money to the exchequer. But he sometimes used his position as discretionary paymaster to line his own pockets.

A system of preferences here again affected the tally-holder's prospects. His chances were good if he was a local baron; they might be good too if he was a local merchant, especially one whose tally was levied on customs arising from his own goods; he might even contrive to be appointed collector, and pay himself. A peremptory writ from the king reinforced a claim. A less-favoured holder might try to discount the tally with the collector, or perhaps hint at a bribe; but he would still be in competition with other claimants. An insignificant pensioner was likely to get only a 'saucy answer'.

If the holder's importuning finally came to naught, as was often the case, he had to take his dishonoured tally back to the exchequer. There the clerks can-celled his original entry in their accounts; and he wearily joined the queue for a fresh tally, probably on a different revenue. Another journey followed. Years might pass before he got his money. Yet all these (and other) imperfections in the system 'do not seem to have disturbed the equanimity of the exchequer'.[40]

The exchequer's accounting for tallies

The exchequer kept its accounts as lists of receipts and payments on separate sheepskin rolls ('pells'). This simple method worked efficiently until the tally of assignment came into use.

[39] J. F. Willard, 'The Crown and its Creditors'. *Eng. Hist. Rev.* (1927), 12. Steel, *Receipt of the Exchequer*, 345.
[40] Ibid. 364. H. Hall, *History of the Customs Revenue*, i. 11, 190. G. L. Harriss, 'Preference', 25.

Not surprisingly, the exchequer could not readily fit entries for these new tallies into its cash accounts, which became endlessly confused. On striking an assignment tally, the clerks entered not only the notional receipt but (as cash was not in fact received) also a notional payment. More trouble came when the tally was finally returned by the customer, etc. for his acquittal. The clerks sometimes took refuge in explanatory glosses and fictitious loans.[41]

Discounting

We may guess that, as tallies circulated so freely, many private firms engaged in discounting; and that the big risks and delays made for stiff rates. But we know little about the details and rates of discounting, presumably in part because canonical rules against usury made explicit mention indiscreet. We do know that the customers' discount charges on tallies (bribes rather than time discount?) were looked on as an abuse of power, and were denounced in popular petitions.[42]

We likewise know little about rates of loan interest. Despite the ban on usury, the king was able to raise loans; and the rich lenders grew richer. Interest must have been allowed in some guise or other. Possibly the exchequer issued loans at a deep discount; in one instance, the lender of £2,703 seems to have paid in only £2,000, the £703 shortfall being described as war expenses. Or a lender might get a seemingly unconnected reward such as a post as tax 'farmer'.[43]

Royal control of sheriffs *via* the tally

In the early Middle Ages, the English kings (notably Henry I, 1100–35) were bent on wresting administrative power from feudal barons, and giving it to royal servants. These included the sheriffs of the counties. Besides their many other duties, sheriffs collected revenues that included certain taxes, receipts from the royal estates, and the 'rich spoils of law' (i.e. fines).

Sometimes the office of sheriff was filled by a powerful baron and became hereditary; but, whenever possible, the king put his own men into these key posts. He used the exchequer as a means of clamping tight controls on them. And the exchequer relied heavily on the tally. (Curiously, the king does not seem to have used this tally system in his southern French domains.[44])

---

[41] H. Jenkinson, 'Medieval Tallies'. 306. C. D. Chandaman, *The English Public Revenue, 1660–88* (Oxford, 1975), 288.

[42] H. Hall, *History of the Customs Revenue*, i. 10.

[43] Steel, *Receipt of the Exchequer*, p. xxxvii, 319; *Cambridge Economic History.*

[44] See n. 47 below.

Twice a year, the sheriff had to present himself at the exchequer to defend his stewardship, i.e. act as 'accountant' for all details of the revenues and expenses of his shire. (The civil servant at the head of a British government department is still its 'accounting officer'.) He then paid in sums that he owed, and was given tallies as receipts; in early days, he might be given separate tallies for individual items of revenue (e.g. on one occasion, the Yorkshire sheriff got 972 at once), but later on he received a collective *dividenda* tally for all petty items. He produced tallies as vouchers for some of his expenses.[45]

Tax and tallies

Throughout Europe, taxes and other dues were levied with the tally's aid. Scandinavia in particular gives proofs that tallies were used when taxes and tithes were gathered. Thus a Finnish court record of 1522 tells how Thomas had to pay a heavy fine for breaking the collector's tally 'with which it is the custom to collect tax'.[46] Again, a French document of 1578 orders villagers near Dijon to stop using tax tallies.[47]

Two interesting questions follow. First, as some taxes had names that resemble 'tally', were these names derived from the tally? Examples are:

> *Tallage*, imposts levied by English kings and feudal superiors. Serfs protested 'they would rather go down to hell than be beaten in this matter of tallage'.[48]
>
> *Tallia*, a Swedish tax.
>
> *La taille*, the vexatious French tax originally levied on ignoble persons to raise funds for e.g. their lord's crusade, and later levied by the king (till the Revolution).

Voltaire tells us that the name *la taille* did indeed come from the 'odious collectors'' practice of marking each payment on a tally;[49] and some later writers find this plausible. But the balance of expert opinion traces the name to an allied stem, *taliare*, to cut (cf. 'tailor'); thus the French king cut (apportioned) the tax total between provinces according to reports on their crops, etc., and

[45] Helen M. Cam, *The Hundred and the Hundred Rolls* (London. 1930), I, *et seq.* Judith A. Green, *Government of England under Henry I* (Cambridge, 1986), 195. *Parliamentary Papers* (1868–9), xxxv. ii. 339. H. Jenkinson, *Archaeologia*, 368; 'Medieval Tallies', 300. Sheriff = shire-reeve. Reeve = steward.

[46] Grandell, *Historiska studies i folkliv*, 12.

[47] J.-J. Hemardinquer, 'La Taille: impat marqué sur un baton', *Bulletin philologique et historique* (1972), 508–11.

[48] H. S. Bennett, *Life on the English Manor* (Cambridge. 1937). 139.

[49] *Larousse*, 'la Taille'; Voltaire, *Oeuvres* (Paris, 1819), xiii. 80; xiv. 371.

so on down to parishes, and then (by 'friendship, party, animosity, and private resentment') to persons.[50]

Second, did the collection process rely on the split form of tally? Probably not. The unsplit tally was better in two ways: it displayed the apportionment of taxes between households, and it served the collector as voucher when he accounted to his superior for all sums due.[51]

Records of as late as 1784 show the procedure still extant in remote villages of the Landes and Pyrenees. The 'coarse and ignorant' inhabitants met in general assembly, and assessed themselves (in kind) according to their means; the collectors, also illiterate, notched the tax roll on a 'baton'.[52] Sweden has hundreds of unsplit tax tallies. A rather fine one, from 1627, looks somewhat like a broadsword. It has a line down the middle of each side. One of the resulting strips lists the payers' marks: alongside each mark, in the other strip, are notches recording the payers' dues. Finland has a planchette of as late as 1820, for day labour on roads, etc., by twenty families. Thanks to such tallies, the villagers could see the fairness (or otherwise) of the sharing between households, the payers were given a receipt before witnesses, and the collector had a complete record.[53]

THE PRIVATE TALLY

The more remote the tally was from a government office, the less likely it was to survive. The PRO has preserved several hundred private tallies (vouchers to accounts); otherwise few remain. However there can be little doubt about the 'extreme popularity' of the private tally. Estates and monasteries found it convenient; some surviving stocks, notched by a reeve when he collected rents from monastery tenants, served to acquit tenants in the eyes of the abbot. Wyclif denounced 'lords who take goods of the poor and pay for them with white sticks'. There is evidence of the tally's common use among traders by the thirteenth century (and presumably it had come into use earlier). Chaucer's characters mention it twice ('so be I faille [to pay] . . . write it upon my taille'). Many tallies, anticipating bills of exchange, were passing from hand to hand at a discount. 'English medieval finance was built on the tally.'[54]

[50] *Oxford English Dictionary*. Adam Smith. *Wealth of Nations* (Dublin, 1776), iii. 307.
[51] Grandell, *Historiska studier i folkliv*, 12.
[52] J.-J. Hemardinquer, 'La Taille'.
[53] Grandell, *Historiska studier i folkliv*, 12.
[54] Jenkinson, 'Medieval Tallies'. 293; *Archaeologia*, 379. Steel, *Receipt of the Exchequer*, p. xxxv. Clanchy, *Memory to Written Record*, 72. 95. Chaucer, Prologue, *Canterbury Tales*, l. 570.

At a time when coins were both scarce and bad, the tally helped to foster the process by which a credit economy flourished even though debt settle ments depended ultimately on barter. A barter system could hardly function well if it consisted only of discrete transactions—if (say) tailor and peasant had to swap a coat for a pig. The tailor might not want a pig that day; and the coat might be worth more than a pig. Dealings became feasible if the tailor sold the coat on credit, and at later dates bought such items of farm produce as he needed, crediting the peasant; tallies enabled the necessary accounting to be done. They likewise enabled merchants to trade with one another on a two-way basis, with the balance swinging from side to side (as in Colonial America, where however ledger accounts kept track of the deals).[55]

Private persons used much the same notch language as the exchequer, but their writing—if any—tended to be terse and less likely to stick to the full and rigid formulas of officialdom.[56] Notches thus might perhaps stand for money or pigs or corn. The users relied on memory and witnesses for the full story.

The tally's everyday use is attested in several ways. It is for instance taken for granted in the matter-of-fact evidence at an 'inquisition' into the wounding of Walter, an estate servant: Walter was lifting a table, and Hugh was cutting tallies ready for use, when Walter tumbled and fell on Hugh's upturned knife.[57] Consider, too, comments by judges, and the tally's contributions to our speech.

Judges and tallies

Tallies featured in legal cases, for instance where a creditor demanded payment for goods or repayment of loan. His stock would then at least support his claim; but it might be accepted, not merely as evidence, but as itself generating liability. Its validity was increased if it bore the debtor's seal (important with illiterates).

In 1294, a judge went out of his way to help a merchant who produced an inadequate tally:

He who demands this debt is a merchant, and therefore if he can give slight proof to support his tally, we will incline to that side . . . Every merchant cannot always have a clerk with him.

---

[55] W. T. Baxter, *The House of Hancock: Business in Boston, 1724–75* (Cambridge, Mass., 1945).
[56] Jenkinson, 'Medieval Tallies', 319.
[57] Ibid., 312.

Again, a creditor in 1310 proffered two sealed tallies to witness a debt due by a parson. When the latter tried to evade liability, he provoked the following argument:

'To that you cannot get: for we have produced tallies sealed with your hand.
'We are not put to confess or deny this tally.'

At which Chief Justice Bereford thundered:

'Are not the tallies sealed with your seal? About what would you tender to make law? For shame!'

But Bereford in a later case disparaged the tally (somewhat inconsistently?), pointing out its defects:

'The tally is a dumb thing and cannot speak . . . The notches too; we cannot tell whether they refer to bullocks or to cows or to what else, and you may score as many otches as you like; and so we hold this to be no deed which a man must answer.'[58]

The tally's imprint on our speech

The wide use of tally is suggested by its many contributions to our everyday speech, e.g.:

To tally, i.e. to match or agree.
Stock. The tally's use as receipt led to 'government stock', 'stock exchange', etc. (But 'stock-in-trade' stems from the other use of 'stock' as 'wealth'.)
Counterfoil, 'counter' probably meaning a control or check.
Score has led to e.g. 'pay off old scores' and 'refused on the score of —'. Its meaning of 'twenty' is said to have come from the herd's habit of counting his beasts by scoring a stick (using the Scandinavian /, ┼┼┼, ✕, and ✳ for 1, 5, 10, and 20). The meanings in sport come from recording cricket runs, etc., with notches; eighteenth-century pictures of cricket matches often show two scorers notching the runs on short sticks.
In the nick of time suggests last moment victory.
Hop-scotch is related.
Indenture, a paper cut zig-zag—an alternative to the wooden tally.

Less common now are 'tallyman' (a trader selling goods on credit, and collecting the price by instalments); 'on tally' (on tick) and 'to live on tally' (outside wedlock).[59]

---

[58] C. H. S. Fifoot, *History and Sources of the Common Law* (London, 1949), 224–46.
[59] *Oxford English Dictionary*; but see K. Thomas, 'Numeracy in Early Modern England', *Trans. Royal Historical Society* (1987), 119.

The decline of the private tally

Jenkinson argued that tallies reached their peak of popularity in the fourteenth century, and that their private use declined thereafter (though the exchequer clung to them, ostensibly because they were necessary for the safety of the king's revenue, but also because the staff had a vested interest in the old ritual). He dated private tallies by their use of Latin or English; he saw many with Latin inscriptions (i.e. early date), only two with English (later date). He ascribed the decline to increased literacy and the coming of paper.[60]

But we may well suppose that the decline was slow, and stretched over centuries. Paper may perhaps have appeared in urban England by the thirteenth century, but it remained an expensive import. In Tudor times, a quire of writing paper (twenty-four sheets) cost a labourer's day wages; and probably the fringes of Scotland and Ireland had not yet heard of it. The invention of printing must have strained supplies of both paper and parchment; one parchment copy of the Gutenberg Bible needed the skins of three hundred sheep.[61]

The tally in many ways compared badly with paper. It was less easy to use and store. And it could hardly be adapted to the needs of the new breed of literate men who were learning to use Arabic numerals, the alphabetical index, cross-references, and then the ledger.[62] Paper's convenience came to outweigh cost, in the eyes at least of substantial merchants. The Yamey volume of accounting pictures shows Renaissance counting-houses in rich detail, but not a single tally.[63]

Yet some lesser folk must have stayed loyal to the tally. Shakespeare would hardly have mentioned it in a poem of personal feeling if it had not been in fairly common use ('nor need I tallies thy dear love to score'). Another of his lines perhaps suggests that, though still familiar, the tally was coming to be looked on as out-worn ('whereas, before, our forefathers had no other books but the score and tally').[64]

Can we regard the tally as being, in any direct sense, the ancestor of double-entry accounts? Clearly not. But the tally did foster credit transactions and multi-sided transfers; and so it must have made merchants familiar with notions that later won better expression as debits and credits.

---

[60] Jenkinson, 'Medieval Tallies', 313.

[61] Coleman, *British Paper Industry*, 4.

[62] K. W. Hoskin and R. H. Macve, 'Accounting and Examination', *Accounting, Organization, and Society* (1986), 105.

[63] B. S. Yamey, *Arte e Contabilita* (Bologna, 1986).

[64] Sonnet 122. *2 Henry VI* IV. vii. 39.

THE CHECKER-BOARD

Despite its merits as a record, the tally was hardly an efficient means of calculating. It became more helpful when it was used alongside the abacus.

The latter has taken several forms, some of which were already familiar in antiquity. It might be no more than a board sprinkled with dust on which lines were scratched ('abacus' possibly comes from Hebrew 'abaq', dust); and pebbles might serve as counters (Latin *calculus* means 'pebble'). By late Norman times, however, it had developed into the superior form (imported from Moorish Spain) of the checker-board (*scaccarium*, a chess-board). This

Fig. 7.4 Checker-board and counters (Hans Schäufelein, parable of the unjust steward, early sixteenth century)

Source: Courtesy of B. S. Yamey, *Arte e Contabilità*, 107.

might literally be a board, or a table-top, or a 'worked reckoning cloth' to be put on a table. It was criss-crossed with suitable lines; calculation was done by moving counters onto and off the resulting spaces. The counters usually were bits of metal like coins.[65]

Rulings

There were several forms of ruling (geared to the Roman numerals). One of 1691 appears in Figure 7.5. The circles represent counters, here for 1,000, 50, and 1, i.e. a total of 1,051. As can be seen, counters were put either on the lines, or (to represent intermediate numbers such as V and L) half-way between lines.[66]

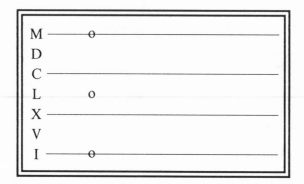

Fig. 7.5

For money arithmetic, some slightly more complex form was useful. Two such forms are shown in Figures 7.6 and 7.7. The first ('the merchants' use') had a horizontal row for each denomination of money:

> *Pence*—lowest row (nearest operator). A counter on the line stood for 1*d.*; above the line, for half a shilling, i.e. 6*d.*
> *Shilling*—next row. A counter on the line and to the right stood for 1*s.*, to the left for 5*s.*; above for half a £, i.e. 10*s.*

and so on for the £ and for scores of £s. The abacus might accordingly appear as in Figure 7.6.

[65] F. P. Barnard, *The Casting-Counter and the Counting Board* (Castle Cary, 1981), 29.
[66] Ibid. 235.

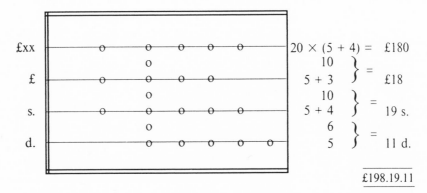

£xx					$20 \times (5 + 4) =$ £180
					10
£					5 + 3 $\}$ = £18
					10
s.					5 + 4 $\}$ = 19 s.
					6
d.					5 $\}$ = 11 d.

£198.19.11

Fig. 7.6

The second form ('the auditor's use', employed at the exchequer) had vertical columns for the denominations; the operator used as many horizontal rows as he found helpful (e.g. for distinguishing revenues from expenses):

Pence—right-hand column; counters stood for 1*d.* if placed low, and for 6*d.* if high.

Shillings—next column; low counters stood for 1*s.*; high counters for 5*s.* (at right) and 10*s.* (at left)

nd so on for £s, etc. The exchequer used seven columns (£10,000, £1,000, ₤100, £20, £1, 1*s.*, 1*d.*),[67] and thus reflected the various sizes of notches on allies, as in Figure 7.7.

£xx	£	s.	d.

20 × 5	10 + 5	10 + 5	6
20 × 4	3	4	5
£180 +	18	19s.	11d.

Fig. 7.7

[67] *Dialogus*, 31.

Calculation technique

To see how addition sums were done on the abacus, we can turn to the description of a tax audit at a German city (adapting it by substituting English money units). A gentleman of standing (the 'reckoner' or 'calculator') had the cloth before him, and a bowl with silver counters. The burgomaster read out the various sums due; for each sum, the calculator placed counters on the appropriate spaces. As soon as there were counters for 12*d.* in the penny space, he took them off and put one counter in the shilling space. As soon as there were counters for 20*s.* on the shilling space, in like manner he took them off and put a counter in the space for £s. A second gentleman examined the vouchers. A prelate read out a duplicate copy of the accounts (to ensure that the church got its share?). When the reckoning was finished, the calculator stated the amount shown on the cloth; the burgomaster was responsible for the accuracy of the result.

Subtraction could be done by removing counters. Even multiplication and division were possible, but only by a skilled abacist.[68]

The counters

Coins could serve as counters. But, soon after AD 1200, the French court took to using special 'casting counters' (*jettons*), and this fashion spread. Persons of refinement might have their own silver pieces, stamped with fanciful designs that illustrated proverbs, verbal conceits, etc. The less affluent used crude pieces made of base metal. Sometimes counters served too as small change.

Though few 'boards' have survived, there are still counters in plenty. One collector tells us that he owned 7,000 and had examined 35,000 others.

From the standpoints of numbers and interest to later collectors, French counters reached a peak under Louis XIV. They were employed until the Revolution (and acquired extra uses as medals and as largesse to be thrown to the poor). But the Revolution brought its simpler decimal units of money, weight, etc.; moreover the old system savoured of royalism. Many counters went to the melting pot.[69]

---

[68] Barnard, *Casting-Counter*, 233; Charles Singer (ed.), *History of Technology*, ii (Oxford, 1957), 766.
[69] Barnard, *Casting-Counter*, 22; J. M. Pullan, *History of the Abacus* (London, 1968), 45; David E. Smith, *History of Mathematics*, ii (New York, 1958).

Decline of the abacus

In Britain, the counting board probably dropped out of use somewhat earlier. Shakespeare still had references to it: Iago speaks scornfully of 'this counter-caster', and an ignoramus 'cannot do it [arithmetic] without compters'.[70]

Two things lessened the need for the abacus. One was cheap paper. The other was the use of Arabic numerals. Europe was slow to accept these. The author of the *Dialogus* knew of them (thanks to the writings of Moorish scholars), but preferred the Roman system. 'Ciphering' was long regarded as a bizarre and mysterious art. Arabic figures had, however, percolated into common use by the seventeenth century, and 'made the elementary rules of arithmetic accessible to every child'. An arithmetic book of 1668 explains manual accounting, but omits this section in its 1699 edition.[71] The Scots exchequer abandoned its board perhaps about 1660.[72] Only in the East has the abacus (in its form of beads on wires) remained popular.

THE MEDIEVAL AUDIT

Manor accounts

A feudal lord could own many manors. His whole estate was often supervised by a steward, and each manor by a reeve. The latter was either appointed from above or elected by his fellow serfs.

The reeve as accountant

One of the reeve's most troublesome tasks was to draft the yearly accounts for his manor. For this work, he relied on his memory, tallies, and perhaps notches on barn-posts. (We are told that some nineteenth-century farmers still kept complicated accounts on tallies, cutting the amounts with a bill-hook 'as fast as you could write them with a pen'.) The reeve's figures were put into writing by trained scribes, who made a round of manors each Michaelmas for this purpose; or the priest might do the writing.

---

[70] *Othello*, I. i. 31; *Winter's Tale* IV. iii. 38.
[71] *Dialogus*, p. xxxvii; Singer, *History of Technology*, 767; Thomas, 'Numeracy', 122.
[72] A. L. Murray, 'Procedure of the Scottish Exchequer', *Scot. Hist. Rev.* 40 (1961), 95.

In form, the reeve's accounts seem the obvious ancestor of the 'account charge and discharge', still used by Scottish solicitors for trust funds, etc. The reeve was charged to deliver, e.g.:

Rents
Sales
Fines receivable

The discharge allowed him such items as:

Tithes
Repairs to castle
The fines of tenants too poor to pay

Then came the balance payable by the reeve for this year, plus any balance due from earlier years. (Sometimes the latter balance prefaced the charge; but that arrangement blurred the current year's results.) A physical inventory of livestock might be appended on the back of the account. Tallies might be attached to the foot of the account, to record payments by the reeve to his lord.

Hearing the accounts

The feast of St Michael (29 September) was the 'season for hearing the accounts'. The reeve at that time faced a whole team of auditors: it might include the steward and (if the manor belonged to a monastery) the cellarer. These men were well informed, and would 'take inquest of the doings which are doubtful'. To help their probings, they brought with them the rolls of the manor, and so could—with seemingly uncanny knowledge—check the current figures with earlier ones. In many surviving accounts, some entries in the scribe's writing are struck out and replaced by entries in an auditor's hand. The reeve used tallies to vouch his outlays, and received a tally when he handed over his balance. If we may judge from the well-known procedures at the exchequer, the manor auditors did the needed sums with the help of a reckoning cloth.

A reeve might be put in the stocks because of his arrears. But sometimes the auditors would forgive a debt because of the reeve's 'weakness and poverty'.[73]

[73] Bennet, *Life on the English Manor*; John Hacker, *Rural Economy and Society in the Duchy of Cornwall* (Cambridge, 1970). *Proceedings of the Society of Antiquaries* (1893–5), 309. P. D. A. Harvey, *Manorial Records*, British Records Association, Archives and the User, No. 5 (1984).

The exchequer audit

Just as many a pub is called 'The Chequers', the principal treasury of England took its name from the checker-board, which was central to its working. An earlier name was 'The Tallies'.

The exchequer was first mentioned in 1110.[74] It was organized in two divisions:

Upper. This was a court of the 'Kings Baron's and Great Men', e.g. the Justiciar (first subject of the realm, entrusted 'with the king's very heart'), Chancellor, Constable, and Treasurer. They made sure that the royal revenue was properly collected, largely by the sheriffs. The Treasurer was the mainstay of the whole exchequer. Fitznigel had himself obtained the post (by purchase); his *Dialogus* lingers affectionately over the procedures, particularly the sheriff's audit. The upper division became also a court of law, popular because it gave prompt judgement over disputed dues, and enabled citizens to appeal against harsh collectors.

Lower. This had the humbler roll of cash office. It was staffed by lesser officials, differing in their duties (Fitznigel tells) 'but alike in their zeal for the king's advantage when justice permits it'. They deputized in their masters' names; thus, when in time the Chancellor stopped attending the meetings, his clerk took his place, eventually coming to be called the Chancellor of the Exchequer and then superseding the Treasurer as chief official; there were likewise two understudy Chamberlains and a Constable. Other officers included four tellers to count the cash, a silver-smith and melter (to assay coins paid in), a tally-cutter, and an usher who went to the royal forests to fetch wood for tallies. Some of these functionaries assisted their masters in the Upper Court when it was in session.[75]

The sheriff's 'farm'

Because trustworthy officials were not always available, medieval kings tended to privatize tax gathering, i.e. to use tax farmers. A sheriff paid a fixed rent—his 'farm' or 'ferm'—for the right to collect certain of his county's taxes, rents of royal manors, etc. (but he also had to collect and hand over some other items). A surplus on his farm was his wages; a deficit had to be made good out of his own pocket. He thus had strong reason to act as 'the hammer of the poor'.[76]

---

[74] Green, *Government of England under Henry I*, 41.

[75] *Dialogus*, p. xxxv *et seq.*; *Dictionary of the Middle Ages* (New York, 1984), 532.

[76] *Cambridge Economic History*, iii (Cambridge, 1963), 437. It is not clear how much the sheriffs could

The king summoned a sheriff ('see, as you love yourself and all that you have, that you be at the exchequer there and then') at Easter and at Michaelmas. The Easter visit was provisional, i.e. the sheriff then paid in about half of his dues on account—the 'sheriff's profer', for which he received a memorandum tally. His accounts were not audited till his Michaelmas visit, when he came back for another profer and then his audit, final payment, and acquittance.[77]

Analogies with chess and criminal courts

On taking his place in the court, the sheriff found himself facing a formidable team that was arrayed on three sides of a table (see Figure 7.8). The table was rather small (10 feet by 5 feet), with a rim to stop the checkers from rolling off. On it was spread a dark cloth 'figured with squares like a chessboard' with lines 1 foot apart. The row of barons overlapped the top of the table. The sheriff sat opposite them; beside him were his assistants

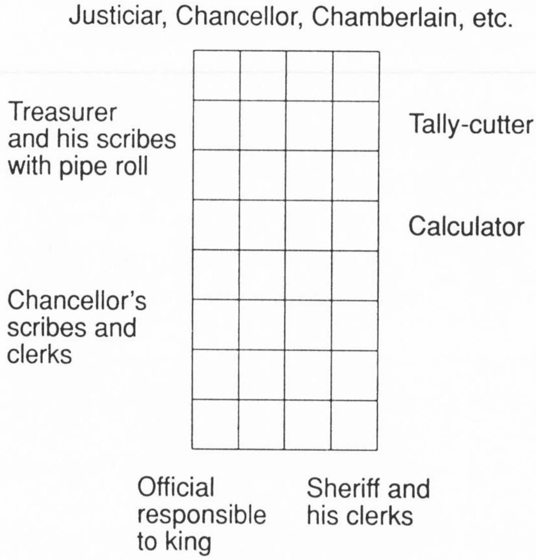

Justiciar, Chancellor, Chamberlain, etc.

Treasurer and his scribes with pipe roll

Tally-cutter

Calculator

Chancellor's scribes and clerks

Official responsible to king

Sheriff and his clerks

Fig. 7.8

involved outlays, yet were prized. An honest sheriff was at least entitled to various small fees and some hospitality. A dishonest sheriff could exact other fees ('the sheriff's welcome'); he could cheat the exchequer; he could commandeer horses and carts; and he could be ambidextrous as a judge, i.e. take bribes from both sides—Morris, *Medieval English Sheriff*, 279.

[77]   *Dialogus*, 79; Hall, *History of the Customs Revenue*; Poole, *Exchequer in the Twelfth Century*.

bailiffs, and clerks with stocks and vouchers). His opponent, the Treasurer,
t on the left side, also with supporters.[78]

Fitznigel relishes the confrontation between Treasurer and sheriff, and the
analogy with a chess game: just as 'on a chessboard, battle is joined between
two kings . . . here too struggle is joined between two persons, to wit, the
Treasurer and the Sheriff who sits at his account, while the rest sit by as
judges to see and decide'.

Fitznigel carries the analogy further by describing the minor officials as
pawns. There were many of these, and there was much duplication of work.
Not only was each item in the sheriff's account checked carefully and entered
in several rolls, but many of the officials were watched over by colleagues; as
Fitznigel puts it, 'a three-fold cord is not easily broken'. Such excessive checking prompts one to wonder whether the officers perhaps were too ill-
educated for accuracy, or were intent on making jobs for hangers-on, or were
prone to corruption. Fitznigel must have permitted himself the same doubts;
when, as 'master' in his dialogue, he has described the officer who acted as
watchdog over the Treasurer, he makes his 'scholar' interject: 'Well then, saving the Treasurer's reverence, this appointment seems to detract from his dig-
nity, since his honour is not absolutely trusted.' At which, the master replies:

God forbid! Say rather that his labour is spared and his security assured. For it is not
because either he or anyone else is not trusted that so many sit at the Exchequer; but
because it is fitting that such great matters and the public affairs under so great a
prince should be entrusted to many great personages, not merely for the King's profit,
but to honour his excellence and royal state.[79]

Audit by ear

Medieval audit procedure had to suit men who were illiterate, i.e. to whom
the ear was more important than the eye; even nobles and monks 'wrote' by
dictating to a scribe, and could 'read' with most understanding by listening to
someone with reading skill. 'Inspecting a document' meant hearing it read.
Auditors accordingly listened as the details of an account were related. (This
presumably explains our rather odd use today of 'auditor'—rather than, say,
'scrutineer'—and of 'to hear from' those who write to us.)[80]

At the sheriff's audit, therefore, most of the court's exalted members sat

---

[78] Madox, *History and Antiquities of the Exchequer*, 105 *et seq.*
[79] *Dialogus*, 29. The rolls were not exact duplicates of one another, e.g. fines levied by different courts
were classed differently in the various rolls. Modern attempts to reconcile the rolls may baffle researchers.
M. H. Mills, *Eng. Hist. Rev.* (1921), 349.
[80] Clanchy, *From Memory to Written Record*, 97, *et seq.*

back and listened to a dialogue between the (attacking) Treasurer and the (defending) sheriff.

The audit ceremony

This can be visualized as follows. The Treasurer has made meticulous preparation; he has brought tallies awaiting matching and each shire's sheepskin records (pipe-rolls, so called because of their shape). Known revenues (e.g. fixed rents) and payments are already entered in the rolls, and blanks are left for the unknown. The Treasurer is supported by his 'lynx-eyed' scribe; next sits the Chancellor's scribe (copying what the other writes), and the Chancellor's clerk to watch that no mistakes are made. Yet another official is directly responsible to the king for another roll; he sits on the sheriff's left. At the table's right is the calculator; he sits at the middle of his side (in front of the £ column) so that his hand can move freely and everyone can see him. Beside him is the tally-cutter. Others present include suppliers, etc., holding tallies from the sheriff; alerted by public notices, they could attend the audit to check that their claims were allowed.[81]

The Treasurer starts by calling the name of the accountant, i.e. the sheriff, who is put under oath, and is charged—almost like a criminal—with having money of the king. The accounting (like that of the manor) follows the system of charge and discharge. The Treasurer carefully dictates from his roll the known amounts of the charge—the farm, arrears from former years, etc.; also the sheriff has to confess his variable revenues (including fines, the chattels of fugitives from justice, of those mutilated for their crimes, and of deceased usurers). His discharge covers fixed payments such as tithes, alms, and the wages of royal servants (e.g. pipers and wolf-takers). It covers also his variable payments. As authority for making these, he may plead custom (e.g. the expenses of trial by ordeal), or he may hand in the royal writs sent to him (e.g. orders to fortify castles, and to give 'honours and succour' to royal guests). Even where the court knows well that such-and-such outlays have been made, it may hotly contest the sheriff's claim if he does not submit writs as authority and vouchers proving payment.[82]

Meantime the calculator—who can perhaps be likened to a slick modern *croupier*—listens to the proceedings, and says the amounts as he flips his counters on and off—a 'confusing and laborious process . . .'

---

[81] *Dialogus*, 18, *et seq.*; *Dictionary of the Middle Ages*; iv. 530; *Parliamentary Papers*, 341; Morris, *Medieval English Sheriff*, 252.

[82] *Dialogus*, 24, *et seq.*; Hall, *History of the Customs Revenue*, 196.

> Tongue, eyes, hand and restless brain
> Work with all their might and main.

He puts out the charge items as heaps of counters, and then the discharge items as heaps on a lower line. In simple cases (no 'blanching'—see below), the lower line is next subtracted from the upper; the sheriff is responsible for the remainder. His stocks for earlier payments are duly matched with foils held by the exchequer.

The above description is oversimplified in various ways. For instance, the sheriff's dealings may be split between his main farm and various minor sections, each of the latter being treated as a separate account charge and discharge. Again, some of the items may be entered by tale (the stated number of pence being accepted without deduction for clipping, forgery, and other faults), or may instead be subject to blanching (deduction for the faults). For the blanching process, the melter takes from the sheriff's cash a random sample of 240 silver pence, melts them over a 'cleansing fire', skims off the impurities, and ends with a silver ingot. This is brought back to the court and weighed. If (say) it is 12*d.* (= 5 per cent) short of a pound weight, and the sheriff's payment is £100 of coin, the heap of counters at his credit is cut down to only £95. Then, in order that the Treasurer can account for the actual number of coins, two tallies are struck—one for the £95 (given to the sheriff), and a shorter 'combustion tally' for £5.[83]

Moreover, doubtful questions continually come up during the audit. Do the rents accord with ancient custom? Has the sheriff acted properly? The Justiciar and other barons resolve these points and declare the law: 'the highest skill at the exchequer does not lie in calculations but in judgements'.[84]

After two days of grilling, the sheriff's ordeal ends. He publicly takes his affidavit that he has made his account to the best of his knowledge and belief. If the balance is adverse, he pays it in; the two halves of his tally are put together, and the payment is recorded in fresh cuts across the splits; if he cannot pay, he is liable to go to the Tower. If a balance is due to him, it is carried forward or set off against any sums due by him on other accounts.[85] Finally 'he is quit' is written in the rolls,[86] and he is 'cast out of court'. His account cannot in future be called in question; like a person discharged by a criminal court, he cannot be tried twice on the same charge.[87]

---

[83] *Dialogus*, 38, 125.
[84] Ibid. 15–30.
[85] Ibid. 21, 126; Hall, *History of the Customs Revenue*, 186.
[86] 'Quietus est'; this gives point to Hamlet's 'he himself might his quietus make with a bare bodkin'.
[87] J. E. D. Binney, *British Public Finance and Administration 1774–92* (Oxford, 1958), 216, 238.

After Fitznigel's time, some details of the procedure changed. Thus the duration of a typical audit rose to seven days; perhaps as a result, the date fixed for an audit might be many months after the fiscal year.[88]

Audit of lesser officials

Much the same procedure was continued further down the official scale, e.g. between a sheriff and minor accountants (such as bailiffs from whom the sheriff exacted a farm for the right to collect part of the revenue).[89] The sheriff had his own 'exchequer', often in the castle of his county town, with an elaborate machinery of records and private tallies.[90]

THE EXCHEQUER TALLY'S SPECTACULAR END

The private tally disappears

After the fourteenth century, as we have seen, substantial merchants used the tally less and less, though petty traders still found it helpful till the eighteenth century or even later. Hogarth's picture of the milk-woman shows her brandishing a tally at her poet-debtor. (Sly milk-women could sometimes, without detection, 'cut dead men'—i.e. two notches for one on the split tally.[91]) A historian, recalling his stay in Paris during the 1830s, tells us:

The baker's man in the morning brought with his basket a bundle of tallies on a ring. The maid produced her counter-tally, and the number of rolls or loaves was marked with a file on tally and counter-tally laid together, just as described in the *Dialogus*.

Such a baker might keep tallies not only for his debtors, but also for his creditors; these supplied wheat, and were later paid by barter (a loaf in return for a kilo of flour).[92]

One comes across stray references to the split tally even in the early twentieth century. It has served as a record of output (e.g. bins filled by Kent hop-pickers), and of timber deliveries to the University of Åbo (Turku). Its use was often associated with dirty materials (e.g. charcoal deliveries in Sweden), presumably because these would soil paper records.

[88] M. H. Mills, *Eng. Hist. Rev.* (1921), 484.
[89] Morris, *Medieval English Sheriff*, 250.
[90] Ibid. 283. Jenkinson, *Archaeologia*, 368; 'Medieval Tallies', 301.
[91] Dorothy Davis, *A History of Shopping* (London, 1966), 217; Thomas, 'Numeracy', 119.
[92] J. H. Ramsey, *Revenues of the Kings of England* (Oxford, 1925). 13; M. Stevelinck in correspondence. The tally was still used in some Kentish hop farms in 1938. The stocks were kept by the tallyman (strung on a cord at his belt) and the foils by the pickers. A notch was scored with a file across both bits for every five bushels—notes by Museum of Kent Rural Life, Maidstone.

The exchequer's late ritual

Far from disappearing, the exchequer tally kept and even increased its importance for some centuries.

The exchequer has given historians much scope for colourful prose. It was 'elephantine in its movements but elephantine in its memory . . . its lethargic ritual concealed a curiously sluggish vitality'. Its ancient custom was 'already a fetish' in the thirteenth century. Nevertheless it ran 'the most efficient system of public finance in Europe'; at it, the English 'showed their systematising genius'.[93]

The exchequer's cutting and notching method persisted with little change for six centuries. A thirteenth-century clerk could have interpreted an eighteenth-century tally (though, as we shall see, he would have been startled by its extended functions). Roman numerals and Latin were used till the end.

However, time brought a shift to new taxes that the sheriff did not collect, and so his half-yearly visits grew less important; nevertheless the antique manner of *viva voce* audit survived (till 1834), with a kind of dress-rehearsal the day before.[94] For other transactions (e.g. day-to-day dealings with tax-collectors and lenders), the tally ritual had by the sixteenth century become as follows. The sum of money received was entered in an account book and then on a strip of parchment—the 'teller's bill'. To prevent fraudulent alteration by the payer, the bill was thrown down a pipe into the tally court, i.e. a room below. Here entries were made in two more books; a tally was struck by two deputy-chamberlains, and a tally-writer put on the narration; then entries and tally were checked and rechecked. The payer could collect his stock on application, usually on a later day. If his payment was a loan, he would at its maturity present his stock; another elaborate ritual followed as the officials sought out the foil, joined it to the stock, and made suitable entries in the rolls.[95]

Given such strict procedures, how are we to explain the stocks that were not returned to the exchequer, and are now prized by antiquarians? Part of the answer may be that, while lenders had good reason to return their tallies at maturity date, other men might have less reason, e.g. a payer of certain kinds of tax, of a fine, or of a fee for a baronetcy. In theory, some of these payers later took their stocks back to the exchequer to have their accounts acquitted; the officials then kept the stock and spliced it with the foil. But a

---

[93] *Dictionary of the Middle Ages*, iv. 531; Jenkinson, *Archaeologia*, 368; Henry Roseveare, *The Treasury* (London, 1969), 21.

[94] Binney, *British Public Finance*, 213.

[95] *Parliamentary Papers* (1835), xxxvii, p. 342.

payer might not bother with this sterile drill; and so stocks remained in private muniments.[96]

Tallies of *sol* and *pro*

At one time or another, the exchequer used perhaps a dozen different kinds of tallies (including e.g. memorandum and combustion—described above). But, for our purposes, the later tallies can still be classed under the two familiar heads:

1. *Tally of receipt.* This was the straightforward acknowledgement of actual in-payment. The first word of the entry in the pell was *solutum* (= paid); hence *sol* tally.

2. *Tally of assignment.* This was the instrument for securing payment from a third party. It usually was still a *sol* tally; the payee was not named, so that transfer was possible. But it might be a *pro* tally; here the inscription stated that it was struck *pro* (= for the benefit of) a named person, on a specified revenue. Such revenue was alienated, i.e. the right to money was transferred to the favoured creditor, who could in his own name sue the revenue receiver. A *pro* tally was clearly less flexible than a *sol* tally, and perhaps less useful to the king as a means of anticipating revenue.[97]

To woo cautious investors and lessen the king's dependence on goldsmiths, yet another kind of assignment tally was devised by exchequer officials early in the reign of Charles II. This was the 'tally of loan', which can perhaps be regarded as the first government stock. It was backed up by a repayment order that carried 6 per cent interest and was negotiable by endorsement. Such tallies were to be cashed in regular sequence from taxes granted by Parliament; but officials at once extended the system to other kinds of revenue that the original Act had not contemplated. The tallies passed from hand to hand, e.g. goldsmiths (whose banking activity was expanding fast in this period) cashed them at a discount.[98]

Climax under Charles II

Charles II inherited an impossible financial position, and needed a growing revenue; yet a hostile Parliament was niggardly in voting him taxes. The

---

[96] Jenkinson, 'Medieval Tallies', 293.

[97] Binney, *British Public Finance*, 224; Chandaman, *English Public Revenue, 1660–88*, 288.

[98] John Clapham, *The Bank of England* (Cambridge, 1944), 11; W. A. Shaw, 'The Treasury Order Book', *Economic Journal* (1906), 37.

exchequer was thus hard-pressed. One of its troubles now seems odd. The revenues of a financial year came in only after some delay, whereas expenditures began immediately. Modern states have learned how to smooth over this temporary shortfall; 'the process seems so easy to the modern mind that we are almost reluctant to acknowledge the difficulty of the problem that beset Charles'.[99]

The tally, particularly the new tally of loan, gave the king an unseen and unsuspected way of creating credit almost at will. He exploited it to the full.

We are lucky in having first-hand accounts of the issues from a high civil servant. Pepys, as secretary to the navy, had to rely on tallies to meet the fleet's needs. The exchequer gave him new tallies which he then tried to turn into cash. His diary has more than eighty references to them, e.g. 'To the exchequer, and there got my tallys for £17,000, the first payment I ever got out of the exchequer . . . and away home with my tallys in a coach, fearful every step of having one fall out or snatched from me' (19 May 1665). His fears were not groundless. On 26 November 1668, a subordinate lost a £1,000 tally. However when Pepys came to his office two days later, he heard to his 'great content' that a porter had found the tally in Holborn, and had brought it in; for which honest act the man was rewarded with twenty shillings.

Charles II at first managed the issues with prudence. But soon, hard-pressed by the demands of war and love, he grew reckless. The issue of tallies rose to a *crescendo*. In consequence, they became hard to cash. Pepys tells how he went to the 'Excise Office where I find that our tallys will not be money in less than sixteen months; which is a sad thing, for the king to pay interest for every penny he spends—and which is strange, the goldsmiths with whom I spoke do declare that they will not be moved to part with their money upon the increase of the consideration by 10 per cent' (21 Jan. 1665). The tally office became overworked, and its ancient form of accounts grew bewilderingly complex; Pepys denounces its clerks as 'lazy rogues . . . Lord, to see what a dull heavy sort of people they are there, would make a man mad' (16 May 1665).

By the 1670s, the royal finances were in great disorder. The debt rose to £1 million, a whole year's revenues. Bankers were 'ground between their angry creditors and an empty exchequer'. The legal limit on interest rates was 6 per cent, but Charles had to pay 20 or even 30 per cent. In 1672, he was forced to suspend all payments of interest for twelve months—the 'stop of the

[99] Shaw, 'Treasury Order Book', 35.

exchequer' by which 'the common faith of a nation was violated', and some goldsmiths were incapacitated.[100]

Tallies and the founding of the Bank of England

Despite this disaster, the exchequer in following decades was still able to issue tallies and notes. But the 'stop' meant that no one would accept these unless they were backed by high interest. Moreover they circulated at a discount. The rate reflected the status of the taxes on which the tallies were secured. It reflected too the king's fortunes: those of William III did not inspire confidence, and so (according to a somewhat jaundiced pamphlet) great numbers of his tallies lay bundled up like faggots in the hands of brokers and stock-jobbers, who 'devoured the King and the army . . . scarce 50% of the money granted by Parliament has come into the hands of the exchequer, and that too late for service, and by driblets'.[101]

Trade was expanding greatly in these years. Traders and Crown both needed a solid establishment that could advance money at a reasonable rate. So there was a strong case for the 'daring idea' of a Bank of England. It was duly founded in 1694.

Tallies were important in its financing. The government wanted to get the flood of tallies off the market; and, after hard bargaining, the Bank agreed to help, on very advantageous terms. Subscribers to its capital ('engrafted stock') could pay four-fifths in tallies, taken at par; the government then paid the Bank 8 per cent interest on the tallies' nominal value. It also instructed the Bank (1696) to buy up other tallies (said by then to be selling on average at a 40 per cent discount), and on these too it paid the Bank 8 per cent interest.[102]

Even after the Bank was founded, tallies played some part in finance. Coins were still scarce, and so 'all great dealings were transacted in tallies, bank bills, and goldsmiths' notes'.[103]

By the eighteenth century, the Crown relied increasingly for its short-term needs on exchequer bills rather than tallies. But it still issued tallies to investors in the national debt. And it experimented with a new form, the annuity tally: lenders got the right to an assignable annuity, for life or a fixed term such as ninety-nine years.[104]

---

[100] John Clapham, *Bank of England*, 12; E. Lipson, *Economic History of England* (London, 1956), iii. 236.
[101] J. Francis, *History of the Bank of England* (London, 1847), 58.
[102] Clapham, *Bank of England*, 47.
[103] A. Andreades, *History of the Bank of England* (London, 1924), 23.
[104] Philip Norman, 'Exchequer Annuity Tallies', *Proc. Archeological Soc.* (1902), 300; Binney, *British Public Finance*, 127.

The end of the exchequer tally

It was obvious by the eighteenth century that the routines of the exchequer, once admirable, had become a confused farce. But they lingered on, even though they had to be buttressed with a parallel system more suited to the times. Clerks from the Bank of England came daily to take charge of the cash transactions and make the effective accounting entries; and payers got a written quittance as well as a stock.

The exchequer could not reform itself even if it had wanted to do so. It was hamstrung by its own rules, which had grown into non-statute law. The tally was the only form of quittance allowed to it. And its officials, now sinecurists who delegated their work, had the strongest reasons to fight change. They were paid fees on all receipts; as the national revenue grew, so did their pickings. A teller was rumoured to earn what was, for the times, the immense income of £30,000 a year.[105]

But, as part of the popular campaign for political reforms, change came at last. An Act of 1782 abolished the sinecures at the exchequer—though still with a reprieve; an indulgent Parliament provided that the Act should not take effect till the death or retiral of the two Chamberlains. These were young patricians (one was still at Eton), and they clung to their offices for another forty-four years, i.e. till 1826. Then methods were reformed also; paper replaced wood as the material for receipts (but still with the old Latin formula). The obsolete accounting routines were abolished soon after—the sheriffs' in 1833, and the exchequer's in 1834.[106]

A fair number of the late tallies are in the PRO. They, and their accompanying accounts, show some odd quirks in state finance. An unknown American in 1805 sent conscience money. The account of an official at Gibraltar includes money spent for the release of captives in Morocco, and (1752, the year of calendar reform) shows deductions from salaries for 'the eleven days in September annihilated by Act of Parliament'. Some tallies suggest extreme dilatoriness in settling accounts; thus an 1825 tally is for transactions in the 1808–14 Spanish campaign; and the executors of a contractor got his 'stipend', for work in Florida during 1767 and 1781, only in 1826.[107]

[105] Binney, *British Public Finance*, 224; *Illustrated London News* (1858), i. 446.
[106] R. L. Poole, *Exchequer in the Twelfth Century*, 91; M. T. Clanchy, 'Burning the Tally Sticks in 1834', *Literacy and Law in Medieval England* (London, forthcoming 1995); Dickens was satirical about the exchequer's reluctance to replace sticks with paper: 'all the red tape in the country grew redder at the bare mention of this bold and original conception', *Speeches and Letters*, ed. K. J. Fielding (Oxford 1964), 204.
[107] PRO F 402/301; British Museum, OA 9443–8.

Parliament blazes

But the tally's story has a postscript of high drama. The exchequer had from time to time used old tallies as firewood. (Clearly it viewed records of wood with disdain; paper and parchment were preserved at some cost.) Between 1826 and 1834, however, more than twice the usual quantity had accumulated in the tally room at the exchequer. Then space was needed for a bankruptcy court, and so in 1834 the Lords of the Treasury ordered most of the tallies ('which my Lords understand to be entirely useless') to be destroyed.

The site chosen for the bonfire was a yard that then lay between Parliament and the Thames; the men in charge were cautioned to be careful as the Parliament building was only wood and plaster. But the Clerk of Works—keen on the up-to-date technology—decided that the new iron stoves under the House of Lords would instead be a safe and proper place for the burning. On the evening of 15 October, two workmen employed by contractors moved the tallies (enough to fill two carts) to the cellars. At 6.30 next morning, they began to stoke the stoves, putting in only some ten tallies at a time, and damping them occasionally with water. But by afternoon they had grown impatient, and were pushing in the tallies as fast as they could. At 5.00 p.m. one witness saw an 'astonishing blaze'; a member of a guided tour in the House of Lords felt the heat through his boots. An hour later, the fabric burst into flames.[108]

The Times reported that

people living nearby were thrown into the utmost confusion and alarm by the sudden breaking out of one of the most terrific conflagrations that has been witnessed for many years past . . . countless numbers swarmed upon the bridges, the wharfs, and even upon the housetops; for the spectacle was one of surpassing though terrific splendour . . . Not even the most zealous exertions could save the edifice from absolute destruction.[109]

The tally did not die tamely.[110]

[108] *Parliamentary Papers* (1835), xxxvii, p. 329.
[109] *Times*, 17 Oct. 1834.
[110] Earlier articles are: R. Roberts, 'A Short History of Tallies', *Accounting Research* (July 1952); W. E. Stone, 'The Tally', *Abacus* (June 1975); R. H. Parker, 'Accounting Basics', in G. Macdonald and B. Rutherford (eds.), *Accounts, Accounting and Accountability* (London, 1989).

ALTERNATIVE ACCOUNTANT

The Spectator, 17 June 1989.

Learning Resources
Centre